WINDOWS® 8.1 FOR SENIORS
QuickSteps®

Marty Matthews

New York   Chicago   San Francisco
Athens   London   Madrid
Mexico City   Milan   New Delhi
Singapore   Sydney   Toronto

Cataloging-in-Publication Data is on file with the
Library of Congress

Windows® 8.1 for Seniors QuickSteps®

1 2 3 4 5 6 7 8 9 0   QVS QVS   10 9 8 7 6 5 4

ISBN   978-0-07-183258-8
MHID   0-07-183258-0

SPONSORING EDITOR / Roger Stewart

EDITORIAL SUPERVISOR / Jody McKenzie

PROJECT MANAGER / Hardik Popli, Cenveo® Publisher Services

ACQUISITIONS COORDINATOR / Amanda Russell

TECHNICAL EDITOR / John Cronan

COPY EDITOR / Lisa McCoy

PROOFREADER / Irina Burns

INDEXER / Valerie Perry

PRODUCTION SUPERVISOR / Jean Bodeaux

COMPOSITION / Cenveo Publisher Services

ILLUSTRATION / Cenveo Publisher Services and Erin Johnson

ART DIRECTOR, COVER / Jeff Weeks

COVER DESIGNER / Pattie Lee

SERIES CREATORS / Marty and Carole Matthews

SERIES DESIGN / Mary McKeon

To Michael, a super son!

About the Author

Marty Matthews "played" with some of the first mainframe computers, and from those to the latest tablets, he has never lost his fascination with computers. He has been a programmer to a software company president. Throughout, he has worked to bring others along with him and help them make the best use of all that computers can do. Toward that end, Marty has written more than 80 books on software and computing subjects, with many becoming bestsellers and receiving many accolades.

His recent books include *Windows 8 QuickSteps, iPad for Seniors QuickSteps, Windows 7 for Seniors QuickSteps,* and *Computing for Seniors QuickSteps.*

Marty and his wife Carole, also a writer, are the co-creators of QuickSteps® books and live on an island northwest of Seattle, Washington.

About the Technical Editor

John Cronan has more than 30 years of computer experience and has been writing and editing computer-related books for more than 20 years. His writings include *Microsoft Office Excel 2010 QuickSteps* and *Microsoft Office Access 2010 QuickSteps.*

Acknowledgments

This book is a team effort of truly talented people. Among them are:

John Cronan, technical editor, who corrected many errors, added many tips and notes, and greatly improved the book. John is also a good friend and an author in his own right. Thanks, John!

Lisa McCoy, copy editor, who added to the readability and understandability of the book while always being a joy to work with. Thanks, Lisa!

Valerie Perry, indexer, who adds so much to the usability of the book, and does so quickly and with much thought. Thanks, Valerie!

Irina Burns, proofreader, who made sure that the words and illustrations actually work to tell a story that makes sense, as well as catching and correcting many last-minute errors. Thanks, Irina!

Hardik Popli, project manager, who greased the wheels and straightened the track to make a smooth production process. Thanks, Harry!

Jody McKenzie, editorial supervisor, who is constantly involved with all aspects of the book and makes sure it is an outstanding product. Thanks, Jody!

Amanda Russell, editorial coordinator, queen of Apple permissions, and a true Wonder Woman, who makes it all happen! She tries hard to keep us on schedule; accounts for all the chapters, pages, and illustrations; and gets everything to the right people. And she does all this with a light touch and a smile in her email voice. Thanks, Amanda!

Roger Stewart, editorial director, who is responsible for making this series and book a reality. He has worked with us for over 25 years and has never lost faith, although I'm sure he questioned it more than once. In the process, he has become a valued friend. Thanks, Roger!

Contents at a Glance

Contents

3   Chapter 3   **Storing Information** 67

4   Chapter 4   **Exploring the Internet** 93

5

6

Introduction

Most of my friends and acquaintances are seniors, as I am, and I have spent a fair amount of time helping them get comfortable with computers in general and with Windows 8 in particular. This book is written for you in a voice without jargon using relevant examples in clear, step-by-step instructions. This book zeros in on only the most important topics and uses brief instructions in plain language, with many color visuals, to clearly lead the reader through the steps necessary to perform a task. In addition, a group of fellow seniors have added their comments about what is being discussed to provide a personalized input on a topic.

QuickSteps® books are recipe books for computer users. They answer the question "how do I…" by providing a quick set of steps to accomplish the most common tasks with a particular operating system or application.

The sets of steps are the central focus of the book. QuickFacts sidebars show how to quickly perform many small functions or tasks that support the primary functions. QuickQuotes provide some of the lessons my senior friends have learned. Notes, Tips, and Cautions augment the steps. The introductions are minimal, and other narrative is kept brief. Numerous full-color illustrations and figures, many with callouts, support the steps.

QuickSteps® books are organized by function and the tasks needed to perform that function. Each function is a chapter. Each task, or "QuickSteps To," contains the steps needed for accomplishing the function, along with the relevant Notes, Tips, Cautions, and screen shots. You can easily find the tasks you want to perform through:

- The table of contents, which lists the functional areas (chapters) and tasks in the order they are presented
- A QuickSteps To list of tasks on the opening page of each chapter

- The index, which provides an alphabetical list of the terms that are used to describe the functions and tasks
- Color-coded tabs for each chapter or functional area, with an index to the tabs in the Contents at a Glance (just before the table of contents)

Conventions Used in This Book

Windows® *8.1 for Seniors QuickSteps*® uses several conventions designed to make the book easier for you to follow. Among these are:

- A ✹ in the table of contents references a QuickFacts sidebar in a chapter.
- A 🙿 indicates a QuickQuotes sidebar by a contributing senior.
- **Bold type** is used for words on the screen that you are to do something with, like "…open the **System** menu, and select **Customize**."
- *Italic type* is used for a word or phrase that deserves special emphasis.
- ***Bold-italic type*** is used for a word or phrase that is being defined.
- <u>Underlined type</u> is used for text that you are to type from the keyboard.
- SMALL CAPITAL LETTERS are used for keys on the keyboard, such as ENTER and SHIFT.
- When you are expected to enter a command, you are told to press the key(s). If you are to enter text or numbers, you are told to type them.

Chapter 1 _____

Getting Started with Windows 8.1

Welcome to Windows 8.1! Over its 25-plus-year life, Windows has come a very long way. Windows 8 and its latest variant, Windows 8.1, are immensely easier to use, extremely more capable, and much more reliable and stable than when they started. Windows is an *operating system* that causes a computer to perform its primary functions, including handling information, working with other devices like printers, and interfacing with the Internet. These operating system functions are used by *applications*, or *apps*, to do what you want on a computer, including email, browsing the Internet, listening to music, reading, writing, shopping, banking, investing, photography, research, genealogy, and game playing, to name just a few.

This book is dedicated to helping you, a senior like me (I'm 72 as I write this), get the most out of Windows 8.1 and your computer. If you are just starting out with Windows 8.1, it is likely that you also have a new computer, so we will begin by looking at your computer and seeing what you have available to you and how to use it. Then we'll start your computer and look at Windows 8.1, explore what it is and does, and how Windows is used. The purpose of this chapter is to help you understand what it is that you have and how to get started using it. Many of the subjects in the chapter will be expanded upon in future chapters.

In this chapter you may feel like you are trying to get a drink from a fire hose. There is a lot of detailed information that is required to cover the three methods of using Windows 8.1: with touch, with a mouse, and with a keyboard. Absorb what you can, but don't worry about remembering every keyboard shortcut or every possible way to move your fingers on a touch screen. Even after 20 years of using Windows and two years of using Windows 8, I can't remember it all. For that reason I have created three tables later in this chapter. Two of these have been repeated at the end of the book and can be removed. They are also available for download from our website QuickSteps.org/tables. Refer to these tables often as you are reading this book and using Windows 8.1 on your own.

 TIP If you print out the tables from our website, it helps the "senior" eyes if the tables are printed in Landscape view (wider than taller).

LOOK AT YOUR COMPUTER

Computers today cover a broad range of devices. In addition to the more common desktop and laptop computers shown in Figure 1-1, there are now tablets, convertibles, and ultrabooks that all run Windows 8.1, which you can see in Figure 1-2. There is actually another category called "detachables" (not shown here) where the screen can be removed from the keyboard, which some people feel are superior to convertibles.

 NOTE In Figure 1-1, I identify several objects as being "pointing devices." In two of the cases, the pointing device is a mouse, while on the laptop, it is a track pad. On touch screens, the pointing device can be your finger. As mentioned later in the text, I use "mouse" as a general term for all pointing devices.

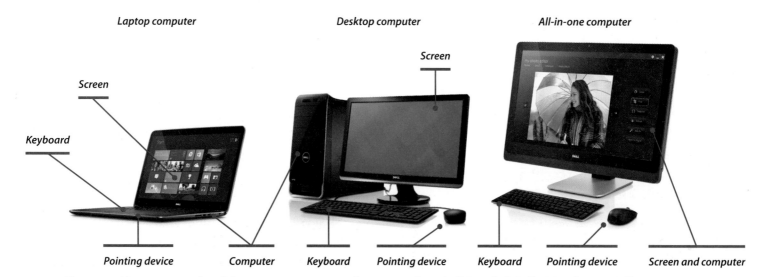

Laptop computer *Desktop computer* *All-in-one computer*

Screen

Screen

Screen

Keyboard

Pointing device *Computer* *Keyboard* *Pointing device* *Keyboard* *Pointing device* *Screen and computer*

Figure 1-1: Here are examples of the more common types of computers from Dell, Inc., their Dell XPS 15 laptop, Dell XPS 8700 desktop, and Dell XPS 27 all-in-one computers. (Courtesy of Dell, Inc.)

Tablet computer   Ultrabook computer   Convertible computer

Figure 1-2: Here are examples of three less common types of computers from Dell, Inc., their Dell Venue 8 Pro tablet, Dell XPS 11 Ultrabook, and Dell XPS 12 Ultrabook convertible computer. (Courtesy of Dell, Inc.)

Review the Types of Personal Computers

In this book, our discussion of Windows 8.1 will cover practically any device that runs Microsoft Windows 8.1, including:

- **Tablets**, which are smaller (7 to 12 inches) handheld screens that are generally operated by touching the screen with either a finger or a stylus, although some have separate keyboards.

- **Convertibles**, which can be used either as a tablet or as a laptop computer with a screen that swings to be either on top of the keyboard, looking like a tablet, or behind the keyboard like a laptop.

- **Detachables**, which are tablets with a separate and independent keyboard, often connected to the tablet using Bluetooth wireless technology.

- **Ultrabooks**, which are laptops that are very thin, lightweight, highly capable, and with a long battery life. The screens on some fold back so they can be used like a thicker tablet.

- **Laptops**, which are like a clamshell with a screen behind the keyboard that closes to be carried around.

- **Desktops**, which are the classic personal computers with a separate computer, screen, keyboard, and mouse.

- **All-in-ones**, or integrated computers, which have large screens (18 to 27 inches), with the major computer components packed in the back of the screen and a separate keyboard and mouse.

Identify the Parts of Your Computer

The laptop, desktop, and all-in-one computers all have the same set of six primary external components, four of which are shown in Figure 1-1. Ultrabooks and convertibles have all but the optical disc, while tablets are just a screen and a pointing device (your finger or a stylus). The primary external components are as follows:

- The **computer** itself processes what is entered on the keyboard, pointed to by the mouse, read from a disc, or received from the Internet and then displays it on the screen.

- The **screen** displays information from the computer.

- The **keyboard** transmits typed information from you to the computer. Replaced with on-screen keyboards on tablets and some other devices.

- A **pointing device**, such as a mouse, stylus, or your finger, allows you to point at and select objects on the screen.

- An **optical disc** drive reads information, music, or videos contained on either a CD (compact disc) or a DVD (digital video disc) into the computer. Smaller devices, including tablets and many ultrabooks, and convertibles do not have optical discs.

- **Connecting receptacles** allow you to connect other devices to a computer, such as a printer, a camera, an external hard drive, a sound system, or a TV.

In addition, all computers have four or five major internal components and many other minor components.

 TIP You don't need to know much about the internal components, just that they are there performing their functions.

- The **central processing unit**, or CPU, does all the real work of the computer, and the technology behind its intelligence is the reason that the huge computers we knew "back in the day," which took up the square footage of half a football field, now can fit in your hand.

- **Memory**, or random access memory (RAM), is used to temporarily store information that the computer is using while it is turned on. When you turn the computer off, the contents of the memory disappear.

- The **hard disk** drive (HDD) is a rotating magnetic disk within your computer that is used to store both programs and information on your computer that you want stored for longer periods. The information on a hard disk remains intact when you turn your computer off. The hard disk is used to store information you write, pictures you take, your email address list, your financial records, and many other pieces of information you don't want to lose.

- **Flash memory** is solid-state memory like regular memory, but it retains its contents when the power is turned off. Flash memory is common in small, chewing-gum-package-size "sticks" that plug into a USB (universal serial bus) receptacle and are called USB flash drives. In tablets and some ultrabook and convertible computers, larger amounts of flash memory are permanently mounted in the computer and called solid-state disks (SSDs) to replace the hard disk because SSDs are smaller, lighter, and faster.

- The **motherboard** is used to plug in the CPU and memory and to connect to the hard disk and various external components. It is the central connecting device joining all of the computer's components.

Use Your Computer

The exact way that a computer is used depends on the computer. Determining this requires that you refer to the information that came with the computer. Here are some general rules of thumb for using a computer:

- **Start the computer** by pressing and releasing a power button, most of which have a symbol similar to the one shown here.

- **Stop the computer** by indicating to the operating system that you want to do so, as explained in the next section. In a real emergency, you often can stop the computer by pressing and holding down the power button. This can be dangerous, however, since if you have not saved the information that is in memory, you might lose it. If you use the operating system to shut down, you will be reminded to save information in memory, or it will automatically be done for you.

- **Insert a disc in an optical drive** by opening the drive. There is normally a button or area that you press to do this. The button is often located on the drive, to its right, or below the drive. When the drive is open, handle a disc only by its edges or center and place it in the tray that has opened. Then press the button again, or gently press the front of the open tray to close it. After several seconds you should see some instructions appear on the screen telling you what to do next, as described in the following section.

- **Connect a printer** or other device to the computer. Most printers and many other devices connect to a computer using a USB connector, shown next, into which a cable from the printer or other device is inserted. In addition to USB connectors, your computer may have slots for memory cards used in cameras and other devices, as well as connectors for audio, video, and external hard disks. These connecting receptacles can be on the front, back, and/or sides of a computer. Your computer instructions will describe these to you.

EXPLORE WINDOWS 8.1

The Windows 8.1 operating system provides the foundation set of instructions that are executed on your computer.

An operating system is the interface between you and the computer hardware. It facilitates your running other programs, such as Microsoft Word, storing a file, printing a document, connecting to the Internet, or retrieving information from a number of sources without you knowing anything about how the hardware works.

Windows 8.1 can be used in three ways:

- **Touch** If you have a multi-touch display screen, you can use one or more fingers on the screen. See "Use Touch" later in this chapter.
- **Mouse** If you have a mouse or other pointing device like a track pad, you can use it. We will refer to all pointing devices as a "mouse." See "Use a Mouse" later in this chapter.
- **Keyboard** If you have a keyboard, it can be used. See "Use the Keyboard" later in this chapter.

In many cases, you will have a choice of two or more of these methods. In this chapter we'll explain each of the methods in depth and define words (in italics and bold type) that will be used throughout the rest of the book, which allow you to choose the method you want to use in a particular case. In this chapter and the beginning page of the next couple of chapters, we'll reinforce this by further describing the options that are available.

Getting into and using Windows 8.1 is not that different from previous versions of Windows, except that there is now a separate Lock screen and you may be able to use touch.

▷▷ Start and Log On to Windows 8.1

To start Windows, simply turn on the computer. Press its power button or push the on/off switch.

When you turn on the computer, you should see the opening Lock screen similar to the one shown next, although it may be customized by the computer manufacturer and have a different background.

6:38
Monday, October 7

From the Lock screen, you need to display the Logon screen where you can enter a password or PIN (personal identification number). To do that:

1. Display the Logon screen with:

   Touch   Move your finger (*swipe*) up from the bottom of the screen.

   Mouse   Point the mouse anywhere on the screen and press the left mouse button (*click*). You can also point on the bottom border of the screen, and press and hold the left mouse button while moving the mouse up toward the top (*drag*).

   Keyboard   Press SHIFT or SPACE or almost any other key.

2. If you see two or more users on the screen:

   Touch   Touch or *tap* your name, picture, or icon, or that of the default user.

   Mouse   Point at and press the left mouse button, or *click* the name, picture, or icon you want.

   Keyboard   Press TAB one or more times to *select* the name, picture, or icon you want, and press ENTER.

3. Enter your password or PIN:

   Touch   Tap the text box where a password or PIN needs to be entered to bring up the touch keyboard, tap the keys needed for your entry, and tap ENTER.

   Mouse   Click the **Ease Of Access** icon ⚙ in the lower-left corner of the screen, click **On-Screen Keyboard**, and click the keys needed for the password. (The on-screen keyboard is different from the touch keyboard, but you can also use the mouse with the touch keyboard after you bring it up with touch. See "Use the Touch Keyboard" later in this chapter.)

   Keyboard   Type your entry and press ENTER.

If you purchased a computer with Windows 8.1 installed on it or you upgraded to Windows 8.1, you will be asked to enter a new user name and password. If someone else installed Windows 8.1 on your computer, he or she should have given you a password. As you will see in Chapter 10, you can change passwords and add users if you wish.

When you have successfully logged on, the Start screen will open, as you see in Figure 1-3.

▷▷ Use a Mouse

A *mouse* is any pointing device—including a track pad, trackball, stylus, or a mouse—with two or more buttons. I assume you are using a two-button mouse. Moving the mouse moves the pointer on the screen.

You can control the mouse with either your left or right hand, in which case, the purpose of the buttons may be switched. (See Chapter 2 to switch the buttons.) This book assumes you are using your right hand to control the mouse and that the left mouse button is also called "*the* mouse button." The right button is always called the "right mouse button." If you switch the buttons, you must change your interpretation of these phrases.

 TIP As is generally true in the computing community, I will use the word "*app*" whenever I am talking about an application or program that can run on a computer. Also, when I use the word "*computer,*" I'm talking about any device, including desktop, laptop, notebook, netbook, or tablet, that can run Windows 8.1. (Smartphones might eventually be included in this statement, but as of now they don't run full Windows 8.1 as described here. Apps do apply to the programs that run on smartphones.)

Figure 1-3: The Start screen provides options for what you want to do next.

The actions of the mouse allow you to:

- **Highlight** an *object* (a button, an icon, a border, etc.) on the screen by pointing to it. *Point* at an object on the screen by moving the mouse until the tip of the pointer is on top of the object.

- **Select** an object on the desktop or start an app on the Start screen by clicking it. *Click* means to point at an object you want to select and quickly press and release the left mouse button.

- **Open** an object such as a folder, or start an app on the desktop, by double-clicking it. *Double-click* means to point at an object you want to open and press and release the mouse button twice in rapid succession.

- **Open** an object's *context menu,* which allows you to do things specific to the object, by right-clicking it. *Right-click* means to point at an object you want to open and quickly press and release the right mouse button.

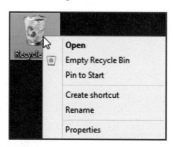

- **Move** an object on the screen by dragging it. *Drag* means to point at an object you want to move, and then press and hold the mouse button while moving the mouse. You will drag the object as you move the mouse. When the object is where you want it, release the mouse button.

Mirror Touch

Windows 8.1 has added several new mouse moves to mirror what can be done with touch:

- **Switch to the Start screen** by moving the mouse to the Windows 8.1 icon ▦, which Microsoft calls (and I will) the *Start button,* in the lower-left corner of the screen while in the desktop or a Windows 8–style application (see discussions of both of these later in this chapter) and clicking the Start button.

- **Switch to a recently opened window** by moving the mouse to the upper-left corner of the screen to display a thumbnail of the most recently opened window, given that one was recently opened, and clicking it to open that window.

- **Open Charms** by moving the mouse to the lower-right or upper-right corner of the screen and then moving the mouse up or down to open the *Charms* pane; any of the Charms themselves can then be clicked to open windows or perform functions. See "Use Charms" later in this chapter.

- **Switch to other open windows** on the Start screen by moving the mouse to either the upper- or lower-left corners of the screen and then moving the mouse down or up to display all of the open windows, any of which can be clicked to be opened.

NOTE If you move the mouse to the upper- or lower-right corners without then moving it up or down and just point to the corners, you briefly get a "ghost" image of the Charms. After moving the pointer up or down, the "full" Charm pane appears, as well as the enlarged time and date box, similar to what is shown in Figure 1-4.

Use Touch

Touch screens have been around for a number of years and supported by previous versions of Windows, but before Windows 8.1, there were relatively few users of them. Modern tablets and touch screens for desktop and laptop computers are changing that. Windows 8.1 and the most recent devices support *multi-touch* where five or more fingers can be sensed at one time. For the most part, touch replaces what you can do with a mouse. The touch motions for the related mouse actions are shown in Table 1-1.

 CAUTION! Do not use anything on a touch screen except a finger or possibly a stylus, if it came with the screen. Especially do not use a pencil or ballpoint pen.

Figure 1-4: Charms provide the primary control device for Windows 8.1 and are brought in from the right edge of the screen.

Table 1-1: Finger Gestures for a Multi-Touch Screen

Gestures	Description
	Select an object on the screen or start an app on the Start screen by touching or *tapping* it once with a single finger, similar to clicking with a mouse.
	Open an object or start an app on the desktop by tapping it twice with a single finger, similar to double-clicking with a mouse.
	Move an object on the screen by holding a finger on an object while moving it in any direction, similar to dragging with the mouse.
	Open an object's *context menu,* which allows you to do things specific to the object, by holding a finger on the object (pressing down and holding a single finger on the object for a moment), waiting for a box to appear, and then releasing the finger, which has the same effect as right-clicking with the mouse.
	Scroll the screen, a window, or a pane by moving a finger up or down or left or right on the screen; a mouse needs to use a scroll bar or a wheel, as described later in this chapter.
	Zoom in (enlarge what is shown on the screen) by placing two fingers on the screen and spreading them apart; a mouse requires zoom controls that are not always present. (Think of this as spreading a tear in a piece of paper apart so you can see what is underneath.)
	Zoom out (reduce in size what is shown on the screen) by bringing two fingers together. (Think of this as gathering together an area so you can see more of what surrounds it.)
	Turn a page by *flicking* one finger in either direction.
	Open windows and controls by *swiping* a finger in from the frame around the screen on to the screen: From the right edge to open Charms (see "Use Charms" later in this chapter). From the left edge to open apps that have been previously started. From the bottom and top in Windows 8–style applications to open controls and other features. See "Use Windows 8–Style Screens" later in this chapter.

Use the Keyboard

While a keyboard can obviously be used to enter text into the computer, it can also be used for many control purposes as an option to using touch or the mouse. This applies to the physical set of keys in a laptop or notebook computer, or the separate device used with a desktop computer. While there is a keyboard that can be displayed on a touch screen, it is primarily for entering text and has limited use in control for the obvious reason that other touch options are available for that. (See "Use the Touch Keyboard" next.)

The general control functions that can be performed with a physical keyboard include the following:

- **Select** an object on the desktop's taskbar (see "Explore the Desktop" later in this chapter) by repeatedly pressing **TAB** or one of the **ARROW** keys until the object is selected.

- **Open** a selected object or start an app by pressing **ENTER**.

- **Open** a selected object's context menu by pressing the context menu key on the lower right of the main section of most keyboards.

Some keys on a physical keyboard perform special control functions, as shown in Table 1-2.

The **WINDOWS** key on the lower left  of most keyboards, between **CTRL** and **ALT**, has taken on greater significance in Windows 8. Table 1-3 shows the **WINDOWS** key assignments.

Table 1-2: Special Control Keys

Keys	Description
ALT+F4	Close a window or an app.
ALT+SHIFT+ARROW KEYS	Move the selected object on the screen in the direction of the arrow keys.
CTRL+TAB	From the Start screen, opens All Apps or Apps view.
CTRL+plus sign key (+)	Zoom in.
CTRL+minus sign key (−)	Zoom out.
CTRL+ALT+DEL	Open system options, including ones for shutting down Windows.
CONTEXT MENU	Open the context menu for a selected object.

Table 1-3: Actions Taken with Various Windows Key Combinations

Key(s)	Description
WINDOWS	Switches to the Start screen from the desktop or Start screen app, and to the desktop from the Start screen once the desktop has been otherwise opened.
WINDOWS+1, 2…	Switches to the desktop and opens the first, second, etc., application on the taskbar.
WINDOWS+B	Switches to the desktop and selects the notification area.
WINDOWS+C	Opens Charms.
WINDOWS+D	Shows the desktop, hiding open windows.
WINDOWS+E	Switches to the desktop and opens File Explorer.
WINDOWS+F	Searches for files.
WINDOWS+H	Opens the Share pane.

Table 1-3: Actions Taken with Various Windows Key Combinations *(Continued)*

WINDOWS+I	Opens the Settings pane.
WINDOWS+K	Opens the Devices pane.
WINDOWS+L	Locks the computer and displays the Lock screen.
WINDOWS+M	Switches to the desktop and minimizes all open windows.
WINDOWS+O	Turns a tablet's autorotate between portrait and landscape on or off.
WINDOWS+P	Opens the settings to display on a second screen.
WINDOWS+Q	Searches for apps.
WINDOWS+R	Switches to the desktop and opens Run.
WINDOWS+U	Switches to the desktop and opens the Ease of Access Center.
WINDOWS+W	Searches for settings.
WINDOWS+X	Opens the System menu.
WINDOWS+Z	In a Windows 8–style window, displays the App bar.
WINDOWS++ **WINDOWS+−**	Opens the screen magnifier and increase or decreases the magnification of the current screen.
WINDOWS+TAB	Switches among Windows 8–style apps.
WINDOWS+HOME	Closes all but the selected window on the desktop. When pressed a second time, it reopens all windows originally open.
WINDOWS+F1	Opens Windows Help.
WINDOWS+PRT SCN	Saves an image of the screen to the Clipboard; +**ALT** saves just the open window.
WINDOWS+UP ARROW	Maximizes the selected window. If this is followed by **WINDOWS+DOWN ARROW**, the window is restored to its original size.
WINDOWS+DOWN ARROW	Minimizes the selected window, unless the window was originally maximized, in which case the window is restored to its original size.
WINDOWS+LEFT ARROW	The selected window fills the left 50 percent of the desktop. If this is followed by **WINDOWS+RIGHT ARROW**, the window is restored to its original size.
WINDOWS+RIGHT ARROW	The selected window fills the right 50 percent of the desktop. If this is followed by **WINDOWS+LEFT ARROW**, the window is restored to its original size.
WINDOWS+SHIFT+UP ARROW	The selected window fills the desktop vertically, but maintains its previous width. If this is followed by **WINDOWS+SHIFT+DOWN ARROW**, the window is restored to its original size.

QuickFacts

Use the Touch Keyboard

If you are using a computer with a touch screen, you can bring a keyboard up on the screen that you can use with touch, as shown next.

There are three ways to bring up the touch keyboard:

- Tap in a text box or text area, such as the text box for entering a password.
- Tap the keyboard icon in the notification area of the desktop.
- Swipe in from the right of the screen to open Charms, tap **Settings**, tap **Keyboard**, and tap **Touch Keyboard And Handwriting Panel**.

The default keyboard that opens is primarily for typing alphabetic letters. If you need to type numbers or special characters, tap the **&123** key in the lower-left corner to bring up this keyboard.

You can get additional special characters by touching the brighter, right-pointing arrow in a circle. The above keyboards are normal or standard keyboards. If you touch the keyboard icon in the lower-right corner of the keyboard, you can select an alternative split keyboard or a handwriting tablet if you have a stylus available. The split keyboard has a key in the lower left, similar to the standard keyboard, to display special characters. The split keyboard also has a unique key, a vertical column of dots that allows you to select the size of the keys.

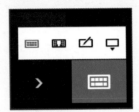

There is actually a second keyboard that can be displayed on the screen, called the On-Screen Keyboard, that is for use with a stylus or a mouse. You can open this keyboard by tapping or clicking the **Ease Of Access** icon in the lower left of the Logon screen and tapping or clicking **On-Screen Keyboard**. It can also be opened through the Ease of Access settings in the Control Panel as discussed in Chapter 2.

The split keyboard can be helpful when holding a tablet, allowing you to use both thumbs to type, like texting on a cell phone.

Review Terms and Conventions

This book is meant for all Windows 8.1 users, including those who have touch, as well as those who have a mouse and keyboard. As a result, I will often use terminology that is not specific, allowing you to choose from among the three techniques. Table 1-4 shows the action terms I will use along with their context and how these

terms should be implemented with a mouse, touch, or a keyboard. If you have the options, you can choose which you want to use.

Often in a list of steps there will be a number of them in succession. For example, to display the Ancestry document written by my father and stored on my computer (see Figure 1-5), I could write:

Table 1-4: Implementing Common Terms with a Mouse, Touch, and a Keyboard

Action Term	With a Mouse	With Touch	With a Keyboard
Select an object on the desktop, in a window or dialog box, or on a menu	**Click** the object	**Tap** the object	Use **TAB** or the **ARROW KEYS** to highlight the object and press **ENTER**
Start an app in the Start screen	**Click** the tile	**Tap** the tile	Select the tile and press **ENTER**
Open an object on the desktop, such as a window or folder	**Double-click** the object	**Double-tap** the object	Select the object and press **ENTER**
Start an app on the desktop	**Double-click** the app	**Double-tap** the app	Select the object and press **ENTER**
Open an object's context menu	**Right-click** the object	**Touch** and hold for a moment, then release	Select the object and press the **CONTEXT MENU** key
Open the App bar for an app	**Right-click** the app	**Touch** and hold for a moment, then release	Select the object and press the **CONTEXT MENU** key
Move an object on the screen	**Drag** the object with the mouse	**Drag** the object with your finger	Select the object and press **ALT+SHIFT+ARROW KEYS**
Switch to the desktop from the Start screen	**Click** the desktop tile	**Tap** the desktop tile	Press **WINDOWS+D**
Switch to the Start screen	**Click** the **Start** button	**Swipe** from the right edge and tap the **Start** button	Press **WINDOWS**
Switch to another running Windows 8–style app	**Point** to the upper-left corner, move down, and click the app	**Swipe** from the left edge until the app opens	Press **WINDOWS+TAB**
Open Charms	**Point** to the lower-right corner and move up	**Swipe** from the right	Press **WINDOWS+C**
Open Apps view	**Click** the down arrow on the Start screen	**Swipe** up from the vertical middle of the Start screen	Press **CTRL+TAB** from the Start screen

From the Start screen, switch to the desktop, start **File Explorer**, open **Libraries**, open **Documents**, open the **Documents** folder, open the **Ancestry** folder, open the **J B Matthews** folder (my father), and open the **Ancestry** document.

Using the mouse, this would be:

From the Start screen, click the desktop tile, click the **File Explorer** icon in the taskbar, click **Libraries**, double-click **Documents**, double-click **Documents**, double-click the

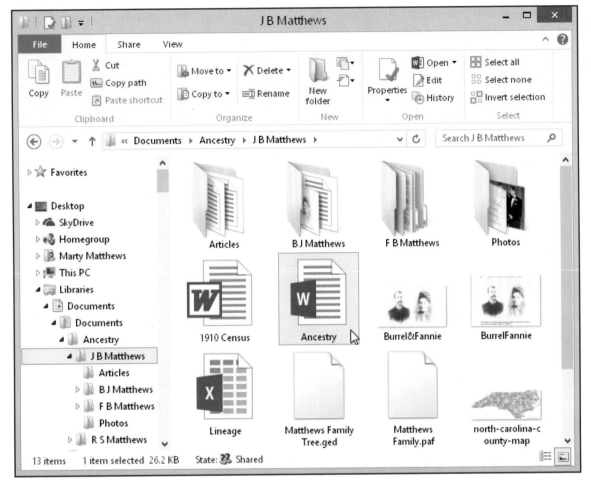

Figure 1-5: Locating and opening a document on your computer can require several steps.

Ancestry folder, double-click the **J B Matthews** folder, and double-click the **Ancestry** document.

Using touch this would be:

From the Start screen, tap the desktop tile, tap the **File Explorer** icon in the taskbar, tap **Libraries**, double-tap **Documents**, double-tap **Documents**, double-tap the **Ancestry** folder, double-tap the **J B Matthews** folder, and double-tap the **Ancestry** document.

To remove the repetitive words and shorten this, I will use the vertical line, or "pipe," character to represent in this case a succession of "open." (The pipe character will mean repeat the last action term or verb spelled out.)

From the Start screen, switch to the desktop, start **File Explorer**, open **Libraries | Documents | Documents | Ancestry** folder **| J B Matthews | Ancestry** document.

This assumes you know when "open" means "click" or "tap" and when it means "double-click" or "double-tap." This will be become second nature after a while, but if you are unsure, click or tap once and if that doesn't work, double-click or double-tap.

> **TIP** Starting an app on the desktop itself requires a double-click or double-tap, unless the app is on the taskbar at the bottom of the screen, in which case, starting the app requires only a single click or tap.

▶▶ Select a Windows View

There are two primary views in Windows 8.1: the *Windows 8–style* interface, which is new to Windows 8, and the *desktop*, which is similar to the desktop in previous versions of Windows and is used with all legacy applications and other functions.

Explore the Windows 8–Style Interface

The Windows 8–style interface uses the entire screen and hides all Windows controls behind the edges of the screen. The Windows 8–style interface is used with applications written for Windows 8 or Windows 8.1 and with the Start screen that opens upon starting Windows 8.1. The concept behind the Windows 8–style is to give the maximum exposure and simplicity to what is being displayed on the screen and not have it be crowded and confused with controls. Figure 1-3 shows this with the Start screen, first by itself, as you see it when you start Windows 8.1. Figure 1-4 shows the Start screen with the *screen edge controls* (or Charms) that can be brought in from

the right side of the screen, as explained in "Use a Mouse" and "Use Touch" earlier in this chapter. See "Use Windows 8–Style Screens" later in this chapter.

Use the Start Screen

The Start screen, shown in Figure 1-3, replaces the Start menu in previous versions of Windows and provides the primary means of starting apps and opening system features. The Start screen displays *tiles* that represent apps or features that can be started or opened. The tiles, which may all be on one large screen or laid out horizontally over several smaller screens, can be customized, as you will see in Chapter 2. To locate and start or open a tile:

- **Touch** If needed due to a smaller screen, move your finger across the screen (*swipe*) from right to left to display the tile you want to open or start and then tap the tile. The speed at which you move your finger will determine how far the tiles move.

- **Mouse** If needed due to a smaller screen, move the mouse pointer to the bottom of the screen and use the horizontal scroll bar that is displayed, as described in "Use Classic Windows" later in this chapter, and then click the tile.

- **Keyboard** Use the scroll keys on the keyboard (**UP**, **DOWN**, **LEFT**, **RIGHT**, **PAGE UP**, **PAGE DOWN**, **HOME**, and **END**) to move a selection box to the tile you want to start and then press **ENTER**.

Use the Desktop

The Windows 8.1 desktop, shown in Figure 1-6, can hold windows and run apps within it. In its simplest form you see a background scene, a bar at the bottom with buttons on the

The Recycle Bin icon opens a folder of deleted files

A desktop icon for an app you can run, or a file or folder you can open

The desktop is used for windows, dialog boxes, and icons

The Start button switches you to the Start screen

The taskbar shows apps that are running and other apps that are "pinned" to it

The mouse pointer shows where the mouse is currently pointing

The notification area holds icons of running system apps and information

Figure 1-6: *The Windows 8.1 desktop provides a workspace to hold windows of running apps and open folders similar to prior versions of Windows.*

left, and the time and date and other icons on the right. There may also be one or two icons in the upper-left area.

The desktop is, in a sense, a special app that you start from the Start screen and can switch between it and other Windows 8.1

apps that are open. At the same time, it's different from Windows 8–style apps in that it has its own controls and acts much like the desktop in older versions of Windows.

To open the desktop from the Start screen:

Tap or click the desktop tile or press **WINDOWS** on a keyboard to display the desktop, as you see in Figure 1-6.

To return to the Start screen from the desktop:

Tap or click the Start button in the lower-left corner of the screen or press **WINDOWS** on a keyboard.

⟩⟩ Explore the Desktop

The desktop provides a place to display and run legacy (Windows 7 and prior) apps or new apps written for the legacy environment:

- The **desktop** itself is the entire screen, except for the taskbar at the bottom. Windows, dialog boxes, and icons, such as the Recycle Bin, are displayed on the desktop. You can store *shortcuts,* which are icons for your favorite apps, on the desktop (see Chapter 2). You can drag windows, dialog boxes, files, and icons around the desktop. Double-click or double-tap an icon on the desktop to open it.

- The **taskbar** across the bottom of the screen contains the active *tasks,* which are icons and titles of the apps that are running on the computer, and folders that are open or "pinned" to it. The taskbar also holds the Start button on the left, and the notification area and Show Desktop button on the right. Click or tap an app on the taskbar to open it.

 NOTE Microsoft and I use the term "pinned" to refer to how apps are kept on the Start screen and on the taskbar. Think of "pinned" as in posting a note to a corkboard with a push pin. In both the Start screen and taskbar, pinning an app there takes a conscious effort to do it and a conscious effort to remove it. You'll see how in Chapter 2.

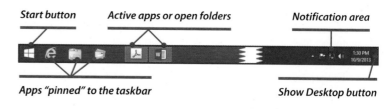

Start button   *Active apps or open folders*   *Notification area*

Apps "pinned" to the taskbar   *Show Desktop button*

 NOTE Your taskbar may have more or fewer objects than those shown here.

- **Desktop icons**, which can be in any number and anywhere on the desktop, are in the upper-left corner of Figure 1-5. Desktop icons represent apps or folders that can be started or opened and moved about the screen. The Recycle Bin is a desktop icon for a folder that contains all of the files that have been deleted since the Recycle Bin was last emptied. Double-click or double-tap a desktop icon to open or start what it refers to.

- The **mouse pointer**, or simply the *pointer* or *mouse,* shows where the mouse is pointing. Move the mouse to move the pointer.

Use the Notification Area

The *notification area* on the right of the taskbar contains the icons of special programs and system features, as well as the time and date:

- **Show hidden icons** Click or tap the up arrow to see the icons of hidden programs, and then click any you wish to open.

- **Open a system feature** Click or tap one of the icons to open a system feature.

- **Set the time and date** Click or tap the time and date area to see a calendar and

an analog clock, and then click or tap **Change Date And Time Settings** (see related Note).

- **Show the desktop**   On the far right of the taskbar is an unmarked rectangular area, which, if you click or tap it, will minimize all open windows and dialog boxes and display the desktop. Clicking or tapping it again restores all open windows and dialog boxes. If the capability called "Aero Peek" has been enabled (you'll see how in Chapter 2), simply moving the mouse over (also known as *mousing over*) this button temporarily makes all open windows and dialog boxes transparent until you move the mouse away.

 NOTE   If you are connected to the Internet, you will never need to set your time and date, even when changing to or from daylight saving time, because Windows automatically synchronizes your computer's time with a local time server.

 NOTE   The icons you have in the notification area will depend on the apps and processes you have running and the system features you have available. The icons can include Keyboard ▦, which opens the touch keyboard; System Messages ▣, which accesses the Action Center; Power ▥ and Wireless ▦, which appear on a tablet or notebook computer; and Speakers, which allows you to control the sound from your computer ◪. You may have Network ▦, which opens the Network and Sharing Center in place of Wireless, and no Power icon if you are using a desktop computer.

▷▷ Use Charms

There is a set of controls available on both the Start screen and the desktop, called "Charms," that are initially hidden.

Open Charms

To open Charms:

- **Touch**   Move your finger from *off* the screen on the far right on to it (*swipe* from the right edge). Charms will open as shown next. Tap a Charm, such as **Settings**, to open it.

- **Mouse**   Move the mouse into the lower-right or upper-right corner of the screen and then move it up or down the right edge. Charms will open as shown with touch. Click a Charm, such as **Settings**, to open it.

- **Keyboard**   Press WINDOWS+C. Charms will open as you saw with touch. Use the arrow keys to highlight a Charm, such as **Settings**, and press ENTER to open it.

Explore Charms

Five Charms are displayed in the pane that opens on the right of the screen:

- **Settings**   Provides a number of primary controls related to the current screen (see Figure 1-7):

    Power   Allows you to shut down the computer, restart it to refresh Windows and/or applications, or put the computer to "sleep" in a very low-power mode where it can be quickly restarted. See "End Your Windows Session" later in this chapter.

    Notifications   Allows you to select how long you want to hide system messages that you receive, such as a security notice.

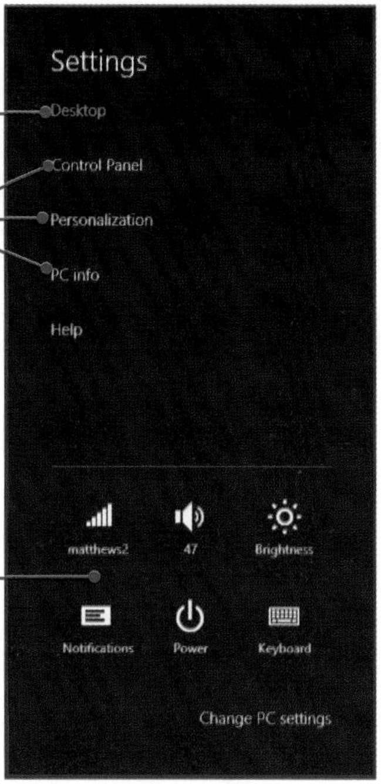

Figure 1-7: *The Settings pane provides controls related to the current screen, as well as those in several general-purpose settings areas.*

Network Displays the status of the network and/or wireless connections you are using.

Sound Allows you to adjust the level of sound being produced or mute it completely.

Screen Allows you to adjust the brightness of your screen, if possible, and turn on or off the ability of a tablet to rotate the screen.

Keyboard Opens the On-Screen Keyboard if a touch screen is available.

Settings Allows you to adjust controls for the current screen.

Help Opens Windows Help; see "Get Help," later in this chapter.

Change PC Settings Opens PC Settings; see Chapter 2.

- **Devices** Controls the devices connected to your computer.

- **Start** Switches between the Start screen and the desktop.

- **Share** Shares apps and their data.

- **Search** Searches for files, applications, and settings.

Use Start Screen Tiles

The Start screen, shown in Figure 1-3, contains tiles for the apps that Microsoft decided would be most useful to you. As you will see in Chapter 2 you can change the order of the tiles and size, as well as add and remove tiles to reflect the apps and functions you want on your Start screen. The tiles on your Start screen are only a subset of the possible tiles you can have there. If you select (tap or click) the down arrow in the lower-left area of the Start screen ⊕ or swipe up from the bottom of the screen, you will open *Apps view*, which displays all the apps on your computer, as you see in Figure 1-8. Any of these apps can be on the Start screen as you will see in Chapter 2. You can also leave them where they are and still use them as if they were on the Start screen.

Start an App

The apps represented by the tiles on the Start screen, such as Calendar, Weather, Word, and Excel, need to be started in order to use them. The method for starting an app depends on where the app icon is located:

- **On the Start screen** Click or tap the app tile.

- **On the desktop** Double-click or double-tap the app icon, or "shortcut."

Figure 1-8: *Apps view displays all the apps installed on your computer, initially in alphabetical order, but you can change this.*

- **Pinned on the desktop's taskbar**   Click or tap the app icon.

- **In the notification area**   Click or tap the app icon.

Close an App

When you are done using an app, you may simply go on to other apps, leaving the original app "running." Actually, it uses very little of the system's resources when you leave it in this way. Eventually, Windows will see that it is not being used and shut it down. If for security or other reasons you want to close or shut down an app, you may do it in several ways:

- An open Windows 8–style app can be closed by dragging the top of the app with a mouse or a finger to the bottom of the screen.

- A Windows 8–style app that is hidden by the desktop can be closed by pointing at the **Start** button in the lower-left corner of the screen and moving the mouse up the left edge of the screen to display the apps that are running. Right-click the app you want to close, and click **Close**. While it's possible to do this with touch, you most frequently end up opening the app instead of closing it.

- An app opened on the desktop can be closed by clicking or tapping the **Close** button in the upper-right corner of the window .

▷▷ Use an App

In Windows 8.1, when apps are started they are displayed in two ways: the classic window similar to those in Windows 7 and earlier versions that use the desktop, and Windows 8–style screens, which are new.

Use Classic Windows

Many of the apps that you will use with Windows 8.1 open a classic window on the desktop, as shown with the Microsoft Word 2013 window in Figure 1-9. This window has a number of features that are common to other desktop windows and that are referred to in the remainder of this book. Not all windows have all of the features shown in the figure, and some windows have features unique to them. Also, some of the details in this window, not described here, are described elsewhere in the book.

- The **Quick Access toolbar** holds tools you often use, such as New Folder for creating a new folder.

- The **details pane** displays the principal objects in the window, such as documents, images, files, folders, and apps.
- The **title bar** is used to drag the window around the desktop, and may contain the name of the app or folder in the window.
- The **Minimize button** decreases the size of the window so that you see it only as a task on the taskbar.
- The **Maximize/Restore button** increases the size of the window so that it fills the screen. When the screen is maximized, this button becomes the **Restore button**, which, when tapped or clicked, returns the screen to its previous size.
- The **Close button** shuts down and/or closes the app, folder, or file in the window.
- The **window border** separates the window from the desktop, and can be used to size the window horizontally or vertically by dragging a border.
- The **sizing handle** in each corner of the window allows it to be sized diagonally, increasing or decreasing the window's height and width together when you drag a handle.
- The **ribbon** contains tools related to the contents of the window. Click or tap a tool to use it. The specific parts of the ribbon are not displayed until one of the related tabs is clicked or tapped.
- **Tabs** allow you to select from several different of groups of ribbon tools.

TIP Double-clicking a window's title bar toggles between maximizing and restoring a window to its previous size.

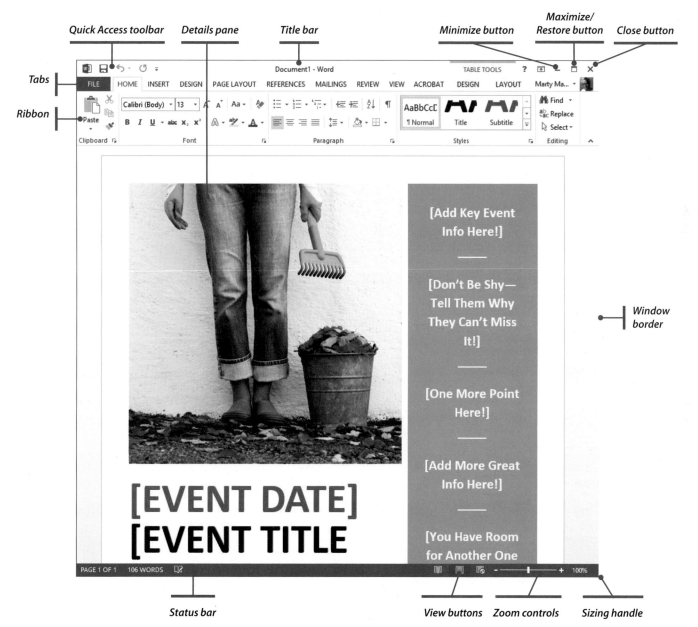

Quick Access toolbar   Details pane   Title bar   Minimize button   Maximize/Restore button   Close button

Tabs

Ribbon

Window border

Status bar   View buttons   Zoom controls   Sizing handle

Figure 1-9: The Microsoft Word 2013 window has many features common to other app windows opened on the desktop.

Use Windows 8–Style Screens

Windows 8–style screens, shown with the Maps app in Figure 1-10, initially fill the entire screen, and its controls are only available when you want them. To display the *App bar* with the controls, as shown in Figure 1-10:

- **Touch** Swipe up from the bottom outside the screen.
- **Mouse** Right-click an inactive area (not a link) of the display.
- **Keyboard** Press WINDOWS+Z.

To hide the App bar and its controls:

- **Touch** Tap in an inactive area of the app.
- **Mouse** Click an inactive area of the app.
- **Keyboard** Press WINDOWS+Z.

The controls on the App bar are unique to the app being run. The controls for Internet Explorer are described in Chapter 4.

 TIP The Settings pane on the right, opened from Charms, provides additional controls and options for an open Windows 8–style app.

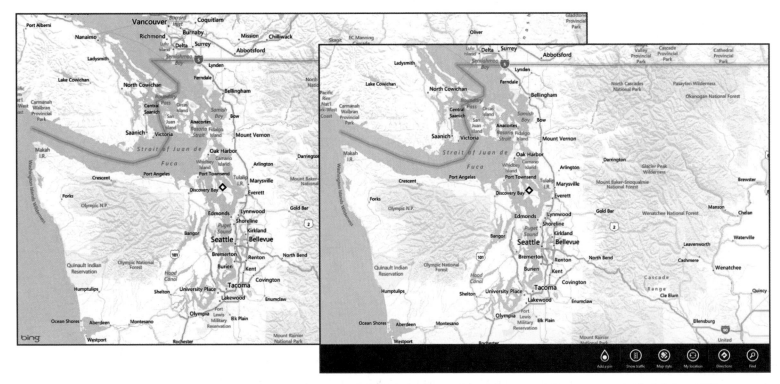

Figure 1-10: Windows 8–style applications initially fill the entire screen with their information without controls, as you see on the left here. When controls are enabled, an App bar appears at the bottom of the screen, and sometimes an options bar at the top.

Navigate the Windows Desktop

When multiple windows and other objects are open on the desktop, navigating among them and displaying the one(s) you want could be difficult. Figure 1-11, for example, shows such a situation. Windows 8.1 has a number of features to handle this:

- **Aero Peek**   To see what's hidden on the screen
- **Aero Shake**   To minimize other open windows
- **Aero Snaps**   To resize and position windows
- **Jump lists**   To see recent files and app options
- **Taskbar previews**   To see what is open in an app

Aero Peek

Aero Peek allows you to see what's hidden on the desktop behind all the open windows. You can do this on a temporary (or "peek") basis or a more long-lasting one.

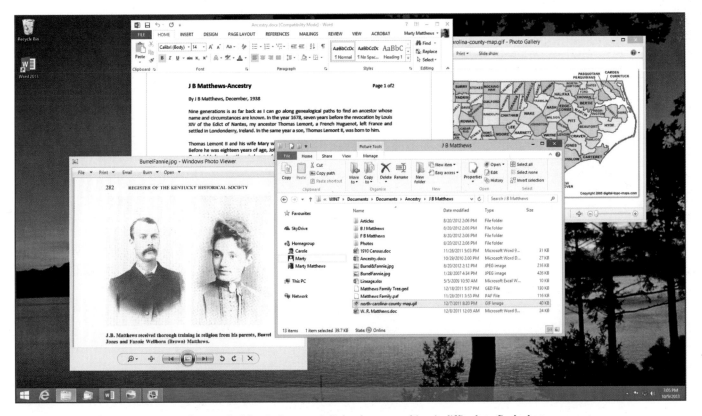

Figure 1-11: A screen can become cluttered with windows and dialog boxes, making it difficult to find what you want.

NOTE If your Aero Peek is off by default, turn it on from the desktop by opening the taskbar's Properties menu (right-clicking or pressing and holding for a moment on the taskbar) and then selecting (clicking or tapping) **Properties**. In the Taskbar Properties dialog box that opens, on the Taskbar tab, select **Use Peek to Preview the Desktop** so it has a check mark, and then select **OK**.

- **Temporarily peek** at the desktop:

  Move the mouse pointer to ("mouse over") the **Show Desktop** area on the far lower-right corner of the taskbar (must be done with the mouse). All the open windows will become transparent ("glass") frames, as you can see in Figure 1-12, and you can then see what was hidden on the desktop, such as the items in the center of Figure 1-12.

- **Return** to the original desktop after a temporary peek:

  Move the mouse pointer away from the Show Desktop area. All the open windows will reappear, as shown in Figure 1-11.

Figure 1-12: With Aero Peek, all open windows become transparent.

- **Hide** all open windows so you can see and work on the desktop:

  Select (click or tap) the **Show Desktop** area on the far right of the taskbar. All the open windows will be hidden, and you can move the mouse around the entire desktop.

- **Unhide** all open windows and return to the original desktop:

  Select (click or tap) the **Show Desktop** area on the far right of the taskbar. All the open windows will be returned to their original position.

Aero Shake

Aero Shake allows you to minimize all open windows except for the one you are "shaking." To "shake" a window:

- Point to the title bar of the window you want to remain open with either the mouse or your finger. Press and hold the mouse button or your finger on the title bar while moving your hand rapidly to the left and then to the right, as if you were shaking it.

  –Or–

- Select the window you want to keep displayed. Press and hold **WINDOWS** while pressing **HOME**.

To return the minimized windows to their original size and position, repeat the same steps.

Aero Snaps

Aero Snaps "snaps" a window to various parts of the screen, a function similar to the Maximize/Restore button (which can still be used) on the title bar of a selected, floating (not already maximized) window, with some useful additions:

- **Maximize** a floating window:

Point within the title bar of a window, not on its edge, and drag it to the top of the screen. The window will be maximized to fill the screen.

–Or–

Press and hold **WINDOWS** while pressing **UP ARROW**.

- **Restore** a maximized window (independent of how it was maximized):

Double-click or double-tap the title bar.

–Or–

Select the window you want to be restored. Press and hold **WINDOWS** while pressing the **DOWN ARROW**.

- **Vertically maximize** a floating window while not spreading it out horizontally:

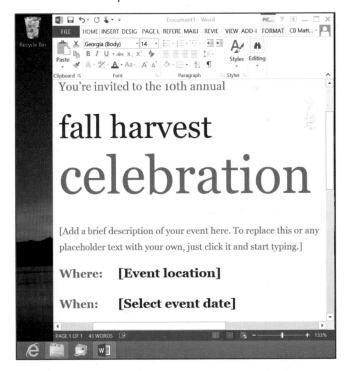

Point to the top or bottom *edge* of a window, and drag it to the corresponding edge of the screen. The window will be vertically maximized.

–Or–

Select the window you want to be maximized. Press and hold **WINDOWS** while pressing **SHIFT+UP ARROW**.

- **Restore** a vertically maximized window:

Point to the top or bottom *edge* of a window, and drag it toward the center of the screen. The window will be resized as you drag it down.

–Or–

Select the window you want to be maximized. Press and hold **WINDOWS** while pressing **SHIFT+DOWN ARROW**.

- **Left-align** a floating window and have it occupy 50 percent of the screen:

Point to the title bar of a window, and drag it to the corresponding edge of the screen. When the mouse pointer (not the window's edge) reaches the edge of the screen, the window will fill the left 50 percent of the screen.

–Or–

Select the window you want to be aligned. Press and hold **WINDOWS** while pressing **LEFT ARROW**.

- **Right-align** a floating window and have it occupy 50 percent of the screen:

Point at the title bar of a window, and drag it to the corresponding edge of the screen. When the mouse pointer reaches the edge of the screen, the window will fill the right 50 percent of the screen.

–Or–

Select the window you want to be aligned. Press and hold **WINDOWS** while pressing the **RIGHT ARROW**.

- **Restore** a window that is filling 50 percent of the screen: Double-click or double-tap the title bar *twice*.

–Or–

Select the window you want to be restored. Press and hold **WINDOWS** while pressing the key opposite to the one used to enlarge it.

–Or–

Point at the title bar of a window, and drag it away from the window edge it was aligned to.

Jump Lists

Jump lists are a context or pop-up menu for application icons on the taskbar. When you right-click or hold your finger on an app icon on the taskbar, a menu will appear above it containing a list of recent files or webpages, as well as options to close the app, pin or unpin it from the taskbar, and open the app with a blank file or webpage.

Taskbar Previews

Taskbar previews are a miniature image, or thumbnail, of an open window attached to a taskbar icon. When you mouse over an icon on the taskbar (there is not a consistent way to do this with touch, but a stylus held a small fraction of an inch off the screen will do it), a thumbnail of the open window or windows related to that icon will temporarily appear, as shown next. If you then move the mouse to the thumbnail, a temporary full-sized image will appear (see Figure 1-13). When you move the mouse off the thumbnail or the icon, the corresponding image

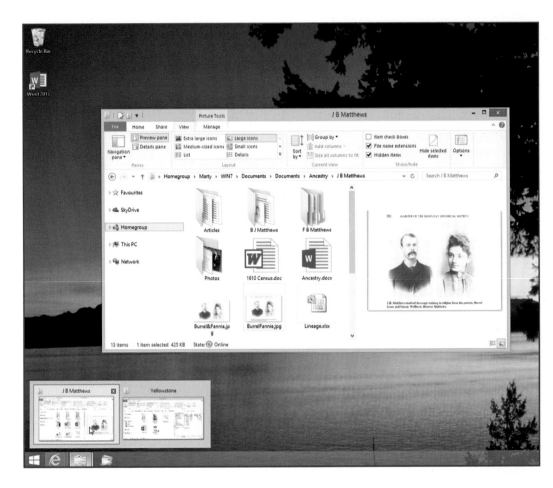

Figure 1-13: The natural instinct is to move the mouse from the thumbnail to the temporary larger window to open it, but that causes both images to disappear. You must click the thumbnail.

will disappear. Open a window by clicking its thumbnail. Close a window by clicking the **Close** button on the thumbnail.

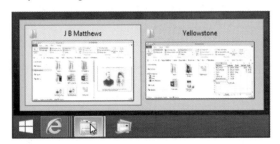

TIP Look at the icons on the taskbar in Figure 1-13. It is obvious by its bright highlight that the File Explorer icon is selected and the one displaying the thumbnails. You can also tell that the Internet Explorer icon, by its lesser highlight and border, has open windows, while Windows Live Mail does not.

✔ QuickFacts

Split a Windows 8.1 App

One of the benefits of the Windows 8–style apps is that they fill the entire screen with their display and information, which is great until you want to look at another app while you are looking at the first app. Windows 8.1 fixed that problem by allowing you split the screen with a Windows 8–style app using only half of the screen. You can run another Windows 8–style app in the other half, or you can display the desktop with one or more windows there, as you can see in Figure 1-14. To split a Windows 8–style app screen:

1. Start the app from the Start screen or Apps view as you normally would.

2. Open the desktop, move the mouse to the lower-left corner, and then move it up the left edge to display the Windows 8–style apps that are running at that moment.

3. Right-click or touch and hold for a moment the app that you want to split to open its context menu.

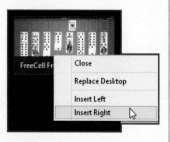

4. Select either **Insert Left** or **Insert Right** to place the app on either the left or right and use up one half of the screen.

5. Repeat the first four steps to display another Windows 8–style app in the other half of the screen or open one or more desktop apps there.

6. If you want to have the app you are displaying take more or less than half of the screen, use the mouse or your finger to drag the three dots in the center of the screen either left or right.

7. Close a split app in the same way you would close any other app.

▷▷ End Your Windows Session

You can end your Windows session from opposite lower corners of the screen in either the desktop or Start screen and in several ways, depending on what you want to do.

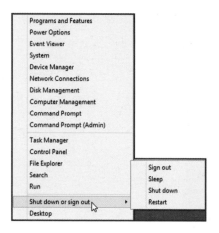

End from the Left

In the lower-left corner of either screen (this cannot be done with touch):

1. Right-click the **Start** button in the lower left or press **WINDOWS+X** to open the System menu (discussed further in Chapter 2).

2. Click **Shut Down Or Sign Out** or use the arrow keys on the keyboard to select that option and press **ENTER** to open the Shut Down menu.

3. Click the Shut Down option you want or use the arrow keys on the keyboard to select the option and press **ENTER**. See "Shut Down Options" later in this chapter.

Figure 1-14: By splitting a Windows 8–style app screen, you can look at two apps at the same time.

End from the Right

On the right side of either screen with touch, the mouse, or the keyboard:

1. Swipe to the left from outside the screen on the right, point the mouse at the lower right or upper right and move the mouse up or down the right edge, or press **WINDOWS+C** to open Charms.

2. Tap, click, or use the arrow keys on the keyboard and press **ENTER** to open **Settings**.

3. Tap, click, or use the arrow keys on the keyboard and press **ENTER** to open **Power**.

4. Tap, click, or use the arrow keys on the keyboard and press **ENTER** to select the Shut Down option you want.

Shut Down Options

The meanings of the various Shut Down options are as follows:

- **Shut Down** Closes all active apps and network connections and signs out all users so that no information is lost, and then turns off the computer (if it is done automatically) or tells you when it is safe for you to turn it off. When you start up the computer, you must reload your apps and data and reestablish your network connection (done by Windows) to get back to where you were when you shut down.

- **Restart** Closes all active apps and network connections and signs out all users so that no information is lost. Windows is then shut down and restarted. This is usually done when there is a problem that restarting Windows will fix or to complete setting up some apps.

- **Sleep** Leaves all active apps, network connections, and your user account active and in memory, but also saves the state of everything on disk. Your computer is then put into a low-power state that allows you to quickly resume working exactly where you were when you left. In a desktop computer, it is left running in this low-power state for as long as you wish. In a mobile computer (laptops, notebooks, netbooks, tablets, and slates), after three hours or if the battery is low, your session is again saved to disk and the computer is turned off. When you restart your computer after an extended "sleep," the settings and apps from the previous session are reloaded.

- **Sign Out** Saves your current settings and status and work of active apps to disk and closes them down so nothing is lost or left running and then asks if someone else would like to sign in. (This is only available from the System menu on the left.)

Resume from Sleep

There are several ways to resume operation after a computer has been put into Sleep mode, which depend on your type of computer, how it was put to sleep, and how long it has been sleeping. A computer can be put into Sleep mode either by your action, as described earlier in this section, by closing the lid on a mobile computer, or as the result of the computer not being used for a period of time, which is controlled in the Power Options (see Chapter 9). The ways to resume include the following:

- Press any key on your keyboard, move the mouse, or touch the screen (if you have a touch screen). This works with most desktop computers and mobile computers that have only been asleep a short time.

- Quickly press and release the power button on your computer. This works with most recent computers of all types. Holding down the computer's power button for very long will, in most cases, either fully turn off the computer or cause it to restart (shut fully down and then restart).

- Open the top. This works with most mobile computers that have a flip top.

TIP There are two distinct schools of thought on whether you should use Sleep or Shut Down when you leave the computer for any length of time. The primary considerations are security and power usage. Older computers used less power running in Sleep mode than the power consumed during shutting down and starting up. New computers have reduced the power consumed during these events, so it is now a toss-up. From a security standpoint, there is no security like having your computer completely turned off. A computer is also fairly secure in Sleep mode, but it is theoretically possible for a hacker to awaken it. The choice becomes a matter of preference. I turn my computers off; my wife leaves hers on.

3. From the Start screen, open **Charms** and select **Settings | Help**. Internet Explorer will open and display an online Windows Help page that will be different depending on what was on the screen when you opened Charms, like what is shown in Figure 1-15 that was opened from the Start screen.

4. Select the option that is correct for you. This will open a series of pages unique to the options you pick.

▷▷ Get Help

Windows 8.1 Help provides both built-in documentation and online assistance that you can use to learn how to work with Windows 8.1. For example, to use Help:

1. From the desktop, open **Charms** and select **Settings | Help**. The Windows Help and Support windows will open.

2. Select the option that is correct for you. This will open a series of options that in turn will open additional windows.

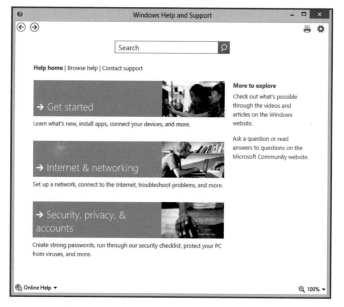

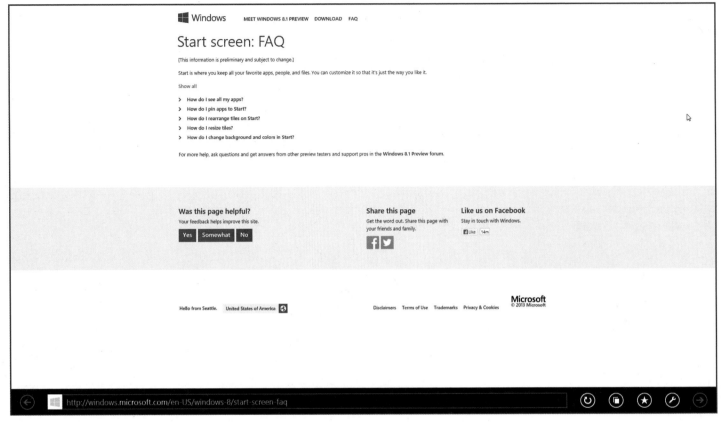

Figure 1-15: The Windows 8.1 Help page provides options for working with what else is on the screen.

Page Picks and Chooses What She Needs to Learn

In truth, there is far more about my computer that I don't know than what I know, but I get along pretty well and can do what I want to do. I started out with the idea that I had to learn all about my computer, but quickly found that was a tall order, and so changed my objective to learning just what I needed to know to do writing, e-mailing, online banking, a small amount of shopping, surfing the Internet, and managing my pictures. It works well and is a great asset ... and I'm always curious about what I don't know and want to know more.

Page G. B., 71, Washington

Chapter 2

Customizing Windows 8.1

Windows 8.1 has many features that can be customized. You can keep the default setup, or you can change the look and feel of the Start screen and desktop, including rearranging, adding, and removing objects, as well as how apps and system features, such as sound, operate. This chapter will explore all of these features.

CHANGE THE LOOK OF WINDOWS 8.1

An important aspect of Windows that leads to your enjoyment and efficient use of it is how it looks. Windows 8.1 provides significant flexibility in this area. You can change how the screen looks, including the Start screen, the desktop, and the Windows apps such as File Explorer.

▶▶ Modify the Start Screen

The Start screen is the focal point of Windows 8.1. It contains *tiles* that represent *apps*, programs or applications such as Internet Explorer and Microsoft Word that you can run on your computer. The Start screen is the primary place where apps are started and control functions are accessed. Because of its central focus, it is very important that it be tailored to your needs, both for efficiency and to reduce possible irritation. The changes you can make to the Start screen are many and include the following:

- Rearrange the tiles so the ones you use most are readily available.
- Add tiles that aren't already shown on the Start screen.

- Remove tiles that you don't often use.
- Change the shape and content of a tile.
- Group tiles that relate to each other.
- Change the Start screen's background.

Rearrange Tiles

Rearranging the tiles is easy—just move them (drag with either the mouse or your finger) where you want them. The tiles on the left should be the ones you use most often, and so you should move the tiles around to facilitate that. Figure 2-1 shows an arrangement that works for me.

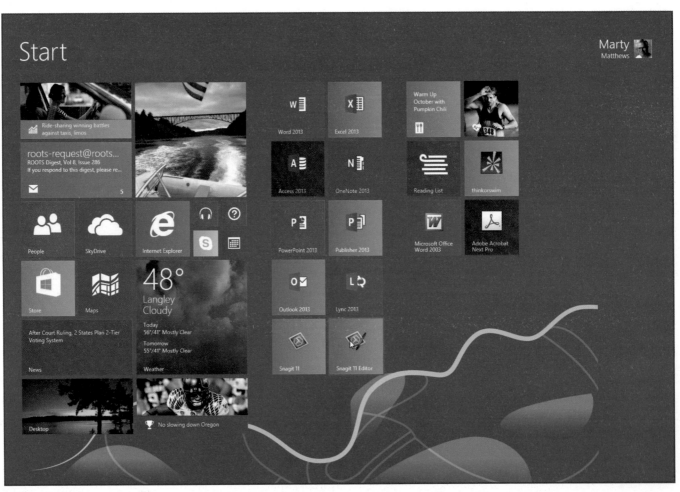

Figure 2-1: The tiles on the Start screen should reflect what you use on the computer, as this does for me.

TIP Have patience while rearranging tiles. They tend to jump into particular spots, not always the one you want them in. Keep trying and they will eventually go where you want them.

Add Tiles

When a new app is installed on your computer, its tile may or may not appear on the Start screen. All apps, though, are displayed in *Apps view* (see Figure 2-2), and you may add those that are not initially there to the Start screen. The tiles that you initially see on the Start screen have been *pinned* there, much as you would put a "sticky note" on some surface or tack something to a corkboard. You can add tiles to the Start screen from the apps that are installed on your computer and shown in Apps view. You can, of course, also install new apps.

Figure 2-2: Apps view displays all the apps installed on your computer.

To pin an already installed app to the Start screen:

1. Open Apps view from the Start screen:

   - **Mouse** Click the down arrow in a circle on the lower-right area of the Start screen.

   - **Touch** Swipe up from the vertical middle of the screen.

   - **Keyboard** Press CTRL+TAB.

2. Open the App bar for the app you want to pin to the Start screen:

   - **Mouse** Right-click the app.

   - **Touch** Press and hold on the app.

   - **Keyboard** Use the arrow keys to select the app and press the CONTEXT MENU key.

The App bar opens with options related to the app, including Pin To Start.

 TIP The contents of the App bar depend on the app selected. Windows 8.1 apps have only Pin To Start and Uninstall, while desktop apps add several desktop-related options.

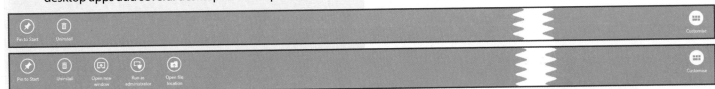

3. Select (tap, click, or use the arrow keys and press ENTER) **Pin To Start**. The app will now appear on the Start screen until you remove it.

To pin a new app to the Start screen:

- Install the new app as you are directed. It will be added automatically to the Apps view, and then you can use the preceding steps to add it to the Start screen.

Remove Tiles

To remove tiles from the Start screen, open the App bar as you did in the last section (by right-clicking, or pressing and swiping down, or using the arrow keys and pressing ENTER) for the app you want to remove and select **Unpin From Start**. To remove several apps at one time, select them all and then select **Unpin From Start**.

 TIP App tiles that you remove from the Start screen with Unpin are still installed on the computer and are available in Apps view. It might make sense to remove all tiles that you don't see an immediate need for and then, as you find you are using some you removed, add them back.

Change Tiles

The tiles on the Start screen can be made larger or smaller and can display real-time information in the tile (called "being live"). For example, the options available for the Weather app allow you to make the tile smaller or larger and to turn off its live display. To change a tile, open the App bar and select the options that you want, as you can see in the Finance tile with live data.

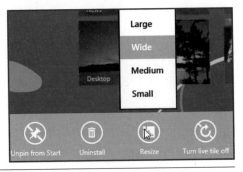

NOTE The available tile sizes are Large, which is a full column and two rows; Wide, which is a full column and one row; Medium, which is half a column and one row; and Small, which is a quarter of a column and half a row.

Customize the Start Screen

The Start screen can be customized by grouping tiles, by naming the groups, by rearranging groups, and by changing the background image and colors on the Start screen.

1. Begin by displaying the Customize option on the right of the App bar:

   - **Mouse**   Right-click a blank area of the screen.
   - **Touch**   Swipe up from outside the bottom of the screen.
   - **Keyboard**   Press WINDOWS+Z.

2. Tap or click **Customize** or press ENTER.

Group Tiles

The Start screen, by default, displays the app tiles in several random groupings. You can change the contents of these groupings by rearranging, adding, and removing tiles, as described earlier in this chapter. You can also create new groups, reorder groups, and name groups, as you can see in Figure 2-3. To create a new group:

1. Add and remove the apps on the Start screen so that you are left with only the apps that you will primarily use.

2. Move (drag) a tile that you want in the new group either to the blank area between groups or to the far right of all groups to establish a new group in that location. A

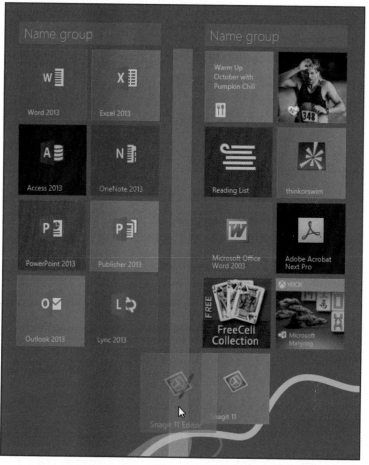

*Figure 2-3: **Grouping and naming tiles on the Start screen will help you find related apps.***

grey vertical bar will appear where the new group will be established as shown in Figure 2-3.

3. Move the remaining tiles that are to be in the new group above, below, or in between existing tiles.

Name Groups

1. While the Start screen is in Customize mode, select the name text box above the group you want to name.

2. Type the name you want, and press **ENTER**.

Reorder Groups

1. When you have created the groups with the tiles you want in each, you can change the left-to-right order of the groups by first zooming out or shrinking the Start screen groups:

   • **Mouse**   By clicking the minimize icon in the far lower-right corner.

   • **Touch**   By bringing two fingers together on the screen.

   • **Keyboard**   By pressing **CTRL**+ minus sign key (–).

2. Drag with the mouse, your finger, or the arrow keys one or more groups on the screen so they are in the order you want them.

TIP When using touch, drag the group to be moved toward the top of the screen and then drag it where you want it, as you see being done with the Microsoft group here:

Change the Start Screen Background

The Start screen can be changed to incorporate one of several patterns and one of a number of color pairs.

1. Open **Charms** and select **Settings | Personalize** near the top of the Settings pane. The Personalize Pane will fill the Settings area on the right of the screen.

TIP You can return to the default background with the settings shown in the next illustration—the mouse is pointing to the default pattern, although yours may have been different.

2. Select several of the pattern choices and several of the color pairs and observe the effect in the portion of the Start screen you can see.

3. Note that one of the pattern choices is your desktop background, the default, or something different if you have previously chosen one. Try it and go back and forth between the desktop and the Start screen. It creates a smooth transition. Figure 2-4 shows my Start screen with the same image I'm using on my desktop.

4. Based on what you have seen, select the pattern and color pair you want to use in the Start screen.

▷▷ Customize the Desktop

Much of the desktop is controlled by the Personalization window, as shown in Figure 2-5. Open it to make many of the

Figure 2-4: You can use your desktop background on your Start screen, the default, or one you have chosen.

changes in this section. (Several of the features controlled in the Personalization window, such as sounds and the mouse pointer, are discussed on their own later in this chapter.)

1. From the Start screen, select the **Desktop** tile to display it. Open the desktop's context menu (right-click or press, hold, and release an area of the desktop without an icon, or press the context menu key on a keyboard).

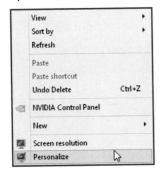

2. Select **Personalize**. The Personalization window opens.

Change the Desktop Themes and Colors

You can use any picture, color, or pattern you want for your desktop background. Windows 8.1 comes with several alternatives, and you can download many more. From the Personalization window:

 TIP You can control many facets of Windows 8.1 just by changing the theme.

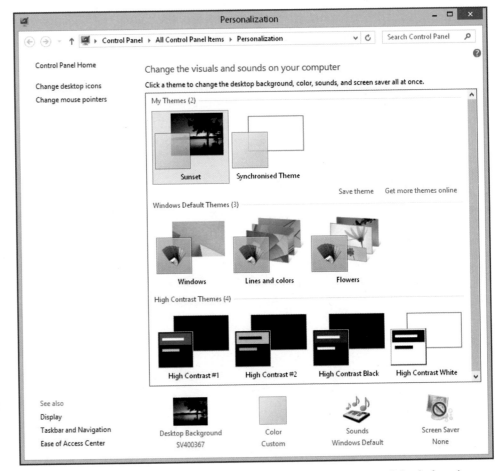

Figure 2-5: *The Personalization window lets you change the appearance of the desktop in Windows 8.1.*

1. Review the themes that are available with Windows 8.1 (or select **Get More Themes Online** to view Microsoft's online library). Select the theme you want to use. With each theme you can select a desktop background and a window color, as well as the sounds used and a screen saver.

2. Select **Desktop Background**. Select the **Picture Location** down arrow, and select a source of pictures (see Figure 2-6),

or select **Browse** and navigate to a location on your computer where you have a picture you want to use (Chapter 3 explains how to navigate on your computer). Select the picture or pictures you want. If you select several pictures, select the time period between changing pictures.

3. Select **Save Changes** to close the Desktop Background window.

4. At the top of the themes list, select **Save Theme** to save any changes to a current theme or to save a new theme.

5. In the Save Theme As dialog box, name the theme, and select **Save**.

 NOTE You can select a new picture and/or theme and almost immediately see the changes on the desktop. If you don't like the changes, select a different picture or theme.

Change the Resolution and Text Size

Depending on your computer and monitor, you can display Windows 8.1 with various resolutions and text sizes. You can select the text and object size for only specific areas of text in the Display window and then go on to adjust the resolution. From the Personalization window:

1. Select **Display** in the lower left. The Display window will appear, as shown in Figure 2-7.

2. Select the size of all items by dragging the slider between Smaller and Larger (Smaller is the default) and/or select the text area down arrow, and select the size you want and whether you want it bold. When you are ready, select **Apply**.

3. Select **Adjust Resolution** in the upper left. If you have more than one display device, select **Identify**. The display's number appears on each screen. In the Display drop-down list, select the display whose resolution you want to change.

4. Select the **Resolution** drop-down arrow. Move the slider up or down to adjust the resolution. (You can try this and if you don't like it, come back and change it.)

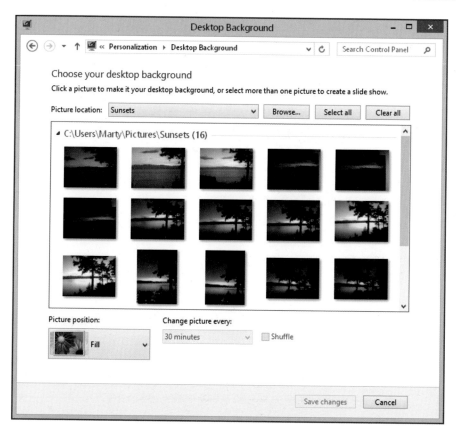

Figure 2-6: *Browse through your photos and see how the ones you like the best look as a desktop background.*

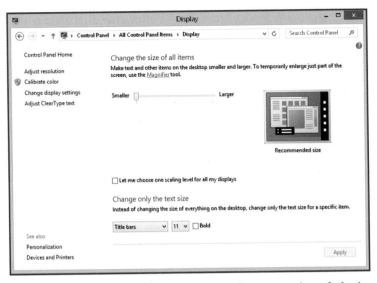

Figure 2-7: *Increasing the text and object size lets you see less of what's on the screen, but what you see is larger and possibly easier to read.*

 TIP Each resolution is tuned to a particular screen style, for example, widescreen (1600 x 900 or above) as dynamically previewed in the upper part of the window.

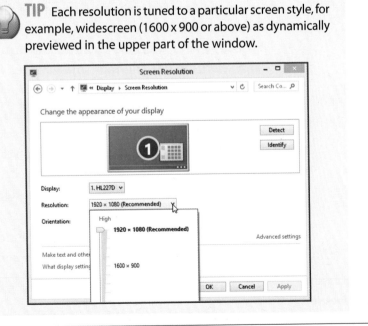

5. Select **Apply** to save any changes, and then select the **Back** arrow in the upper-left area until you are back to the Personalization window.

NOTE The Advanced Settings link at the right of the Screen Resolution window provides access to settings that are specific to your display hardware.

Alter the Appearance of Objects

You can alter the appearance of windows, icons, and dialog boxes, changing their shapes and colors, as well as the font used in those objects. From the Personalization window:

1. Select **Color** at the bottom center of the window. The Color And Appearance window will open.

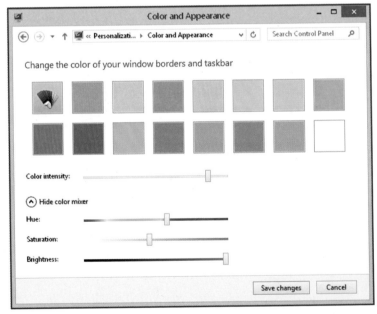

2. Select a different color scheme, if desired; change the color intensity; or mix your own color (click **Show Color Mixer**).

3. Select **Save Changes** to return to the Personalization window and select **Close** in the upper-right corner to close it.

Add App Icons to the Desktop

When you first use Windows 8.1, you will only have a couple of icons on the desktop, including the Recycle Bin, which is the only one Windows puts there by default. Some computer manufacturers may include additional icons. The purpose of having app icons on the desktop, called *shortcuts,* is to be able to easily start the apps by double-selecting their icons. You can have Windows app icons as well as other app icons on the desktop.

Add Windows App Icons

To add Windows app icons, such as for User's Files, to the desktop and customize them:

1. Open the desktop's context menu, and select **Personalize** to open the Personalization window.

2. Select **Change Desktop Icons** on the upper left to open the Desktop Icon Settings dialog box.

3. Select up to five icons that you want to have on the desktop. For example, you might add User's Files. The others you probably use less often, and they can be accessed quickly from the Start screen.

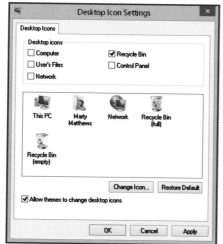

4. To customize a Windows app icon, select the icon and select **Change Icon**. A dialog box will appear displaying alternative icons.

5. Select the alternative you want, and select **OK**.

6. When you are satisfied with the Windows app icons you have selected and/or changed, select **OK**. Your new icon will appear on the desktop.

7. Select **Close** to close the Personalization window.

Add Other App Icons

To add other app icons to the desktop:

1. Select the **Start** screen and open Apps view.

2. Open the App bar for the app and its icon you want on the desktop, and select **Open File Location**.

3. Open the context menu for the highlighted file and select **Send To | Desktop (Create Shortcut)**. The app's icon will appear on the desktop.

Change Desktop Icons

When you have the icons that you want on the desktop, you can change the size of the icons, their order, and their alignment through the desktop's context menu.

Open the desktop's context menu, and select **View** to open the View submenu.

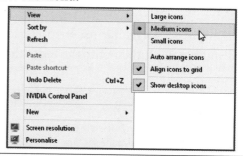

Resize Icons

Windows 8.1 gives you the choice of three different sizes of icons. The size you choose is a function of both the resolution you are using on your display and your personal preference. By default (the way Windows is set up when first used), your icons will be medium size. From the View submenu:

Select each of the sizes to see which is best for you.

Align Icons

You can move desktop icons where you want them; by default, Windows 8.1 will align your icons to an invisible grid. If you don't like that, from the View submenu:

Select **Align Icons To Grid** to clear the check mark and allow any arrangement on the desktop that you want.

If you should move your icons around and then change your mind, reopen the View submenu and:

Select **Align Icons To Grid** to reselect it. Your icons will jump to the invisible grid and be aligned.

Arrange Icons

By default, there is no particular order to the icons on the desktop, and you can move them into the order that suits you.

However, you can have Windows arrange and sort the icons in several ways. From the View submenu:

Select **Auto Arrange Icons**. By default, the icons will be placed in a column alphabetically by name, except that the system icons (Computer, Recycle Bin, Internet Explorer, User's Files, Control Panel, and Network) will be at the top.

If you want to change the order in which Windows 8.1 arranges desktop icons:

1. Open the desktop's context menu, and select **Sort By** to open that submenu.
2. Select one of the options to have the icons sorted in that manner.

Rename Desktop Icons

When you add app icons to the desktop, they may have the word "Shortcut" in their names, or they may have names that are not meaningful to you. To rename desktop icons:

1. Open the app icon's context menu, and select **Rename**.
2. Type the new name that you want to use, and press **ENTER**.

▷▷ Change the Taskbar

The taskbar at the bottom of the Windows 8.1 desktop screen has five standard areas: the Start button, pinned apps on the left, running apps in the middle, and the notification area and the Show Desktop button on the right. You can change the taskbar by moving and sizing it and by changing its properties.

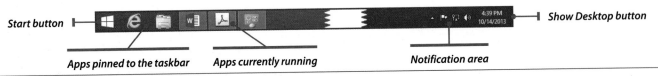

Start button — Apps pinned to the taskbar — Apps currently running — Notification area — Show Desktop button

Figure 2-8: A taskbar can be moved to any of the four sides of the screen.

Move and Size the Taskbar

You can move the taskbar to any of the four sides of the screen. Do this by dragging any empty area of the taskbar to another edge. For example, Figure 2-8 shows the taskbar moved to the right edge of the screen.

You can size the taskbar by moving the inner edge (the top edge when the taskbar is on the bottom) in or out. Here is a taskbar at double its normal size.

In either case, the taskbar must be unlocked. See "Change Taskbar Properties," next, to do this.

▷▷ Change Taskbar Properties

A number of taskbar features can be changed through the Taskbar And Navigation Properties dialog box (see Figure 2-9).

Open Taskbar Properties

Open the taskbar's context menu, and select **Properties**. The Taskbar Properties dialog box appears with the Taskbar tab selected. (Select **Apply** to test a change without closing the dialog box.)

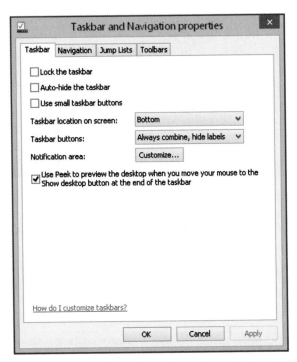

Figure 2-9: You will use the taskbar often, so it should look and behave the way you want.

Unlock the Taskbar

Your taskbar may be locked, which will prevent it from being moved or resized. If yours is locked, you should unlock it for the work in this chapter.

Select **Lock The Taskbar** to remove the check mark and unlock the taskbar.

Hide the Taskbar

Hiding the taskbar means that it is not displayed unless you move the mouse to the edge of the screen containing the taskbar. By default, it is displayed.

Select **Auto-Hide The Taskbar** to select the check box and hide the taskbar.

Use Small Buttons

If you want to conserve desktop space and you have good eyesight, you can make the taskbar about half as tall as it is by default.

Select **Use Small Taskbar Buttons** to select the check box and make the icons smaller.

Customize Taskbar Buttons

There are three choices for customizing taskbar buttons:

- Always combine similar items and hide the labels, such as app names. This is the default.
- Combine similar items when the taskbar is full, but display the labels.
- Never combine similar items under any circumstances and display the labels. This option was used in the tall taskbar illustration earlier in this chapter.

For example, combining similar items puts all Microsoft Word documents in one icon or all Internet pages in one icon so that they take up less room on the taskbar. By default, similar items are combined.

Select the **Taskbar Buttons** down arrow, and make your choice.

Use Aero Peek

As you saw in Chapter 1, Aero Peek allows you to see the desktop and what is under the open windows on the screen when you move the mouse to the Show Desktop button on the far right of the taskbar. If yours is turned off (not checked):

Select **Use Peek** to add the check mark and turn on this capability.

Close Taskbar Properties

After you've made any of these changes to the taskbar, select **OK** to enable them and close the Taskbar And Navigation Properties dialog box.

▷▷ Change the Notification Area

The notification area on the right of the taskbar can also be changed through the Taskbar And Navigation Properties dialog box (see "Change Taskbar Properties" for instructions on displaying the dialog box). The notification area, which can get crowded at times, contains app icons put there by Windows and other apps. You can control which icons are displayed along with their notifications, which icons are hidden while their notifications

are displayed, or which icons are not there at all. To change the notification area:

Select **Customize** opposite Notification Area on the Taskbar tab. The Notification Area Icons window will appear, as shown in Figure 2-10.

Customize Notification Icons

To customize the behavior of icons in the notification area:

Select the drop-down list opposite the icon you want to change, and select the behavior you want.

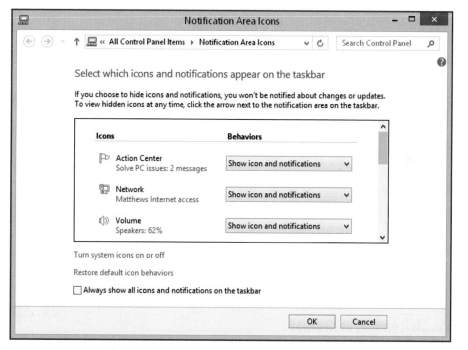

*Figure 2-10: **Turn off the notification area icons that are not useful to you.***

Display System Icons

Up to six system icons—Keyboard (on computers with touch), Action Center, Network, Volume, Power (on mobile computers), and Clock—are shown in the notification area by default. You can turn them off if you wish.

1. Select **Turn System Icons On Or Off**.
2. Select the drop-down list opposite an icon name, and select **Off** to not display it.
3. When you have made the changes you want, select **OK**.

Close Taskbar Properties

After you've made any of these changes to the notification area, select **OK** to enable them and close the Notification Area Icons window. Select **OK** again to close the Taskbar Properties dialog box.

Permanently Pin Icons to the Taskbar

Windows 8.1 provides the ability to permanently "pin," or attach, frequently used app icons to the taskbar starting from the left. Once there, the icons are visible (unless you hide the taskbar), and the related app can be started by selecting it with a single click or tap until you unpin it. By default, Windows 8.1 has two icons pinned to the taskbar: Internet Explorer and File Explorer. You can pin additional icons, you can remove those that are currently pinned, and you can rearrange the current icons.

Pin an Icon to the Taskbar

After you have used Windows 8.1 for a while, you may find that you use an app more often than others and would like to have it more immediately available on the desktop. This is what pinning to the taskbar is for. You can do that by either:

Locating the app icon in File Explorer, the Start screen, or on the desktop; opening its context menu; and selecting **Pin To Taskbar**.

–Or–

Starting a desktop app in any of the ways described in Chapter 1. When it has started, open its icon on the taskbar's context menu, and select **Pin This Program To Taskbar**.

> **NOTE** You can pin a file or folder to the File Explorer icon on the taskbar by opening File Explorer, navigating to the file or folder, and moving it to the File Explorer icon on the taskbar. Access the pinned file or folder by opening the File Explorer icon's context menu and selecting it.

Remove an Icon Pinned to the Taskbar

To remove an app icon pinned to the taskbar:

Open the icon's context menu and select **Unpin This Program From Taskbar**.

Rearrange Icons Pinned to the Taskbar

The icons that are pinned to the taskbar can be moved around and placed in any order.

Drag icons pinned to the taskbar to where you want them.

Change the File Explorer Layout

File Explorer is used to locate and access files stored on your computer. The discussion about using File Explorer is the main focus of Chapter 3. Here, where we're talking about customizing the look and feel of Windows 8.1, we'll briefly talk about customizing

File Explorer. The File Explorer window shown in Figure 2-11 (as well as the image in Chapter 1) has a full set of panes turned on. By default, the preview pane is not visible. You can turn these panes on and turn other panes off using the File Explorer ribbon.

The ribbon has five tabs (four of which are shown in Figure 2-11). The File, Home, and Share tabs will be discussed in Chapter 3. Here we'll talk about changing the app's layout using the View tab.

TIP If you don't see a ribbon at the top of your File Explorer, as shown in Figure 2-11, it may be turned off. You can turn it on by selecting the downward-pointing arrowhead on upper-right area next to the question mark.

Open File Explorer

File Explorer can be opened in either the Start screen or the desktop, both of which take you to File Explorer on the desktop. By default, though, File Explorer is not pinned to the Start screen, so you must use Apps view.

From the Start screen, open Apps view, move the screen contents until you see File Explorer on the far right of the screen, and then select it.

–Or–

On the left of the taskbar on the desktop, select the **File Explorer** icon.

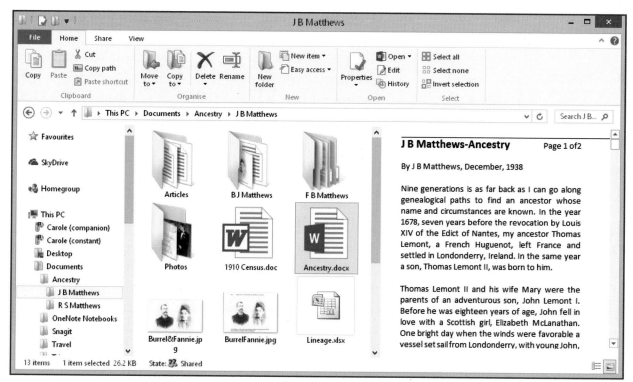

*Figure 2-11: **Windows 8 added a ribbon to File Explorer, giving it a new ease of customization.***

Change Panes

File Explorer can display up to three panes containing up to four sets of information. The left pane can only be the navigation pane displaying disk drives and folders, but you can turn it on or off. The center pane is the subject pane and is always present. The right pane, which is turned off by default, can display either of two panes when it is on: either the preview of a document, where it is called the "preview pane" or detailed information about the document where it is called the "details pane."

1. Select the **View** tab at the top of File Explorer.

2. Select **Navigation Pane** on the left of the View ribbon to open its menu.

3. If there is a check mark next to Navigation Pane in the menu, select it to close the pane. If there is no check mark, select it to display the pane.

4. If the preview pane is not displayed (not highlighted in the ribbon), select **Preview Pane** to display it, or if it is displayed, select **Preview Pane** to close the pane.

5. If the details pane is not displayed (not highlighted in the ribbon), select **Details Pane** to display it, or if it is displayed, select **Details Pane** to close the pane.

Change Icons

The manner that File Explorer uses to represent files and folders has a number of options, including lists, tiles, and icons, and the icons can take several sizes, as you can see in the Layout area of the ribbon.

> Select each of the options in the layout area of the File Explorer's ribbon to see what it looks like, and then select the one you want to use.

NAVIGATE IN WINDOWS 8.1

Windows 8 introduced a number of new ways to navigate both within the operating system as well as around the screen, as you have seen in this and the first chapter. Some of this is the result of enhancing touch, and another part is the result of enabling the mouse or keyboard to do what can be done with touch. For example, a major new command element in Windows 8 is Charms. With touch, Charms is opened by swiping in from outside the right side of the display. To do the same thing with the mouse, you move it to the bottom-right or top-right corners or press **WINDOWS+C** on the keyboard. Windows 8.1 has given you some control over this corner navigation, as well as how the Start screen is used.

▷▷ Change Corner Navigation

By default in Windows 8.1, when you move the mouse to the top-right corner, Charms opens, or when you move the mouse to the top-left corner, recent apps that you have used are displayed. You can change some of the navigation properties through both Charms and through the Taskbar And Navigation Properties dialog box on the desktop.

1. Open Charms and select **Settings | Change PC Settings | PC And Devices | Corners And Edges**.

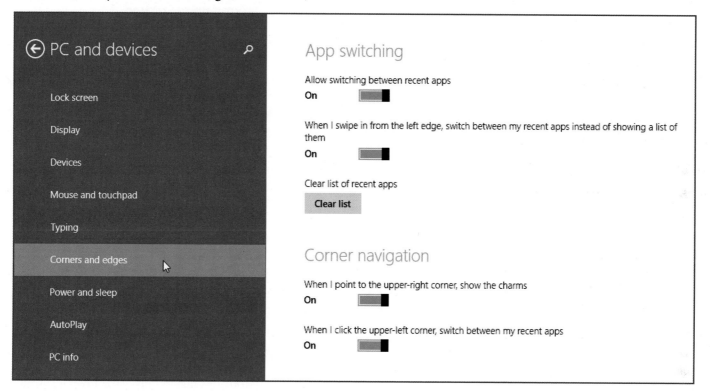

This allows you to:

- Turn on or off switching between recent apps. It is on by default. When this is off, pointing in the top-left or bottom-left corners or swiping in from outside the left edge of the screen does nothing.

- Turn on or off switching between recent apps by swiping in from outside the left edge of the screen. It is on by default. When this is off, swiping in from the left just displays your recent apps.

- Turn on or off showing Charms when you move the mouse to the top-right corner of the screen. It is on by default. When this is off, moving the mouse to the top-right corner does nothing.

- Turn on or off switching between recent apps when you click in the top-left corner. It is on by default. When this is off, nothing is displayed when you point or click in the top-left corner.

2. Open the Taskbar And Navigation Properties dialog box by right-clicking or pressing and holding on the taskbar and then selecting **Properties | Navigation**. The Corner Navigation area allows you to:

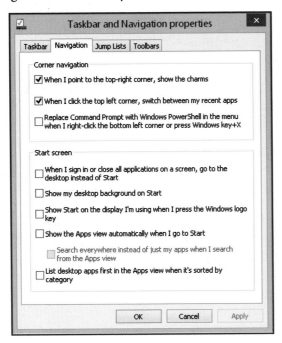

- Turn on or off showing Charms when you move the mouse to the top-right corner of the screen. It is on by default. When this is off, moving the mouse to the top-right corner does nothing.

- Turn on or off switching between recent apps when you click in the top-left corner. It is on by default. When this is off, nothing is displayed when you point or click in the top-left corner.

- Turn on or off replacing Command Prompt with Windows PowerShell in the System menu opened by right-clicking the bottom-left corner of the screen. This for super-techies who want to control Windows using typed commands.

 QuickFacts

Open the Desktop upon Starting

When you start Windows 8.1, the default is to open the Start screen. Some people who have come to Windows 8.1 from prior versions of Windows and primarily use the Windows desktop would like to go directly to the desktop and not the Start screen. Windows 8.1 now allows you to do that in the lower part of the Navigation tab of the Taskbar And Navigation Properties dialog box. Here are the options, slightly reworded for clarity. Select the first option to open the desktop upon starting.

- Go to the desktop when you start Windows or close all apps. This is off by default, and you go to the Start screen in those situations.

- Show the desktop background on the Start screen. This is off by default, and the background on the Start screen is independently controlled.

- Show the Start screen on a selected display when two displays are connected. This is off by default, and the Start screen is shown on both displays.

- Show the Apps view in place of the Start screen when the Start screen would normally be shown. This off by default, and the Start screen is shown.

- Show desktop apps first in Apps view when it is sorted by category, as shown in Figure 2-12. This off by default, and normally Apps view is sorted alphabetically by name.

CONTROL HOW WINDOWS 8.1 OPERATES

How Windows 8.1 operates is probably at least as important to you as how it looks. Windows 8.1 has a number of controls that allow you to customize its operation. The primary container, actually a folder, that provides access to these controls is the Control Panel, which has been in the last several versions of

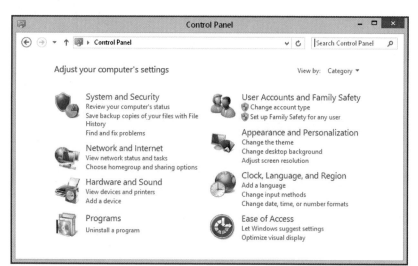

Figure 2-12: **Category view provides a hierarchy of windows that leads you to the settings you want to change.**

Windows. Windows 8.1 has two other sets of controls, some of which are the same: the Windows 8.1 PC Settings app, and the System menu, opened by right-clicking the Start button in the lower-left corner of the screen or by pressing **WINDOWS+X** (it cannot be opened with touch). We'll begin by looking at the Control Panel and some of its controls, and then take a look at PC Settings and the System menu.

▷▷ Use the Control Panel

The Control Panel is a facility for customizing many of the functions in Windows. The individual components of the Control Panel are discussed throughout this book (several in this chapter); this section is an introduction to the Control Panel itself.

Open the Control Panel

To open the Control Panel:

1. In the Start screen, begin typing <u>Control Panel</u>. The Search pane will open displaying the Control Panel app.

   –Or–

   In the Start screen, open Apps view, and move the screen contents until you see Control Panel (under Windows System).

2. Select **Control Panel**. The Control Panel is displayed. By default, it will be in Category view as shown in Figure 2-12.

   –Or–

   From either the Start screen or the desktop, right-click the Start button in the bottom-left corner or press **WINDOWS+X** to open the System menu and select **Control Panel**.

   –Or–

   From the desktop, open Charms and select **Settings | Control Panel**.

Switch the Control Panel View

The Control Panel has three views: the default Category view, shown in Figure 2-12, which groups Control Panel functions; and Large and Small Icons views (Figure 2-13 shows Large Icons view), which shows all the Control Panel components in one window. (Mobile computers will show additional hardware devices unique to them.)

- When in Category view, select the **View By** down arrow on the right, and select either **Large Icons** or **Small Icons**.
- When in Large or Small Icons view, select the **View By** down arrow on the right, and select **Category** to switch back to that view.

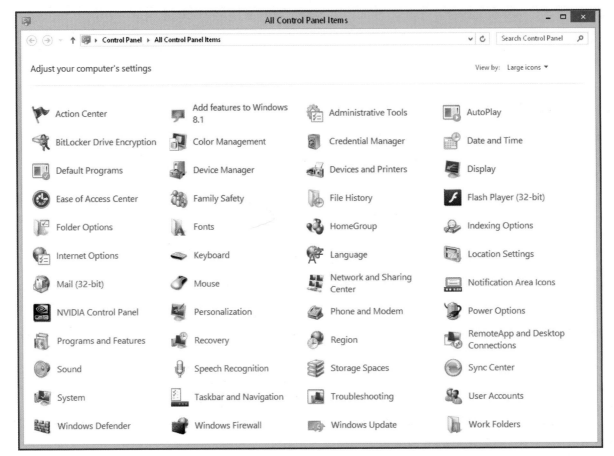

*Figure 2-13: **The Control Panel's Large Icons view shows all of the components in the Control Panel.***

Open a Control Panel Category

Category view groups components into categories that must be opened to see the individual components, although some subcategories are listed.

Select a category to open a window for it, where you can either select a task you want to do or open a Control Panel component represented by an icon, as you can see in Figure 2-14 for the Hardware And Sound category on a tablet PC.

Open a Control Panel Component

When Category view's secondary windows are opened, as in the previous step, the icons for individual Control Panel components are displayed. In either Large or Small Icons view, these component icons are directly displayed. To open a component:

Select the component's icon.

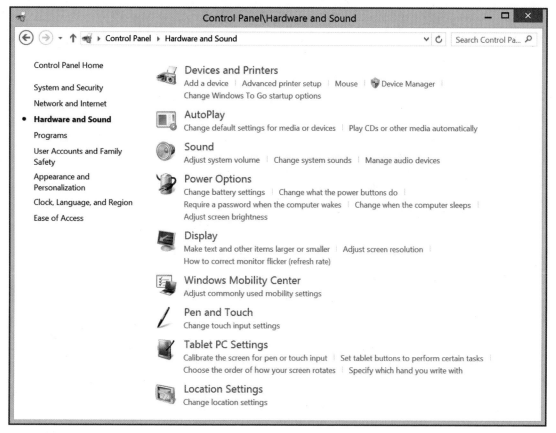

Figure 2-14: **The beauty of the Control Panel's Category view is that components spread around in an icon view are grouped together.**

⊳⊳ Set and Use the Date and Time

Many Control Panel components are also available from other locations. For example, the Control Panel's Date And Time component opens the same dialog box that appears when you select the time and date in the lower-right corner of the desktop and then select **Change Date And Time Settings**. The time

and date may seem simple enough, but significant capability lies behind these basic numbers.

1. Move the mouse until your cursor is on the time in the notification area. The current day and date will appear.

---

2. Select the time or date. The full calendar and clock appear.

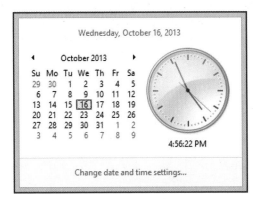

3. Select **Change Date And Time Settings**. The Date And Time dialog box will appear, as shown in Figure 2-15.

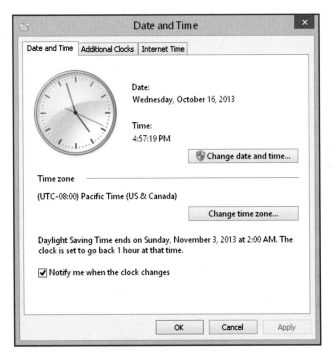

*Figure 2-15: **Setting the date and time is normally automated using an Internet time server.***

4. With the Date And Time tab selected, select **Change Date And Time**. The Date And Time Settings dialog box appears.

 NOTE The blue and yellow shield on the Change Date And Time button tells you that the function being selected requires administrator permission. You must be signed on as an administrator, or have a password for an administrator, to change the date and time.

5. Use the arrows on the left and right on the top of the calendar to change the month. Or, select the month to display the year, use the arrows to change the year, select the month, and then select a day.

6. Double-click or double-tap an element of time (hour, minute, second, A.M./P.M.), and use the spinner to change the selected time element. Select **OK** to close the Date And Time Settings dialog box.

7. Select **Change Time Zone**, select the **Time Zone** down arrow, and select your time zone.

8. Where applicable, select **Automatically Adjust Clock For Daylight Saving Time** if it isn't already selected and you want Windows 8.1 to do that. Select **OK** to close the Time Zone Settings dialog box.

9. Select the **Additional Clocks** tab to add one or two clocks with different time zones. Select the first **Show This Clock** check box, open the drop-down list box, and select a time zone. Enter a display name, and repeat for a second additional clock, if desired. (The additional times will appear when you point to the time in the notification area.) Select **OK** when done.

10. Select the **Internet Time** tab and see how your computer's time is currently being synchronized. If you want to change that, select **Change Settings**.

11. Select **Synchronize With An Internet Time Server** if it isn't already selected, open the drop-down list, select a time server, and select **Update Now**. Once turned on, Windows will check the time every seven days. Select **OK** to close the Internet Time Settings dialog box.

12. Select **OK** to close the Date And Time dialog box.

▷▷ Change Ease-of-Access Settings

Ease-of-access settings provide alternatives to the normal way the mouse and keyboard are used, as well as some settings that make the screen more readable and sounds more understandable.

1. Open the desktop's context menu, select **Personalize**, and select **Ease Of Access Center** in the lower-left area. The Ease Of Access Center window will open, as shown in Figure 2-16.

–Or–

Press **WINDOWS+U**.

NOTE If Always Scan This Section is selected and if you have speakers and a sound card, Windows 8.1 will scan and read aloud the four options in the "Quick Access to Common Tools" section.

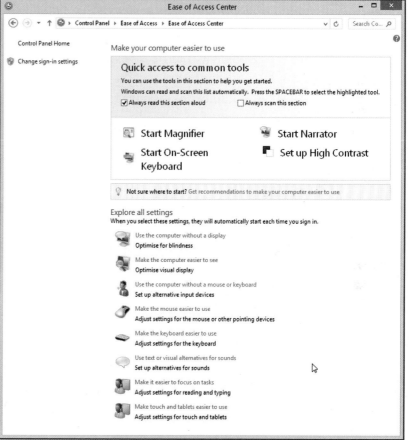

Figure 2-16: Ease-of-access settings let you work with Windows 8.1 and your apps in ways that facilitate use with various physical limitations.

TIP You can also turn on the most common ease-of-access options from the Windows 8.1 logon screen by selecting the **Ease Of Access** icon in the lower-left corner of that screen.

2. Select the options you want to use in the common tools area at the top (see Table 2-1 for a description). You can also turn the options on or off using the keyboard shortcuts shown.

3. Select any of the blue text links in the lower part of the window to review, and possibly change, the ease-of-access settings that apply to various areas of the computer. Within links there are a number of assistive tools, shown in Table 2-2, that can be turned on, either in these links or with the keyboard shortcuts shown.

4. When you have set up the accessibility options you want, select **Close**.

Table 2-1: Ease-of-Access Reading Tools

Option	Description	Keyboard Shortcut
Magnifier	Enlarges a part of the screen around the mouse.	
On-Screen Keyboard	Displays an image of a keyboard on the screen, the keys of which can be selected with the mouse.	
Narrator	Reads aloud selected text on the screen.	
High Contrast	Uses high-contrast colors and special fonts to make the screen easy to use.	Press left **SHIFT**+left **ALT**+and **PRINT SCREEN** all together.

Table 2-2: Ease-of-Access Typing Tools

Option	Description	Keyboard Shortcut
Mouse Keys	Uses the numeric keypad to move the mouse around the screen.	Press left **ALT**+left SHIFT+NUM LOCK.
Sticky Keys	Simulates pressing a pair of keys, such as **CTRL+A**, by pressing one key at a time. The keys **SHIFT**, **CTRL**, and **ALT** "stick" down until a second key is pressed. This is interpreted as two keys pressed together.	Press either **SHIFT** key five times in succession.
Filter Keys	Enables you to press a key twice in rapid succession and have it interpreted as a single keystroke; also slows down the rate at which the key is repeated if it is held down.	Hold down the right **SHIFT** key for eight seconds.
Toggle Keys	Hear a tone when **CAPS LOCK**, **NUM LOCK**, or **SCROLL LOCK** is turned on. You must first turn this on by opening the Ease of Access Center | Make The Keyboard Easier To Use | Turn On Toggle Keys.	Hold down the **NUM LOCK** key for five seconds.

▷▷ Customize the Mouse

The mouse lets you interact with the screen and point on, select, and drag objects. You also can start and stop apps and close Windows using the mouse. While you can use Windows without a mouse, many people prefer it, making it important that the mouse operates in the most comfortable way possible.

Switch Buttons and Pointers

Change the way the mouse works through the Control Panel
Mouse component.

1. Open the Control Panel as described earlier.

2. In Category view, select **Hardware And Sound**, and under
   Devices And Printers, select **Mouse**.

   –Or–

   In Large or Small Icons view, select **Mouse**.

   Either way, the Mouse Properties dialog box will appear.

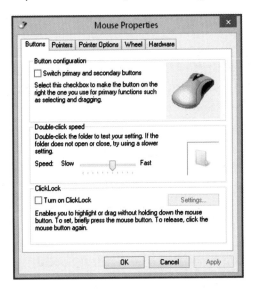

3. If you want to use the mouse with your left hand, select
   Switch Primary And Secondary Buttons.

4. Double-click the folder in the middle-right area of the
   Buttons tab. If the folder opens, your double-click speed
   is okay. If not, drag the **Speed** slider until the folder opens
   when you comfortably double-click it.

5. Select the options you want to use on the **Buttons**, **Pointer
   Options**, **Wheel**, and **Hardware** tabs.

6. Select the **Pointers** tab. If you want to change the way the
   pointer looks, select a different scheme (see "Use a Different
   Mouse Pointer" next in this chapter).

7. When you have set up the mouse the way you want, select
   OK.

Use a Different Mouse Pointer

If it is difficult for you to see the mouse pointer, you can change
how it looks and behaves in the Mouse Properties dialog box.
From the Mouse Properties Pointers tab:

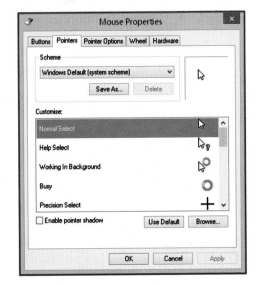

1. Select the **Scheme** down arrow, and choose the scheme you want to use.

2. If you want to customize a particular mouse pointer, select that pointer, select **Browse**, locate/preview and select the pointer you want to use, and select **Open**.

3. Select **OK** to close the Mouse Properties dialog box.

Customize the Keyboard

Depending on your computer and what you do with it, a keyboard may be important. The Keyboard option on the Control Panel allows you to change the length of the delay before a key that is held down is repeated and the rate at which the key is repeated.

1. From the Control Panel in Category view, select **Large** or **Small Icons** view, and then select **Keyboard**. The Keyboard Properties dialog box appears.

NOTE Some keyboards use their own dialog boxes.

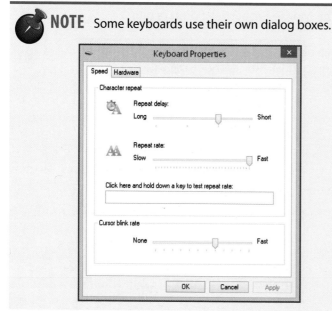

2. Select the text box in the middle of the dialog box, and press a character key to see how long you wait before the key is repeated and how fast the repeated character appears.

3. Move the **Repeat Delay** slider in the direction desired, and then test the repetition again.

4. Move the **Repeat Rate** slider in the direction desired, and then test the repetition again.

5. Move the **Cursor Blink Rate** slider in the direction desired, and observe the blink rate.

6. When you have set up the keyboard the way you want, select **OK**.

Change Sounds

Windows 8.1 uses sounds to alert and entertain you. Through Control Panel's Sound component, you can select the sound scheme you want.

Configure Your Speakers

1. In the Control Panel's Category view, select **Hardware And Sound**, and then select **Sound**.

   –Or–

   In Large or Small Icons view, select **Sound**.

   In either case, the Sound dialog box appears.

2. Select **Speakers | Configure** in the lower-left corner, select your configuration in the Audio Channels list, and select **Test** to test your setup. When you are ready, select **Next**.

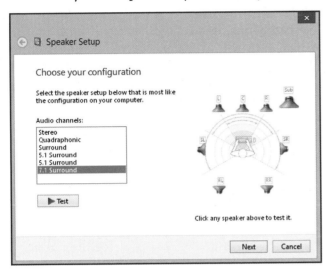

3. If you select a configuration that has more speakers than you actually have—for example, if you have a subwoofer and a pair of speakers—you must select the first 5.1 Surround configuration and select **Next**. Then select the speakers that aren't present—the Center and Side Pair in this example— and select **Next**. Select the speakers that are full-range speakers, and select **Next**. When you are done, select **Finish**.

4. Open (double-click or double-tap) **Speakers**, select the **Levels** tab, and move the slider(s) in the direction desired to set the volume. Select **OK** to close the Speakers Properties dialog box.

Select the Sounds Windows 8.1 Plays

You can select the sounds that are played when various events occur, such as a critical stop or Windows shutdown, in the Sound dialog box. If your Sound dialog box is not open, from the Personalization window, select Sounds.

1. In the Sound dialog box, select the **Sounds** tab. Select the **Sound Scheme** down arrow, and select one of the options.

2. Select a **Program Events** option and select **Test** to hear its current sound played.

3. Select the **Sounds** down arrow to select a different sound for the event. Select **Test** to hear the sound.

4. When you have made all the changes you want to the association of sounds and events, select **Save As** to save your changes as a new scheme. Type a name for the new scheme, and select **OK**.

5. When you are ready, select **OK** to close the Sound dialog box.

 CAUTION! Changing the format used for dates and times might affect other apps, such as Excel.

Change Regional Settings

Windows 8.1 lets you determine how numbers, dates, currency, and time are displayed and used, as well as the languages that will be used. Choosing a primary language and locale sets all the other settings. You can customize these options through the Regional And Language Options component in the Control Panel.

1. In the Control Panel Category view, select **Clock, Language, And Region**, and then select **Language**.

   –Or–

   In Large or Small Icons view, select **Language**.

   In either case, the Language window will open.

2. Verify that you want to use the language shown. If not, select **Add A Language** | *<the language>* | **Open** | *<the specific country using the language>* | **Add**.

3. Select **Change Date, Time, Or Number Formats** to open the Region dialog box.

4. Customize the date and time formats by selecting the down arrow associated with each setting and selecting the option that you want.

5. Select **Additional Settings** and then go to the individual tabs for numbers, currency, time, and date; and set how you want these items displayed. Select **OK** when you are done.

6. Review the **Location** and **Administrative** tabs, and make any desired changes.

7. When you have set up the regional settings the way you want, select **OK**. Close the Language window.

⫸ Consider Additional Sets of Controls

As was mentioned earlier in the chapter, while the Control Panel is the primary location to find Windows 8.1 controls and settings, there are two new facilities that also offer controls: PC Settings, a Windows 8–style app, and the System menu.

Review PC Settings

PC Settings, shown in Figure 2-17, only shares some settings with the Control Panel, and even the settings in Ease of Use do not fully duplicate those in the Control Panel. Most of the PC Setting's controls are discussed in later chapters. Here, simply familiarize yourself with the options.

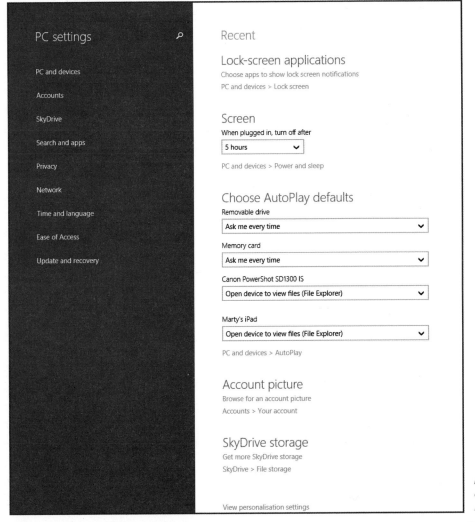

1. Open **Charms** and select **Settings | Change PC Settings**. The PC Settings window will open. The initial screen displays the area where you have recently made changes to these settings and has an option, View Recently Used Settings, to view them.

2. Select each of the options in the left column and review the related settings on the right. Many of these will be discussed in later chapters.

Look at the System Menu

The System menu, shown next, is aimed at advanced users, although anybody can use it. Some of the options are contained in the Control Panel, while others, including Disk Management, Event Viewer, Computer Management, and Disk Management, are hidden in Administrative Tools. Many of the remaining options are available in Apps view. A number of the options

Figure 2-17: **PC Settings is an attempt to replace the Control Panel, but it still has a ways to go.**

will be described later in the book. (The Mobility Center is not on desktop computers.)

Programs and Features
Mobility Center
Power Options
Event Viewer
System
Device Manager
Network Connections
Disk Management
Computer Management
Command Prompt
Command Prompt (Admin)

Task Manager
Control Panel
File Explorer
Search
Run

Shut down or sign out ▸
Desktop

⁹⁹ QuickQuotes

Bobbi Finds Programs and Folders

I often have several programs and folders open on my computer, and with earlier versions of Windows I would have difficulty finding something that I was working on or getting to an icon on my desktop. Now with Aero Peek I can immediately see what's on my desktop, and using taskbar previews I can easily see and choose from among the several documents I might have open in Word or several Internet sites I have open in Internet Explorer. I think these features are a real asset.

Bobbi S., 72, Washington

Chapter 3

Storing Information

The information on your computer—documents, email, photographs, music, and apps—are stored in *files*. So that your files are organized and more easily found, they are kept in *folders*, and folders can be placed in other folders for further organization. For example, a folder labeled "Animals," which is contained in the Pictures folder, contains separate folders for Birds, Pets, and Swallows. The Pets folder contains photos of the pets we've recently had. Such a set of files and folders is shown in Figure 3-1.

In this chapter you'll see how to create, use, and manage files and folders like these. The term "objects" is used to refer to any mix of files, folders, and disk drives.

USE THE WINDOWS FILE SYSTEM

The tool that Windows 8.1 provides to locate and work with files and folders is *File Explorer* (often called "Explorer," not to be confused with Internet Explorer discussed in Chapter 4). File Explorer has a number of components and features, many of which are shown in Figure 3-1 and described in Table 3-1. Much of this chapter is spent exploring these items and how they are used.

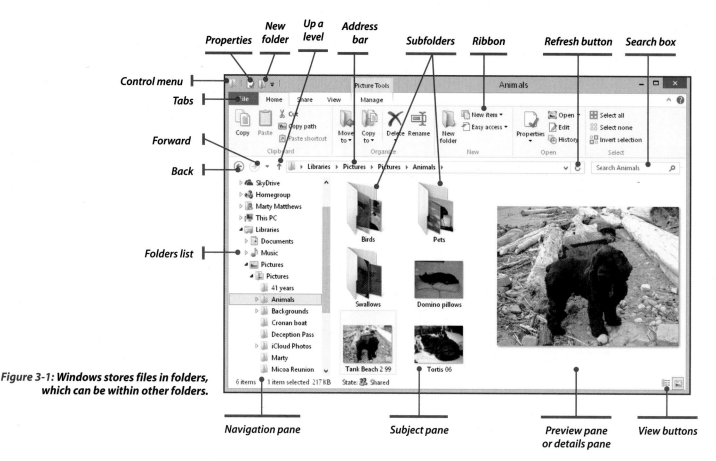

Control menu, Tabs, Forward, Back, Folders list

Properties, New folder, Up a level, Address bar, Subfolders, Ribbon, Refresh button, Search box

Navigation pane, Subject pane, Preview pane or details pane, View buttons

Figure 3-1: Windows stores files in folders, which can be within other folders.

Open File Explorer

The easiest way to open File Explorer is from the desktop.

1. Start your computer, if it's not running, and log on to Windows if necessary.

2. From the Start screen, select the desktop, and on the desktop, select **File Explorer**, third from the left on the taskbar.

3. The File Explorer will open. If it isn't already selected, select **This PC** in the navigation pane to display your major folders, drives, and network locations in the subject pane, as shown in Figure 3-2. You can:

- **Open** (double-click or double-tap) a folder in the subject pane to display its contents so that you can see and work with them.

- **Select** (click or tap) an object within the subject pane to get information about it in the details pane, preview it in the preview pane, or use the ribbon tools with that object.

Table 3-1: File Explorer Components

Component	Function
Control menu	Displays controls for sizing and moving the window with a keyboard
Properties	Displays the properties of the selected object in the subject pane
New Folder	Creates a new folder in the folder displayed in the subject pane
Up a level	Moves the view (the contents of the subject pane) up to the containing folder
Address bar	Displays the location of what is being shown in the subject pane
Subfolders	Shows folders that are within other folders
Ribbon	Contains tools to work with the selected object in the subject pane
Refresh button	Updates what is displayed by the address bar
Search box	Provides for the entry of text you want to search for within the content in the subject pane
View buttons	Allows you to quickly select between Details and Large Icons views
Preview pane or details pane	Displays the contents of the object selected in the subject pane, or it displays details about the object selected in the subject pane
Subject pane	Displays the objects stored at the address shown in the address bar
Navigation pane	Facilitates moving around among the objects you have available
Folders list	Shows the hierarchy of disk drives and folders on your computer
Back and Forward buttons	Displays an object either previously displayed or next in the hierarchy
Tabs	Selects from several different groups of ribbon tools

 NOTE There are several reasons that your File Explorer– This PC window will look different from Figure 3-2. You may have more than one disk drive or disk partition and no, fewer, or more network connections. It also may be that your settings are different, which we'll discuss later in this chapter.

There are three alternative ways of opening File Explorer:

- From the lower-left corner of either the Start screen or the desktop, open (right-click) the **Start** button to open the System menu and select **File Explorer**.

 NOTE As was mentioned in Chapter 2, the System menu can't be opened using touch. You could add the On-Screen Keyboard app to the Start screen. Then, after opening it, you could press **WINDOWS+X** to open the System menu.

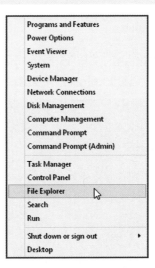

- From the Start screen, select the down arrow on the lower-left corner of the screen, swipe up from the vertical middle of the screen, or press **CTRL+TAB** to open Apps view. From

Figure 3-2: Windows 8.1 displaying This PC shows you everything you can access on your computer.

here, under Windows System, you open File Explorer by selecting either **File Explorer** or **This PC**.

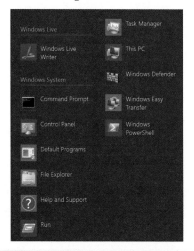

Change the File Explorer Layout

As you see in Figure 3-2, the File Explorer window has several different panes that you may want to use. You can turn them on or off through the ribbon's View tab.

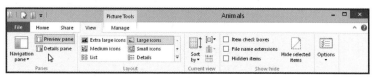

Open Layout Options

In File Explorer, select **View** on the ribbon tabs. The Panes options are displayed for turning on or off the navigation, preview, and details panes. By default, the navigation pane is on, the subject is always on, and the others are off.

Turn On the Preview Pane

With the View tab displayed, select **Preview Pane**.

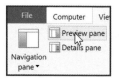

Turn On the Details Pane

In the View tab, select **Details Pane**.

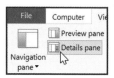

Turn Off the Navigation Pane

In the View tab, select **Navigation Pane**, and then select **Navigation Pane** a second time from the menu.

Customize File Explorer

You can customize how File Explorer looks and determine which features are available with the ribbon.

1. If File Explorer is not already open, select the desktop and select **File Explorer**.

Figure 3-3: File Explorer's ribbon changes to provide commands for what is selected in the subject pane.

2. Select **This PC | Pictures**, and then open a folder of photos in the subject pane. That folder should open, as you can see in Figure 3-3.

3. Select one of the pictures. The ribbon changes to something like this:

These ribbon options are specific to the file selected. Selecting other types of files would have generated different options.

Look at the File Explorer Ribbon

The File Explorer ribbon has at least three tabs and can have five or more, as you can see in Figure 3-3. Each tab is opened

by selecting the tab above the ribbon. When you open Explorer either from the desktop taskbar or in Apps view, the Computer tab is displayed and This PC is selected in the navigation pane. When you select any other folder in either the navigation pane or subject pane, the Home tab replaces the Computer tab. The functions that you can perform with each of the tabs and their ribbon include the following:

- **File tab** provides options for the Windows file system. The first option opens a new window to give you two or more copies of File Explorer on the desktop. The second and third options are for accessing and controlling Windows without using the normal Windows interface. The command prompt is touched on in Chapter 5, but generally, these options are beyond the scope of this book. Delete History allows you to delete the list of recent places you have visited in the file system (shown when you first open the File tab) and to delete recent entries made in the address bar. Help opens the Windows Help system, and Close closes File Explorer, both of which are also available in the tab and title bars, respectively.

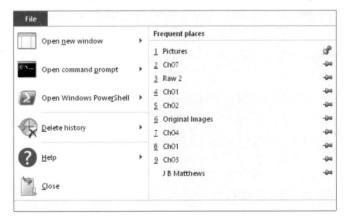

TIP Selecting the push pin on the list of frequent places will keep the entry on the list until you select the push pin again.

 TIP After opening the File tab, you can close it and return to Explorer by selecting the File tab a second time.

- **Home tab**, which is shown in several earlier figures, allows you to perform operations on the object you have selected, such as Cut, Copy, Paste, Delete, and Rename, as well as Move, Copy, Open, and Edit. You also can perform folder-related operations, such as New Folder, Select All, and Invert Selection. Most of these options are discussed later in this chapter.

- **Share tab** allows you to email, burn to disc, print, and fax an object you have selected. You can also compress one or more objects to make them both easier to store and send over the Internet by selecting them and then selecting **Zip**. You can select who and how you want to share the selected objects, turn off sharing, and set up advanced sharing properties. Controlling sharing is discussed in Chapter 8.

- **View tab**, as you saw earlier, allows you to turn the various panes on and off. It also lets you determine how objects are displayed in File Explorer. Figure 3-3 shows objects displayed as large icons, just one of the eight views. You can also sort and group the items in the subject pane and add and size columns in the Details view. You can add a check box and display file extensions (like .doc for older Word files), as well as hide objects and display hidden objects. Options, on the right of the ribbon, opens the Folder Options dialog box discussed later in this chapter.

Point on each of the other seven view choices, ending with Details to see what they are like. In the Details view, which is shown in Figure 3-4, you can:

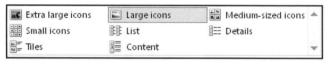

1. Select **Name** at the top of the left column in the subject pane. The contents of the subject pane will be sorted alphanumerically by name. Select **Name** again, and the contents will be sorted by name in the opposite direction.

2. Select one of the other column headings, and then select the same column heading again to see the contents sorted that way, first in one direction, and then in the other. The Sort By option on the View ribbon tab performs the same purpose.

 TIP Point on a column heading and select the down arrow on its right to see filtering options.

3. Move the mouse pointer or your finger until it is between two columns and drag it left or right to dynamically size the column.

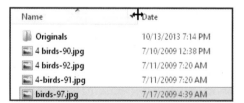

- **Computer tab**, shown in Figure 3-2, provides options for working with the file system and storage devices on your computer and computers networked with yours. These are discussed later on in this chapter and later in this book.

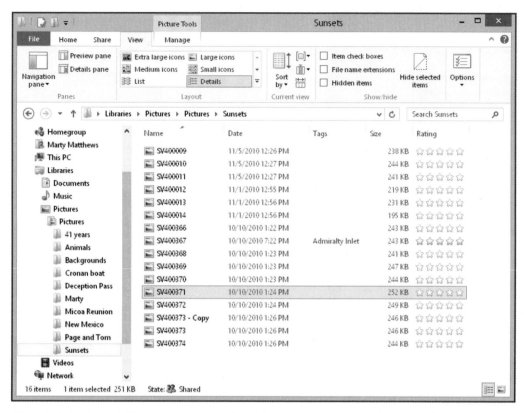

Figure 3-4: Folder Details view gives you further information about the objects in a folder.

 NOTE The Picture Tools Manage tab in Figures 3-1, 3-3, and 3-4 is called a "contextual tab," since it only appears in context with the selected object—in this case, a picture. It provides options for working with the selected object, such as rotating a picture and creating a slide show.

Examine Folder Options

The Folder Options dialog box provides the means to change the way that the Explorer displays and handles files and folders, and could be the reason that your screen looks different from

Figure 3-2. You open Folder Options from the Explorer's View ribbon.

1. Select the top of the **Options** icon on the right end of the View ribbon. The Folder Options dialog box will appear with the General tab displayed, as shown in Figure 3-5. This allows you to:

 NOTE Some options on the ribbon are split in two parts: selecting the icon opens a dialog box; selecting the label and down arrow opens a menu.

Figure 3-5: Folder Options allows you to determine how folders look and behave.

Figure 3-6: There are a number of options in the way that Explorer can display folder and file information.

- Open a new window for each folder you open.

- Use a single click in place of a double click to open a window on the desktop.

- If you choose single click, you can also determine whether to permanently underline an icon title, as in an Internet browser, or underline an icon only when you point on it.

- Display more or fewer folders in the navigation pane. Show All Folders is not on by default, but I recommend that you select it to get a more understandable view of your system.

2. Select the **View** tab, which is shown in Figure 3-6. This gives you a number of options that determine what is displayed for the current folder and allow you to apply these changes to all folders. The default settings generally work for most people.

3. When you are ready, select **OK** to close the Folder Options dialog box. (The Search tab will be discussed under "Search for Apps and Files" later in this chapter.)

LOCATE AND USE FILES AND FOLDERS

The purpose of a file system, of course, is to locate and use the files and folders on your computer. Within your computer, there is a storage hierarchy that starts with storage devices, such as disk drives, that are divided into areas called folders, each of which may be divided again into subareas or subfolders. Each of these contains files, which can be documents, pictures, music, and other data. Figure 3-1 showed folders containing subfolders and eventually containing files. Figure 3-7 shows several disk drives, which in turn contain folders. File Explorer contains a number of tools for locating; opening; and using disk drives, folders, and files.

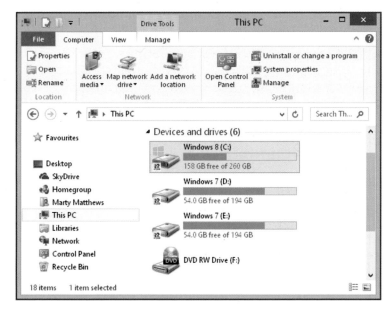

Figure 3-7: Your computer stores information in a hierarchy of disk drives and folders.

Identify Storage Devices

Files and folders are stored on various physical storage devices, including hard disk drives, solid-state drives, CD and DVD drives, memory cards and sticks, and universal serial bus (USB) flash memory. You will have some, but not necessarily all, of the following:

- Primary floppy disk, labeled "A:" (most computers no longer have a floppy drive)
- Primary hard disk, labeled "C:"
- CD or DVD drive, labeled "D:"
- Other storage devices, labeled "E:" and then "F:" and so on

Your primary hard disk is always labeled "C:" Other drives have flexible labeling. Often, the CD or DVD drive will be drive "D:," but if you have a second hard disk drive, it may be labeled "D," as you see in Figure 3-7.

▷▷ Select and Open Drives and Folders

When you open File Explorer and display the items in This PC, you see the disk drives and other storage devices on your computer, as well as several folders, including Libraries, your own user folder, and those for SkyDrive and the Control Panel as you saw in the navigation pane of Figure 3-7. To work with these drives and folders, you must select and open them.

1. In either the Start screen or the desktop, right-click the **Start** button to open the System menu, and select **File Explorer** to open it and display This PC and your local disk drives.

2. In the subject pane (right pane), select disk **(C:)**. Disk (C:) will be highlighted.

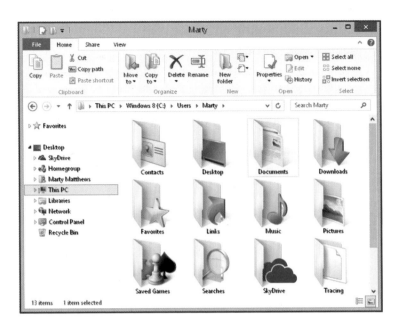

Figure 3-8: Opening a drive or folder will open it in the subject pane.

3. Open (double-click/tap) disk **(C:)**. Disk (C:) will open, and its folders will be displayed in the subject pane.

4. Open **Users** to open that folder and display your folder along with a Public folder.

5. Open your personal folder (the folder with your name on it). The subject pane displays the files and folders in your folder. This will include Contacts, Desktop, Documents, Music, Pictures, and others, as shown in Figure 3-8.

6. Keep opening each folder until you see the contents you are looking for.

▷▷ Navigate Folders and Disks

Opening File Explorer and navigating through several folders— beginning with your hard disk—to find a file you want is fine.

However, if you want to quickly go to another folder or file, you won't want to have to start with your hard disk every single time. The Windows 8.1 File Explorer gives you three ways to do this: through the Libraries folder in the navigation pane, using the folder tree in the navigation pane, or using the address bar.

Navigate Using Libraries

The Libraries folder gives you direct access to the four primary content folders within your personal folder, as shown next. By selecting a library in the navigation pane and then opening folders within the subject pane, you can move around the folders and files within your personal folder. For example, given the folder structure shown in Figure 3-1, here are the steps to open the Animals folder.

1. From the desktop taskbar, open **File Explorer**, and then open the **Libraries** folder.

2. In the navigation pane, select the right-pointing triangle or arrow opposite the Pictures library to open it.

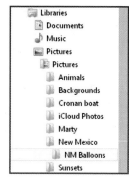

3. Still in the navigation pane, select the right-pointing arrow opposite **Pictures** to open it and then select another enclosed folder to open it in the subject pane.

Navigate Using Folders

The portion of the navigation pane starting with This PC is a folder tree that contains all the disk drives, folders, and files on your computer in a tree, or hierarchical, structure. To open the same folder structure as you did with Libraries:

1. From the System menu, select **File Explorer**, opening This PC in the navigation pane.

2. In the navigation pane, select the right-pointing arrow opposite the (**C:**) disk drive to open it.

3. Still in the navigation pane, select the right-pointing arrow opposite **Users** to open it.

4. Repeat step 3 to open your personal folder and then the Pictures folder.

5. Finally, select the folder (NM Balloons here) that you want to open in the subject pane, as shown in Figure 3-9

Navigate Using the Address Bar

Windows 8.1 gives you another way to quickly navigate through your drives and folders by selecting segments of a folder address in the address bar.

By selecting the folder icon on the left end of the address bar, you can see how this same address looked in versions of Windows before Windows 7 and use the address bar as it was in the past.

C:\Users\Marty\Pictures\New Mexico\NM Balloons

With Windows 8.1, if you select any segment of the address, you will open that level in the subject pane. If you select the arrow to the right of the segment, it displays a drop-down list of subfolders that you can jump to. By successively selecting segments and their subordinate folders, you can easily move

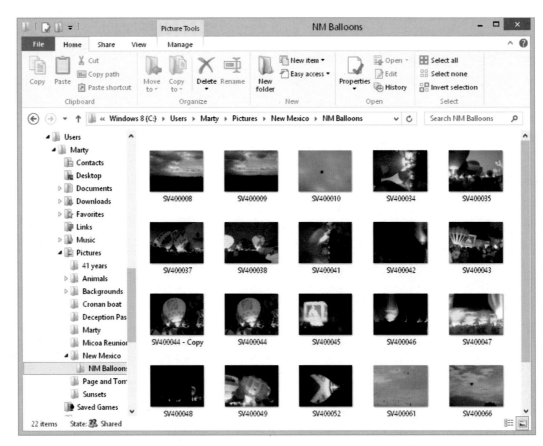

Figure 3-9: Libraries saves a couple of steps, but at the cost of possible confusion.

throughout the storage space on your computer and beyond to any network you are connected to.

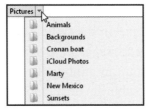

TIP The small down arrowhead between the Forward button and the up arrow displays the list of folders that you have recently looked at. The up arrow moves the *focus* (what is shown in the subject pane) up one level. For example, if the NM Balloons folder is open in the subject pane and you select the up arrow, the New Mexico folder will become the focus displayed in the subject pane.

Create New Folders

While you could store all your files within one of the ready-made folders—such as Documents, Music, or Pictures—you will probably want to make your files easier to find by creating several subfolders.

For example, to create a Windows 8.1 Notes folder:

1. From the desktop taskbar, open **File Explorer | Libraries | Documents**, and open the folder that will contain your Notes folder. Make sure nothing is selected.

2. In the Home ribbon (if it isn't displayed, select the **Home** tab), select **New Folder**. A new folder will appear with its name ("New Folder") highlighted.

3. Type the name of the folder, such as <u>Windows 8 Notes</u>, and press **ENTER**. Open your new folder to view it (you will see it's empty).

As alternatives to selecting New Folder on the Home ribbon, you can select **New Folder** on the right end of the Quick Access toolbar (shown next), or open the context menu (right-click or touch and hold for a moment on a blank area) for the subject pane of File Explorer and then select **New | Folder**.

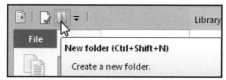

Rename and Delete Files and Folders

Sometimes, a file or folder needs to be renamed or deleted (whether it was created by you or by an application) because you may no longer need it or for any number of reasons.

Rename a File or Folder

With the file or folder in view but not selected, to rename it:

- In the subject pane, slowly select the name twice (don't double-select), type the new name, and press **ENTER**.

  –Or–

- In either the navigation or subject pane, open the context menu for the file or folder, select **Rename**, type the new name, and press **ENTER**.

Delete a File or Folder to the Recycle Bin

With the file or folder in view in either the navigation or subject pane, to delete it:

- Select the icon for the file or folder and press **DELETE** or click **Delete** on the Home tab.

  –Or–

- Open the context menu for the icon and select **Delete**.

Recover a Deleted File or Folder

To recover a file or folder that has been deleted:

- Open the **Recycle Bin** on the desktop to display it. Select the object to be restored, and select **Restore The Selected Items** in the Recycle Bin Tools tab.

  –Or–

- Open the context menu for the file or folder icon, and select **Restore**.

Permanently Delete a File or Folder

If you're sure you want to permanently delete a file or folder:

- Select the icon, press and hold **SHIFT** while pressing **DELETE**, and select **Yes** to confirm the permanent deletion.

–Or–

- Open the context menu for the icon, and press and hold **SHIFT** while selecting **Delete | Yes** to confirm the permanent deletion.

Select Multiple Files and Folders

Often, you will want to do one or more operations—such as copy, move, or delete—on several files and/or folders at the same time. To select several files or folders from the subject pane of an Explorer window:

- Move the mouse pointer or your finger to the upper-left area, just outside of the top and leftmost object. Then drag the mouse or your finger to the lower-right area, just outside of the bottom and rightmost object, creating a shading across the objects.

–Or–

- Select the first object, and press and hold **CTRL** while selecting the remaining objects, if the objects are noncontiguous (not adjacent to each other). If the objects are contiguous, select the first object, press and hold **SHIFT**, and select the last object.

Use the Recycle Bin

If you do a normal delete operation in Explorer or the desktop, the deleted item or items will go into the Recycle Bin. Should you change your mind about the deletion, you can reclaim an item from the Recycle Bin, as explained in "Rename and Delete Files and Folders" earlier in this chapter.

The Recycle Bin is a special folder that can contain both files and folders. You can open it and see its contents as you would any other folder by opening its desktop icon or by selecting it in the navigation pane of the File Explorer. Figure 3-10 shows a Recycle Bin after deleting several files. What make the Recycle Bin special are the special options in the ribbon:

- **Empty Recycle Bin** Permanently removes all of the contents of the Recycle Bin.
- **Restore All Items** Returns all the contents to their original folders, in effect, "undeleting" all of the contents.
- **Restore The Selected Items** Returns the selected items to their original folders.
- **Recycle Bin Properties** Allows you to set the maximum size of the Recycle Bin so it doesn't take up all your disk space.

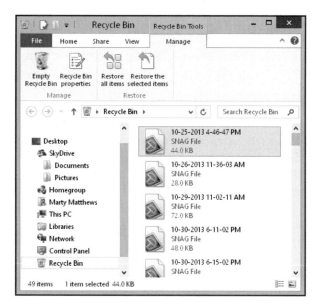

Figure 3-10: The Recycle Bin holds deleted items so that you can recover them until you empty it.

1. With the Recycle Bin open in File Explorer, select **Recycle Bin Properties**. The Recycle Bin Properties dialog box will appear, as you can see here.

2. If you have multiple hard disks, select the drive you want to use for the Recycle Bin. When Custom Size is selected, select the size, and type the number of megabytes you want to use ("7419" megabytes is 7.4 gigabytes).

3. If you don't want to use the Recycle Bin, select **Don't Move Files To The Recycle Bin**. This is strongly discouraged since this means that files will be permanently deleted with no hope of recovery.

4. If you want to see a deletion confirmation message, select that check box to check it.

5. When you are ready, select **OK** to close the dialog box.

▷▷ Create Shortcuts

A shortcut is a link to a file or folder that allows you to quickly open the file or folder from places other than where it is stored. For example, you can start a program from the desktop even though the actual program file is stored in some other folder. To create a shortcut:

1. In File Explorer, locate the folder or file for which you want to create a shortcut. If it is a program file (one identified as an "application," or with an .exe extension), drag it to a different folder, for example, from a folder to the desktop.

2. If it is any other file or folder:

    With a mouse, hold down the right mouse button while moving the file or folder to a different folder and then release the right mouse button.

    With touch, hold your finger on the object until a rectangle appears, then immediately move the file or folder to a different folder and release your finger.

In either case, a context menu should appear. Select **Create Shortcuts Here**.

TIP You may want to have the folders tree visible in the navigation pane and have the destination folder visible so you can drag to it the icon for which you want to create a shortcut.

–Or–

1. In File Explorer, open the folder in which you want to create a shortcut.
2. In a blank area in the subject pane of the folder, open the context menu (right-click or touch and hold until the rectangle appears) and select **New | Shortcut**.

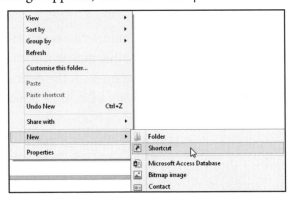

3. In the dialog box that appears, select **Browse** and use the folder tree to locate and select the file or folder for which you want to make a shortcut.
4. Select **OK | Next**. Type a name for the shortcut, and select **Finish**.

NOTE You can tell if an object is a shortcut in two ways: "Shortcut" may be in its title (unless you've renamed it), and an upward-pointing arrow is in the lower-left corner of the icon, like this:

Copy and Move Files and Folders

Copying and moving files and folders are similar actions, and can be done with the mouse, with touch, with the mouse or touch and a menu, and with the keyboard.

NOTE To use touch and the keyboard—for example, holding down **CTRL** or **SHIFT** while moving a file, as in a few places later—you need to use the On-Screen Keyboard app, not the default touch keyboard whose icon is in the notification area of the taskbar. Open the On-Screen Keyboard app from Apps view in the Windows Ease Of Access section.

Copy with the Mouse or Touch

- Copy any file or folder to another folder on the *same* disk by holding down **CTRL** while dragging it.
- Copy any file or folder to another folder on a *different* disk by dragging it.

Move with the Mouse or Touch

- Move a file that is not an app or any folder to another folder on the *same* disk by dragging it.
- Move a file that is not an app or any folder to another folder on a *different* disk by holding down **SHIFT** while dragging it.
- Move an app file to another folder on the same or a different disk by holding down **SHIFT** while dragging it. (Note that program files generally need to be installed and remain in a given location, and moving them may cause them not to run.)

Copy and Move with the Mouse or Touch and a Menu

- To copy and move with a mouse and a menu, hold down the right mouse button while dragging the file or folder. When you release the right mouse button, a context menu opens.

- To copy and move with touch and a menu, touch and hold the object to be moved until you see a rectangle, then drag the file or folder. When you release your finger, a context menu opens.

- In the context menu that opens, you can choose whether to copy, move, or create a shortcut (see "Create Shortcuts" in this chapter).

Copy and Move with the Keyboard

Copying and moving with the keyboard is done with three sets of keys:

- **CTRL+C** ("Copy") copies the selected item to the Windows Clipboard.

- **CTRL+X** ("Cut") moves the selected item to the Windows Clipboard, deleting it from its original location.

- **CTRL+V** ("Paste") copies the current contents of the Windows Clipboard to the currently open folder. You can repeatedly paste the same Clipboard contents to any additional folders you want to by opening them and pressing **CTRL+V** again.

To copy a file or folder from one folder to another using the keyboard:

1. In File Explorer, open the disk and folder containing the file or folder to be copied.

2. Use **TAB** and the arrow keys to select the file or folder, and press **CTRL+C** to copy the file or folder to the Clipboard.

3. Use **TAB**, the arrow keys, and **ENTER** to open the disk and folder that is to be the destination of the copied item.

4. Press **CTRL+V** to paste the file or folder into the destination folder.

 TIP You can also use the Cut, Copy, and Paste commands in the object's context menu (by opening the context menu for the object) or from the Home tab in the File Explorer ribbon.

 TIP There is a unique command in File Explorer's Home tab | Clipboard group, **Copy Path**, that can be used to document where a file or folder is stored or that you can use to repeatedly access a particular folder.

▷▷ Search for Apps and Files

With large and, possibly several, hard disks, it is often difficult to find apps, files, settings, and information on the Internet. Windows 8.1's search features address that issue. It has search facilities on both the Start screen and the desktop.

Search from the Start Screen

The Windows 8.1 Start screen search is a global search for apps, files (including music and pictures), and settings on your computer, as well as information and websites on the Internet. As you see at the top of the Search pane, it is "Everywhere."

1. From the Start screen (anywhere on it—there is not a specific search box), type all or part of the app or filename. (With touch, you need to open **Charms** and select **Search** to get the touch keyboard, unless you have the On-Screen Keyboard app displayed.) As you type, the Windows 8.1 Search screen will open and start displaying items that match some or all of what you typed, as you can see in Figure 3-11.

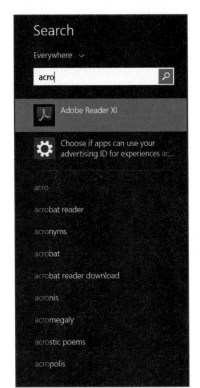

Figure 3-11: *You may need to refine your search criteria to get only the files you are looking for.*

Search from the Desktop

The desktop provides two separate search capabilities, one in the File Explorer for files and apps on your computer, and one in Internet Explorer to search for websites and information on the Internet. The Internet Explorer will be discussed in Chapter 4. Here, we'll discuss the File Explorer's search capabilities.

1. Begin a File Explorer search by selecting what you are going to search in the navigation pane. For example, if you select This PC, you will search everything on your computer. To refine the search, you might limit it to Libraries or a particular disk drive or folder.

2. In the File Explorer Search text box on the right and opposite the address bar, type all or part of the file or folder name, keyword, or phrase you want to find. As you type, File Explorer will start displaying the files and folders that match some or all of what you typed, as you can see in Figure 3-12.

2. If you want to narrow the search—for example, to just files—select the **Everywhere** down arrow and select **Files** in the drop-down menu. Only files will be displayed matching some or all of what you typed.

3. If you see the file or app you are searching for, select it, and if it is a file, it will be displayed in the program that is related to it (Photo for photos, Video for videos, Word for Word documents, and so on). If it is an app, it will start.

4. If you want to further refine your search, type more information into the Search pane's text box.

Figure 3-12: *The File Explorer Search ribbon provides a number of options to refine a search.*

NOTE The touch keyboard does not appear when you touch the File Explorer Search text box. You have to touch the icon in the notification area to display it.

3. If you see the file or folder you are searching for, double-select it. It will be displayed in File Explorer (if a folder) or in the program that created it or that can display it (if a file).

4. Select **Search Again In** on the left of the Search ribbon, and select one of several specific locations in which to search.

5. To filter the search results, select one or more of the options in the Refine area of the Search ribbon. These let you filter the search results by the date it was modified, the kind of file (such as email, Word document, picture, and so on), the size of the file, and other properties (such as type, name, folder path, and tags).

6. You can recall searches you have previously done by selecting **Recent Searches**, and in Advanced Options, you can control where and how searches are performed. The Advanced Options are the same as the options available in the Folder Options dialog box Search tab opened from the View ribbon.

 **QuickFacts**

Create Files

Files are usually created by applications or by copying existing files; however, Windows has an additional file-creation capability that creates an empty file for a particular application.

1 In the desktop, select File Explorer in the taskbar, and open the folder in which you want to create the new file.

2. Open the context menu for the subject pane in File Explorer, and select **New**. A menu of all the file types that can be created by the registered applications on your computer will appear.

–Or–

Select **New Item** in the New area of the Home ribbon. The same menu of file types will open.

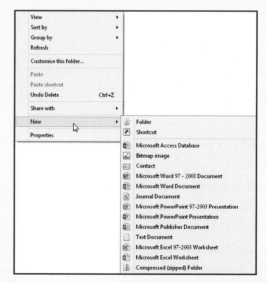

3. Select the file type you want to create. Name the file, and if you want to work on the file, open it in its application.

7. To change search options, select one of the items in the Options area of the Search ribbon. If you want to save the search, select **Save Search** on the ribbon, select the folder in which you want to store the file, type the filename, and select **Save**. If you don't select another folder, saved searches are available in the Searches folder by default. Saved searches also appear under Favorites | Recent Places | Searches in the navigation pane.

8. When you are done, close File Explorer.

Zip Files and Folders

Windows 8.1 has a way to compress files and folders called "zipping." *Zipped* files have the extension .zip and are compatible with a number of programs. Zipped files are smaller (take up less room on a disk) and are transmitted over the Internet faster.

Create a Zipped Folder

You can create a new zipped folder and drag files to it.

1. Open the System menu and select **File Explorer** to display This PC.

2. Navigate to the folder that you want to contain the zipped folder.

3. Open the context menu for the subject pane, and select **New | Compressed (Zipped) Folder**. The zipped folder will appear.

4. Select the folder name, type a new name, press **ENTER**, and drag files and folders into it to compress them.

Send Files or Folders to a Zipped Folder

1. In File Explorer, select the files and/or folders you want zipped.

2. Open the context menu for the selected objects, select **Send To | Compressed (Zipped) Folder**. A new zipped folder will appear containing the original files and/or folders, now compressed.

 TIP When you zip a group of files, open the context menu for the file whose name you want to give to the zip folder, and then select **Send To**. The file's name will automatically be given to the zip folder.

Extract Zipped Files and Folders

To unzip a file or folder, simply move it out of the zipped folder, or you can extract all of a zipped folder's contents.

1. Open the context menu for a zipped folder, and select **Extract All**. The Extract Compressed (Zipped) Folders dialog box will appear.

2. Enter or browse to the location where you want the extracted files and folders, and select **Extract**.

3. Close File Explorer when you are done.

Back Up Files and Folders with File History

Backing up copies important files and folders on your disk and writes them on another device, such as another hard disk, an external hard disk, a recordable CD or DVD, or a USB flash drive, or to the "cloud" (the term used for offsite, Internet-connected storage). Many third-party apps fulfill the function of backing up and restoring files and folders. In Windows 8.1, the backing up and restoring function is done with the File History app.

File History automatically backs up the files that are in your libraries, contacts, and favorites folders, as well as on your desktop. This is done periodically so you can not only restore the most recent copy of a file, but also get a copy of a file as of a particular date. To set up and use File History, you need to do the following:

- Set up a drive on which to store your File History
- Determine which files you want to include in File History
- Determine the frequency of saving files and how long to keep them
- Turn on File History
- Restore files from File History

Start and Set Up File History

1. Open the System menu and select **Control Panel** to display it. In Category view, select **System And Security | File History**. The File History window will open.

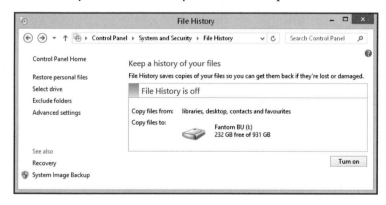

2. Select **Select Drive**. A list of the drives that you have available on your computer will be displayed, excluding the system drive you are using for Windows 8.1.

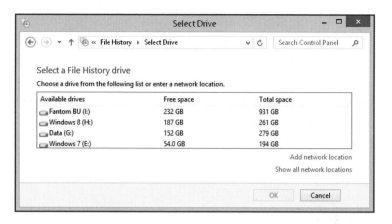

3. Select a local drive on which to store your file history (if possible, back up to an external drive), or select **Add Network Location**.

4. If you chose to save on a network, open the network computer with the drive you want to use to see a list of drives. Open the drive you want to use. Select an existing folder or select **New Folder**, type a name for it, and select **Select Folder**. You are returned to the Select Drive window where the network drive now appears on the list of destination drives. Select it.

5. Select **OK** to return to the File History window. Select **Exclude Folders** to determine what you don't want backed up.

6. Select **Add** to open the Select Folder window. Open the Favorites and Libraries folders to locate and select the folders you don't want backed up. When you have selected a folder you don't want backed up, select **Select Folder**. Repeat this step as necessary. When you are finished, select **Save Changes**. You are returned to the File History window.

7. Select **Advanced Settings** and review the defaults shown next. Select each of the drop-down lists to see the options and select any changes that you wish to make. When you are ready, select **Save Changes**.

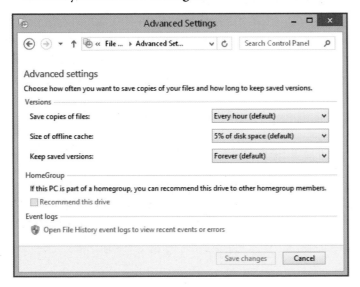

8. Back in the File History window, select **Turn On** to start saving the File History. If you are part of a HomeGroup, you are asked if you want to recommend the drive you selected to your HomeGroup. Select either **Yes** or **No**. You will see a message that the initial File History is being created.

Restore from File History

If you have used File History for a while and you encounter a situation where you need or want to use one or more of the files that have been backed up, you can restore those files with the File History app.

1. Open the System menu and select **Control Panel** to display it. In Category view, select **System And Security | File History**. The File History window will open.

2. Select **Restore Personal Files** to open the Home – File History window shown in Figure 3-13.

3. Open the folders, locate and select the file(s) you want to restore, and select the circular arrow button at the bottom of the window to restore the files to their original location.

   –Or–

   Open the context menu for the file(s) you want to restore and select either **Restore**, to restore the file to its original location, or **Restore To** to specify the folder in which you want to restore the file.

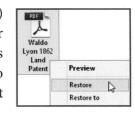

4. If you select Restore To, the Restore To window will open allowing you to select the folder (or create a new one) in

Figure 3-13: File History gives you access to a number of copies of your files over a period of time—a history of your files.

which you want to restore the file. When you have located the folder, select **Select Folder**. The folder will open showing you the file that was restored.

5. Close any or all of the windows that have been opened.

 NOTE System and program files will not be backed up with the automatic File History app.

 ## Write Files and Folders to Other Devices

You may find that you want to get one or more files or folders off your computer, either to give to someone you are not networked with, or to store them somewhere safer than your computer, like a bank safe deposit box. With Windows 8.1, you can copy files and folders to other devices, including writable CDs and DVDs, USB flash drives (these look like a small pack of gum), and memory cards of various types, like those used in many cameras.

Write to CDs or DVDs

To write to CDs or DVDs, you must have a CD or DVD in or connected to your computer and you must have blank media.

1. Place a blank recordable disc (a CD in this example) in the drive and close the door. A message will appear asking you to "Tap to choose what happens with blank CDs." Tap or click this message to open a dialog box asking if you want to burn files to a disc using File Explorer or burn an audio CD using Windows Media Player, or take no action.

2. Select **Burn Files To Disc**. Type a name for the disc. You will be shown two formatting options based on how you want to use the disc:

- **Like A USB Flash Drive**   This format, called *Live File System*, can only be read on a computer with Windows XP or newer versions of the Windows operating systems. This option allows you to add one file or folder to the CD or DVD at a time, like you would with a hard disk or a USB flash drive. You can leave the disc in the drive and drag data to it whenever you want and delete previously added objects.

- **With A CD/DVD Player**   This format, called *Mastered*, can be read by most computers, including older Windows and Apple computers and most stand-alone CD and DVD players. To use this format, you must gather all the files in one place and then burn them all at one time. Use this format for music and video files that you want to play on automobile or stand-alone devices, such as MP3 and video players.

 TIP The Live File System that lets you use CD-R/DVD-R discs like CD-RW/DVD-RW discs is a capability that you can use like an additional hard disk.

3. Select the option you want and then select **Next**. The disc will be formatted and, depending on the option you chose, you will be given the choice to open Media Player, open File Explorer, or take no action. For this discussion, assume that you want to write normal files to the CD, so choose opening the File Explorer. In the subject pane of this File Explorer, you'll see the words "Drag files to this folder to add them to the disc."

4. Right-click or press and hold for a moment the File Explorer icon on the taskbar to open another File Explorer window. Locate in the navigation pane of the new window the folders that contain the files you want on the CD or DVD so that these files are displayed in the subject pane of the new window.

5. With either your mouse or finger, drag the files that you want from the subject pane of the new window to the subject pane of the original window that you opened in step 3, which is the CD/DVD drive, as shown in Figure 3-14.

   • If you are using the Live File System format, as you drag the objects to the drive, they will be immediately written

on the disc. When you have written all the files you want to the disc, in the navigation pane, open the context menu for the drive and select **Close Session**. After the "Closing Session" message above the notification area disappears and is replaced by "Disc Ready," you can remove the disc from the drive and insert it at a later time to resume adding or removing files and folders.

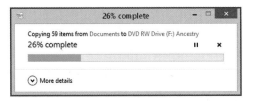

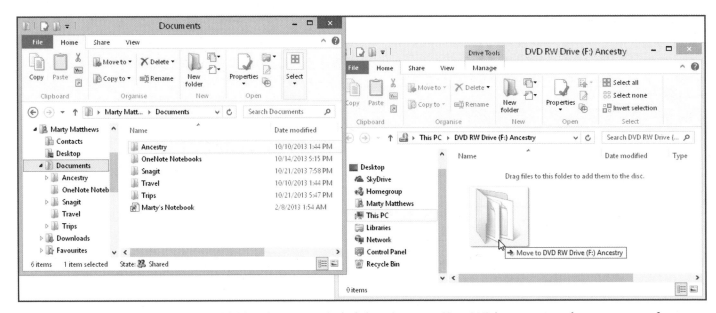

Figure 3-14: Periodically copying files and folders that are particularly important to a CD or DVD is very easy and can protect you from losing the contents.

- If you are using the Mastered format, drag all the objects you want written on the disc to the drive. When all files and folders are in the drive's subject pane, in the navigation pane, open the context menu for the drive and select **Burn To Disc**. You can confirm or change the title, select a recording speed, and then click **Next**. When the burn is complete, the disc will be ejected, and you can choose to burn the same files to another disc. In any case, select **Finish**. The temporary files will be erased, which might take a few minutes.

6. When you are done, select **Close** to close File Explorer.

Write to USB or Other Memory Devices

Writing to a USB flash drive or to a memory card is exactly the same as copying and moving files and folders between two disk drives.

1. Plug the USB flash drive or memory card into your computer. As you saw with CDs/DVDs, you'll get a message about a removable disk that, when tapped, will ask if you want to open the File Explorer.

2. Tap or click this message to open File Explorer, which will identify the device you have inserted so you can copy or move files to it.

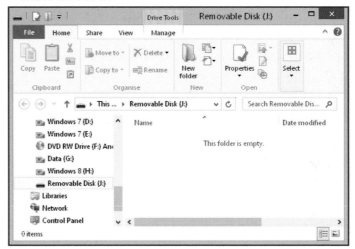

3. Open the drives and folders until you can see the files and folders in the subject pane that you want on the memory device.

4. Scroll the navigation pane so you can again see the "Removable Disk."

5. Drag the files and folders from the subject pane to the Removable Disk in the navigation pane, as you can see in Figure 3-15.

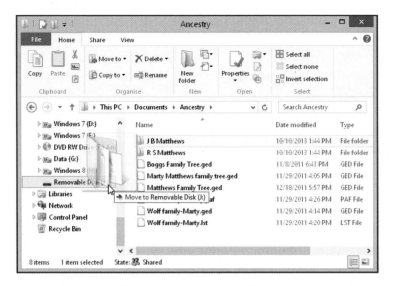

Figure 3-15: Putting files and folders on a USB flash drive or memory card is an easy way to transport them if you are not connected by a network or the Internet.

Tom Works on Excel and PDF Documents

Computers are not second-nature to me, but I find them extremely important in communicating in today's world. I am more productive and, in some ways, better able to grasp the implications of data than previously, when I was buried in the details of generating information myself on a manual spreadsheet.

I mainly use the Internet and email, but I use other programs as well. For instance, as a member of a nonprofit organization for seven years, I receive budgets and financial statements created in Excel from our treasurer. The treasurer attaches the information to an email, and I download it and look at it with Excel. Now I know only the basics about using Excel, but I can read an Excel worksheet just fine, and reading the worksheets allows me to concentrate on the financials of the organization rather than on the steps in creating them. I add comments to the email and return it to the treasurer. This has been an effective and worthwhile way to quickly communicate with other board members.

In a similar way, I can read a PDF document with Acrobat Reader—for free. I don't have to purchase Acrobat Pro or another program that might have been used to create that document.

Tom B., 82, Washington

QuickSteps to...

Chapter 4

Exploring the Internet

The Internet provides a major means for worldwide communication between both individuals and organizations, as well as a major means for locating and sharing information. For many, having access to the Internet is the primary reason for having a computer. To use the Internet, you must have a connection to it using one of the many communications services that are now available, and you need two apps on your computer:

- An **Internet browser** to access the World Wide Web, read the news, look at the weather, use social networking, track your portfolio, watch movies, and shop, among many other things.

- An **Internet mail** app to send and receive email, maintain an address book, and keep track of your appointments.

This chapter will discuss connecting to the Internet, exploring it with Windows 8.1's Internet browser. The following chapter will discuss Internet mail.

CONNECT TO THE INTERNET

You can connect to the Internet using a telephone line, a cable TV connection, a satellite link, or a wireless link. Across these various types of connections there are a myriad of speeds, degrees of reliability, and costs. The most important factor is what is available to you at the location where you want to use it. In an urban area, you have a number of alternatives from landline phone companies, cell phone companies, and cable TV companies, all with options. As you move away from the urban area, your alternatives will decrease to a telephone dial-up connection and/or a satellite link. With a telephone line, you can connect with a *dial-up* connection, a *DSL* (digital subscriber line) connection, or a high-speed fiber-optic connection. DSL, cable, fiber-optic, and some wireless connections are called *broadband* connections and offer higher speeds and are always on. You must have access to at least one of these forms of communication in order to connect to the Internet. You may need to also set up the Internet connection itself.

In addition to the direct connections that you contract for with a telephone, cable, satellite, or cellular company, you can connect to the Internet through one of two wireless connections:

- **Wi-Fi**, which got its origins from "wireless fidelity" but today really doesn't stand for anything. Wi-Fi *hotspots* are areas where the signals can be received and are set up by organizations such as coffee shops, airports, hotels, or other establishments for their customers, or you can easily have Wi-Fi in your home. You may or may not need a passcode to use a Wi-Fi hotspot (you should have one in your home), and you may or may not have to pay for it.

- **3G/4G data plan** through a cell phone company allows you to connect to the Internet anywhere the company has service. In some cases, you have a choice between Wi-Fi and 3G/4G service. Wi-Fi is generally cheaper, but 3G/4G is often, but not necessarily, faster. To set up and use 3G/4G, you need to seek out the instructions of the cell phone company.

▷▷ Establish an Internet Connection

With most forms of Internet connections, you have a choice of speed and ancillary services, such as the number of free email accounts and possibly a personal website. Also, depending on

the type of connection, you may need dedicated equipment, such as a modem, DSL router, or satellite receiving equipment, which may or may not be included in the price. Ask friends and neighbors about what are the best local Internet connections. Contact your local phone company and cable TV provider and ask them about their Internet offering and how much they cost, not just initially, but after 6 and 12 months of use (many companies offer low introductory prices to get you hooked). The speed of information coming over the Internet to you (*download* speed) should be from 2 to 10 megabits per second (Mbps), while the speed of information going from you to the Internet (*upload* speed) should be 1 to 3 Mbps. This should cost you somewhere between $25 and $100 a month, depending on the speed, the type of service, and your location. Obviously, faster is better, but it generally costs more.

TIP Often, setup, installation, and equipment charges for an Internet connection are waived or reduced if you sign a one- or two-year contract and/or prepay for a year or two of service.

Set Up Communications

To set up the communications link between your computer and the Internet, you must first choose and contract for a connection. The Internet service provider (ISP) that provides this service normally will help you set it up.

NOTE To connect to the Internet, you need to have an account with an ISP who will help you establish a user name and password for your account and give you an email address, the type of mail server (POP3, IMAP, or HTTP), and the names of the incoming and outgoing mail servers (such as mail.anisp.net).

A broadband connection—made with a DSL phone line, a cable TV connection, a fiber-optic cable, a satellite connection, or a high-speed wireless connection, is normally made with a device called a *router* that connects to your computer or to a local area network (LAN), which allows several computers on the network to use the same connection. This broadband connection is always on and connected to the Internet. If your computer is turned on and has this connection, there is nothing else you need to do to use it other than start your Internet browser or email app.

Establish a Wi-Fi Connection

When you start a computer in a Wi-Fi (wireless) hotspot, the wireless icon on the right of the taskbar will be dark and have an attention asterisk like this: ▦. This is telling you that you need to set up Wi-Fi. To do that:

1. Select the wireless icon to see a list of Wi-Fi networks that are available at your location, as shown in Figure 4-1.

2. Select the wireless network you want to use. This may open the Security dialog box.

3. If needed, enter the network security key and select **Next**. You will be connected to the network and, in most cases, to the Internet.

Figure 4-1: Many locations have a number of Wi-Fi networks, necessitating knowing which you should use.

Establish a 3G/4G Wireless Connection

Establish a contract with a cellular provider, such as Verizon, Sprint, T-Mobile, or AT&T, and, in communication with them, make sure your device has the necessary transceiver installed and is set up to use their service. Most cellular providers are very helpful in getting you up and running (you're going to be paying them for at least the next two years).

Once you are connected to the Internet, it doesn't matter the type of connection or whether it is wired or wireless, other than the facts that some connections are faster and more reliable than others, and Wi-Fi may be free, but cellular never is.

Explore Windows 8.1's Internet Browser

Windows 8.1 comes with Microsoft's Internet Explorer (IE), version 11 in two flavors: the first is a Windows 8–style app that is started by selecting the **Internet Explorer** tile ![e] on the Start screen. The second is a desktop app that is started by selecting the **Internet Explorer** icon ![e] on the desktop taskbar. Both of these options allow you to go anywhere on the Internet and use all of its resources, but there are some differences.

Discover Start Screen IE 11

Internet Explorer from the Start screen fills the screen, displaying the content of the webpage. When you first open the Start screen IE, there is a command bar with the address box and other controls at the bottom, as you can see on the left in Figure 4-2. Selecting a blank or inactive area on the webpage will close the command bar and its controls, allowing the full screen to be used by the webpage, as shown in the middle of Figure 4-2. The command bar can be restored by right-clicking an inactive area of the screen, selecting the narrow address bar at the bottom of the screen with the three dots, or swiping down from the top or up from the bottom of the screen. When you do that, if you have viewed other websites, a bar of sites you have visited will appear on top of the address bar as you can see on the right in Figure 4-2.

Discover Desktop IE 11

Desktop IE 11 is similar to Internet Explorer in previous versions of Windows. It is inside a window with a set of controls at the top, as you can see in Figure 4-3. You can add toolbars, but the minimum window always has a title bar containing an address box on the left, one or more tabs for

different webpages in the center, and a set of controls on the right and far left.

> **TIP** In most circumstances, once you have installed an Internet connection, it is automatically set up and you have nothing more to do to use it other than start your browser. The easiest way to check that is to try to connect to the Internet as described in the previous section. If you do that and you do not connect to the Internet, you need to contact your ISP, who can probably help you.

USE THE WORLD WIDE WEB

The **World Wide Web** (or just the **Web**) is the sum of all the websites in the world—examples of which are the Wall Street Journal (which is shown in Figures 4-2 and 4-3), Google, and The New York Times. The World Wide Web is what you can access with a **web browser**, such as Internet Explorer.

> **NOTE** For the sake of writing convenience and because Windows 8.1 comes with Internet Explorer, this book assumes you are using Internet Explorer to access the Internet. Other browsers, such as Mozilla Firefox (mozilla.com) and Google Chrome (google.com/chrome), also work fine.

Browse the Internet

Browsing the Internet refers to using a browser, like Internet Explorer, to go from one website to another. You can browse to a site by directly entering a site address, navigating to a site from another site, or using the browser controls. First, of course, you have to start the browser, as described earlier in this chapter.

Figure 4-2: *The Start screen Internet Explorer can give the entire screen to a webpage (center), display a command bar at the bottom (left), or display both the command bar and a tab bar of visited sites (right).*

Enter a Site Directly

To go directly to a site:

1. Start your browser and select the existing address, or ***uniform resource locator** (URL),* in the command bar (at the bottom of the screen in Start screen IE or at the top of the window in desktop IE).

2. Type the address of the site you want to open, as shown (Start screen IE on the left and desktop IE on the right),

and either select **Go/Go To** (the right-pointing arrow on the right) or press **ENTER** in either version of IE.

Figure 4-3: The desktop Internet Explorer always offers a set of controls for you to use on the Internet.

TIP The on-screen keyboard that appears when the command bar is tapped changes the label of the **ENTER** key to **GO**. The right-pointing arrow in the address bar of desktop IE is called "Go To," but the same arrow in the address bar of Start screen IE is called "Go."

Use Site Navigation

Site navigation uses a combination of links and menus on one webpage to locate and open another webpage, either in the same site or in another site.

• **Links** are words, phrases, sentences, or graphics that always have an open hand displayed when the mouse pointer is moved over them and, when selected, take you to another location. They are often a different color or underlined—if not initially, then when you move the mouse pointer to them.

- **Menus** contain one or a few words in a horizontal list, vertical list, or both that always have an open hand displayed when the mouse pointer is moved over them and, when selected, take you to another location.

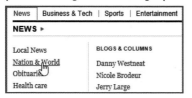

Use Browser Navigation

Browser navigation uses the controls within your browser to go to another location. Both versions of Internet Explorer 11 have two controls not discussed elsewhere that are used for navigation:

- **Back** and **Forward** buttons take you to the next or previous page in the stack of pages you have viewed most recently. Moving your mouse over these buttons will display a tooltip showing you the name of the page the button will take you to.
- **Pages recently entered** button displays a drop-down list of webpages that you have recently entered into the address box, as well as a list of sites you recently visited.

The desktop IE has these controls to the left of and within the command/address bar, as shown here:

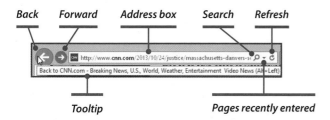

Tooltip   *Pages recently entered*

TIP Open the context menu for a *highlighted* Back or Forward button to open a drop-down menu of recent pages you have visited going in the direction of the button.

Start screen IE has these controls split, with Back and Forward on either end of the command bar, as shown next, and the recently entered sites appearing when you start to enter an address, as shown second.

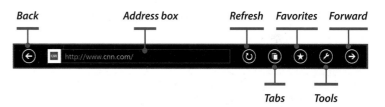

TIP To view a page shown on Start screen IE in desktop IE, select **Page Tools | View In The Desktop**.

Search the Internet

You can search the Internet in two ways: by using the search facility built into Internet Explorer and by using an independent search facility on the Web.

Search from Internet Explorer

To use Internet Explorer's search facility, in either version, select the contents of the address box and begin typing what you want to search for. What happens next depends on what you typed.

As you are typing, IE looks at sites you have recently visited and, if a possible match is found, a site is suggested and others are listed. If what you have typed does not look like a site—for example, "San Francisco Restaurants"—the Bing search site will open with the results of the search, as you can see in Figure 4-4.

When you see a site you want to visit, select the link to go to that site.

Search from an Internet Site

There are many independent Internet search sites. The most popular is Google.

1. In either version of Internet Explorer, select the current address in the address box, type google.com, and either select **Go/Go To** (the right-pointing arrow on the right) or press **ENTER**.

2. In the text box, type what you want to search for, and select **Google Search**. The resulting websites are shown in a full webpage, as illustrated in Figure 4-5.

3. Select the link of your choice to go to that site.

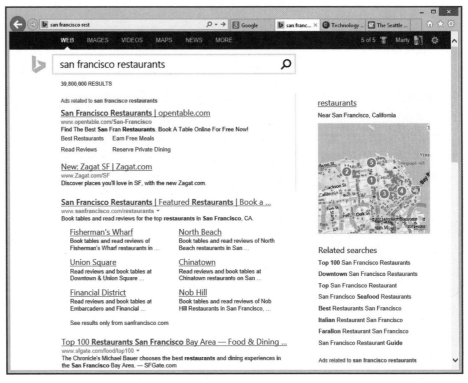

Figure 4-4: The results of a search using Internet Explorer's address box.

 TIP When you enter search criteria, place quotation marks around certain keywords or phrases to get only results that match those words exactly.

▶▶ Save a Favorite Site

Sometimes, you visit a site that you would like to return to quickly or often. Both versions of Internet Explorer have the ability to save sites for easy retrieval.

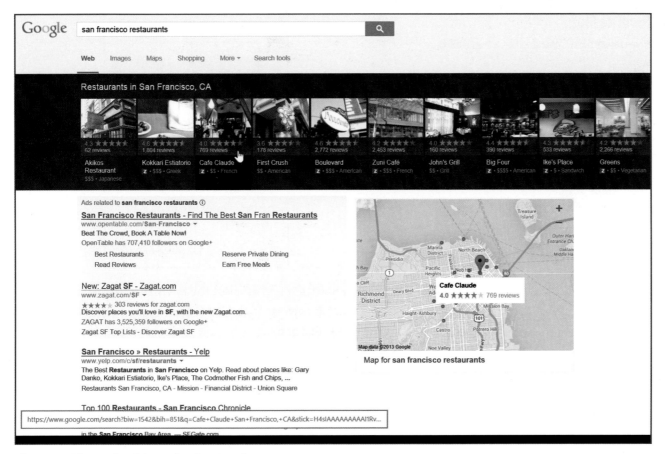

Figure 4-5: The results of a search using Google.

Add a Desktop Favorite Site

In desktop IE 11, you save the site to a list called "Favorites."

1. In Internet Explorer, open the webpage you want to add to your Favorites list, and make sure its correct address (URL) is in the address box.

2. Select the **Favorites** icon in the middle of the three icons on the right of the tab row.

3. Select **Add To Favorites**. The Add A Favorite dialog box appears. Adjust the name as needed in the text box (you may want to type a name you will readily associate with that site), and select **Add**.

Add a Start Screen Favorite Site

In Start screen IE 11, you can also save a site to Favorites.

1. In Internet Explorer, open the webpage you want to add to your Favorites list, and make sure its correct address (URL) is in the address box.

2. Select the **Favorites** icon on the command bar.

3. The Favorites bar will open. Select **Add To Favorites** to open the dialog box, adjust the name as desired, and select **Add** to add the current site to Favorites.

> **TIP** Start screen IE has a new feature that relates to Favorites. It is the new Reading List app and the ability to save websites to the Reading List to look at later. You can add a site you have open in Start screen IE by selecting **Favorites | Share** (on the far-right area of the Favorites bar), and then selecting **Reading List**. You can then come back later and select Reading List from the Start screen to read the sites you have posted there.

In Start screen IE, select the **Favorites** icon on the right of the tab row, scroll the list to the left, and select the site you want to open.

> **TIP** In desktop IE, if the status bar is turned on (open the context menu in the blank area on the right of the tab row and select **Status Bar**), there is a Zoom button and menu in the lower-right corner of the Internet Explorer window. Select the down arrow to open the menu and select a level of magnification, or select **Zoom In** or **Zoom Out** to iterate through the levels, or select the current level to increase the magnification one level. On a touch screen, pinch or spread your fingers.

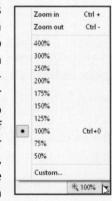

Open a Favorite Site

To open a favorite site you have saved:

In desktop IE, select the **Favorites** icon on the right of the tab row, ensure the **Favorites** tab is selected, scroll the list up if needed, and select the site you want to open.

Change Your Home Page

When you open either version of Internet Explorer, a webpage is automatically displayed. This page is called your ***home page***. When IE starts, you can have it open several pages in addition to the home page, with the additional pages available through tabs (see "Use Tabs" in this chapter).

To change the home page and the other pages initially opened in either version of IE:

1. In desktop Internet Explorer, directly enter or browse to the site you want as your home page. If you want additional pages, open them in separate tabs.

2. Open the context menu for the Home Page icon, and select **Add Or Change Home Page**. The Add Or Change Home Page dialog box will appear.

3. Select:
   - **Use This Webpage As Your Only Home Page** if you wish to have only a single home page.
   - **Add This Webpage To Your Home Page Tabs** if you wish to have several home pages on different tabs.
   - **Use The Current Tab Set As Your Home Page** if you want all the current tabs to appear when you start Internet Explorer or select the Home Page icon (this option is only available if you have two or more tabs open).

4. Select **Yes** to complete your home page selection and close the dialog box.

NOTE You can only set the home page or pages in the desktop version of IE, but the home page(s) you set there will normally be reflected in the Start screen version.

YOU can also change the home page by selecting the **Tools** icon on the far right in desktop IE, selecting **Internet Options** to open the dialog box, and making the desired changes at the top of the General tab.

TIP You can open the home page in its own tab instead of replacing the current tab by holding down **CTRL** while selecting the Home icon.

⊳⊳ Use Tabs

Both versions of Internet Explorer allow you to have several webpages open at one time and easily switch among them by selecting the tab associated with the page. In desktop IE, the tabs reside on the ***tab row***, immediately above the displayed webpage, which also includes the address box, as shown in Figure 4-6.

In Start screen IE, the tabs, shown in Figure 4-7, reside in a separate bar that opens above the command bar when you swipe down from the top of the screen or right-click a blank area of the screen.

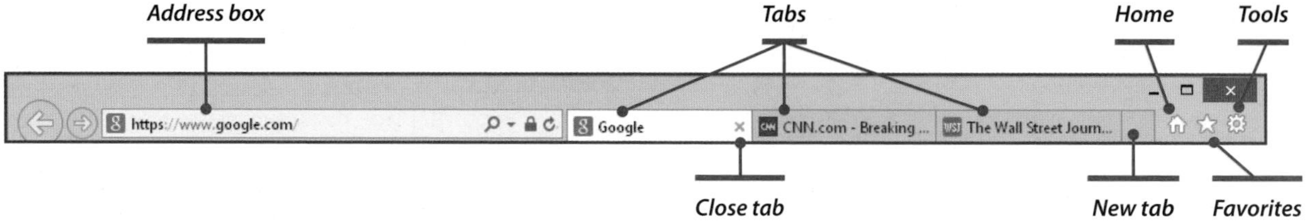

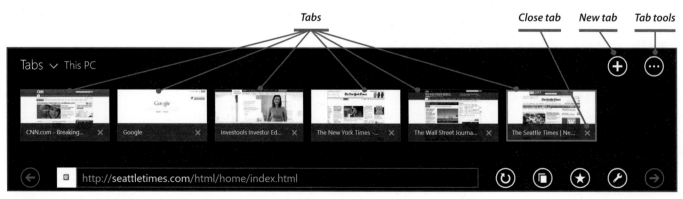

Figure 4-6 labels (top image): Address box · Tabs · Home · Tools · Close tab · New tab · Favorites

Figure 4-6: Tabs allow you to quickly switch among several websites.

Open Pages in a New Tab

To open a page in a new tab instead of opening the page in an existing tab:

1. Open Internet Explorer with at least one webpage displayed.

2. Open the tab bar in Start screen IE and then, in either version, select **New Tab** on the right end of the tab row or bar (or press **CTRL+T**) and open a new webpage in any of the ways described earlier in this chapter.

   –Or–

   Type a web address in the address box, and press **ALT+ENTER**. (If you just press **ENTER**, you'll open a page in the same tab.)

–Or–

Hold down **CTRL** while selecting a link in an open page. (If you just select the link, you'll open a page in the same tab.) Then select the new tab to open the page.

3. Repeat any of the alternatives in step 2 as needed to open additional pages.

Switch Among Tabs

To switch among open tabs:

In Start screen IE, open the tab bar and in either version, select the tab of the page you want to open.

–Or–

Figure 4-7 labels (bottom image): Tabs · Close tab · New tab · Tab tools

Tabs ⌄ This PC

CNN.com - Breaking... | Google | Investools Investor Ed... | The New York Times -... | The Wall Street Journa... | The Seattle Times | Ne...

http://seattletimes.com/html/home/index.html

Figure 4-7: Start screen IE tabs must be specifically displayed to use them.

Press **CTRL+TAB** to switch to the next tab to the right, or press **CTRL+ SHIFT+TAB** to switch to the next tab to the left.

–Or–

Press **CTRL+***n*, where *n* is a number from one to eight to switch to one of the first eight tabs numbered from the left in the order they were opened. You can also press **CTRL+9** to switch to the last tab that was opened, shown on the right of the tab row.

 NOTE To use **CTRL+***n* to switch among Internet Explorer's tabs, you need to use a number key on the top of the main keyboard, *not* on the numeric keypad on the right.

Close Tabs

To close one or more tabs:

In Start screen IE, open the tab bar and select the **x** on the right of the tab of the page you want to close. In desktop IE, select the tab and then select the **x**.

–Or–

Press **CTRL+W** to close the current page and its tab.

–Or–

Open the context menu for the tab of the page you want to close, and select **Close Tab** on the context menu; or select **Close Other Tabs** to close all of the pages except the one you selected.

 TIP In desktop IE, press just the **ALT** key to view Internet Explorer's menus.

▷▷ Organize Favorite Sites

You will probably find that you have a number of favorite sites and it is becoming hard to find the one you want. Internet Explorer on the desktop provides two places to store your favorite sites: a Favorites list, which is presented to you in the form of a menu you can open, and a Favorites bar, which can be displayed at all times. Start screen IE provides a Favorites bar. There are several ways to organize your favorite sites in desktop IE. Start screen IE will mirror your desktop organization.

Rearrange the Favorites List

The items on your Favorites list are displayed in the order you added them, unless you move them to a new location.

In desktop IE, select the **Favorites** icon, locate the site you want to reposition, and move it to the location in the list where you want it. If you go to Start screen IE and open Favorites, you will see your change reflected there.

Create New Folders

Desktop Internet Explorer comes with at least one default folder for the Favorites bar. The computer's manufacturer may have added more folders, and you can add your own within the Favorites list.

1. In desktop IE, select the **Favorites** icon, select the **Add To Favorites** down arrow, and select **Organize Favorites** to open the Organize Favorites dialog box, shown in Figure 4-8.

2. Select **New Folder**, type the name for the folder, and press **ENTER**.

3. Move the desired site links to the new folder, move the folder to where you want it on the list, and then select **Close**.

Figure 4-8: *As with files, organizing your favorite websites helps you easily find what you want.*

Put Favorites in Folders

You can put a site in either your own folders (see "Create New Folders") or the default ones when you initially add it to your Favorites list.

1. Open the webpage you want in your Favorites list, and make sure its correct address or URL is in the address box.

2. Select the **Favorites** icon, select **Add To Favorites**, adjust the name as needed in the text box, select the **Create In** down arrow, select the folder to use, and select **Add**.

Add a Site to the Favorites Bar

In desktop IE, you can turn on the Favorites bar by opening the context menu for any of the three icons (Home, Favorites, and Tools) on the right of the tab row and selecting **Favorites Bar**. By default, the Favorites bar may have several sites on it, but you can delete those and add others.

Open the site you want to add to the Favorites bar. If the Favorites bar is open, select the **Add To Favorites Bar** button on the left of the Favorites bar.

–Or–

Select **Favorites**, select the **Add To Favorites** down arrow, and select **Add To Favorites Bar**.

–Or–

Drag a site's icon from the address box to the Favorites bar, and drag the site icon within the Favorites bar to where you want it.

Access Favorite Folders in Start Screen IE

As was said earlier, Start screen IE Favorites mirrors desktop IE Favorites, and that applies to folders and the Favorites bar. With Start screen IE open, right-click or swipe up from the bottom to open the command bar and select the Favorites icon on the right to open Favorites, as you saw earlier in this chapter. On the left, select either the word **Favorites** or the down arrow to open the list of folders you have and select the folder you want to open. Return to the display of all your favorites by selecting **All.**

Access Web History

Internet Explorer on the desktop keeps a history of the websites you visit, and you can use that history to return to a site. You can set the length of time to keep sites in that history, and you can clear your history.

Use Web History

To use the Web History feature:

1. In desktop IE, select the **Favorites** icon, and select the **History** tab; or press CTRL+H to open the History pane.

2. Select the down arrow opposite **View By Date** in the History tab to select how you want the history sorted. Depending on what you select, you will be able to further specify the type of history you want to view. For example, if

you leave the default View By Date, you can then select the day and website you want to open, as shown in Figure 4-9.

Delete and Set History

You can set the length of time to keep your Internet history, and you can clear this history.

1. In desktop IE, select the **Tools** icon at the right end of the tab row, and select **Internet Options**.

   In the General tab, under Browsing History, select **Delete** to open the Delete Browsing History dialog box. If needed, select the **History** check box to delete your browsing history. Select any other check box to delete that information, although you should keep the Preserve Favorites Website Data check box selected to *keep* that information (it is a confusing dialog box). Select **Delete**.

   –Or–

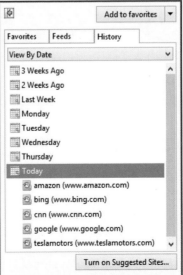

Figure 4-9: The Web History feature allows you to find a site that you visited in the recent past.

In the General tab of the Internet Options dialog box, under Browsing History, select **Settings | History** and use the **Days** spinner to set the number of days to keep your Web History. Select **OK**. The default is 20 days.

2. Select **OK** again to close the Internet Options dialog box.

Control Internet Security

Internet Explorer on the desktop allows you to control three aspects of Internet security. You can categorize sites by the degree to which you trust them, determine how you want to handle cookies placed on your computer by websites, and set and use ratings to control the content of websites that can be viewed. These controls are found in the Internet Options dialog box.

In desktop IE, select the **Tools** icon and select **Internet Options**.

 NOTE The settings that you make in desktop IE also apply to Start screen IE.

Categorize Websites

Desktop IE allows you to categorize websites into zones: Internet (sites that are not classified in one of the other ways), Local Intranet, Trusted Sites, and Restricted Sites (as shown in Figure 4-10).

From the Internet Options dialog box:

1. Select the **Security** tab and select the **Internet** zone. Note its definition and security level.

2. Adjust the level of security you want for this zone. Select **OK** when you are finished.

3. Select each of the other zones, where you can identify either groups or individual sites you want in that zone.

 NOTE Protected Mode—which you can turn on or off at the bottom of the Security tab—is what produces the messages that tell you a program is trying to run in Internet Explorer or that software is trying install itself on your computer. In most cases, you can select a bar at the top of the Internet Explorer window if you want to run the program or install the software. You can also open the notice at the bottom of Internet Explorer to open the Security tab and turn off Protected Mode (clear the **Enable Protected Mode** check box).

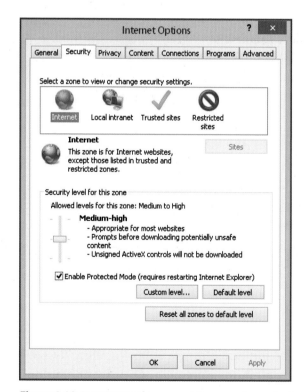

Figure 4-10: Internet Explorer provides a way to control security with zones and determine what can be done within those zones.

Handle Cookies

Cookies are small pieces of data that websites store on your computer so that they can remind themselves of who you are. These can save you from having to constantly enter your name and ID. Cookies can also be dangerous, however, letting people into your computer where they can potentially do damage. Internet Explorer on the desktop lets you determine the types and sources of cookies you will allow and what those cookies can do on your computer.

From the Internet Options dialog box:

1. Select the **Privacy** tab and select a privacy setting by moving the slider up or down.

2. Select **Advanced** to open the Advanced Privacy Settings dialog box. If you wish, select **Override Automatic Cookie Handling**, and select the settings you want to use.

3. Select **OK** to return to the Internet Options dialog box.

4. In the lower part of the Privacy tab, you can turn off the pop-up blocker, which is on by default (it is recommended that you leave it on). If you have a site that you frequently use that needs pop-ups, select **Settings**, enter the site address (URL), and select **Add | Close**.

5. At the bottom of the Privacy tab, you can determine how to handle InPrivate Filtering and Browsing. See the Note on InPrivate Browsing later in this chapter.

Control Content

You can control the content that Internet Explorer displays.

From the Internet Options dialog box:

1. Select the **Content** tab and select **Family Safety**. You must have one or more Child accounts on the computer in order to set parental controls. Select **Accounts** to establish one if needed.

2. With a Child account, select **Manage Setting On The Family Safety Website**. Select the child you want to control to open the Family Safety Settings window, shown in Figure 4-11.

3. Select each of the categories (Activity Reporting, Web Filtering, Time Limits, and so on) to review their purpose and then select the setting that is correct in your case.

4. When you are done, select **Close** twice to first close the Internet Explorer window and then the Family Safety window, and finally select **OK** to close the Internet Options dialog box. (Other parts of this dialog box are discussed elsewhere in this book.)

> **NOTE** Both versions of Internet Explorer have a way to more safely browse and view websites, called *InPrivate*. Open this in Start screen IE by opening the tab bar and selecting **Tab Tools | New InPrivate Tab** . In desktop IE, select the **Tools** icon and then select **Safety | InPrivate Browsing**. This opens a separate browser window with InPrivate identified in the address box in either desktop or Start screen IE. While you are in this window, your browsing history, temporary Internet files, and cookies are not stored on your computer, preventing anyone looking at your computer from seeing where you have browsed. In addition, with the desktop's ActiveX Filtering, also opened from Safety in Tools, you can limit what information about you is passed on to Internet content providers.

▷▷ Copy Internet Information

You may occasionally find something on the Internet that you want to copy—a picture, some text, or a webpage.

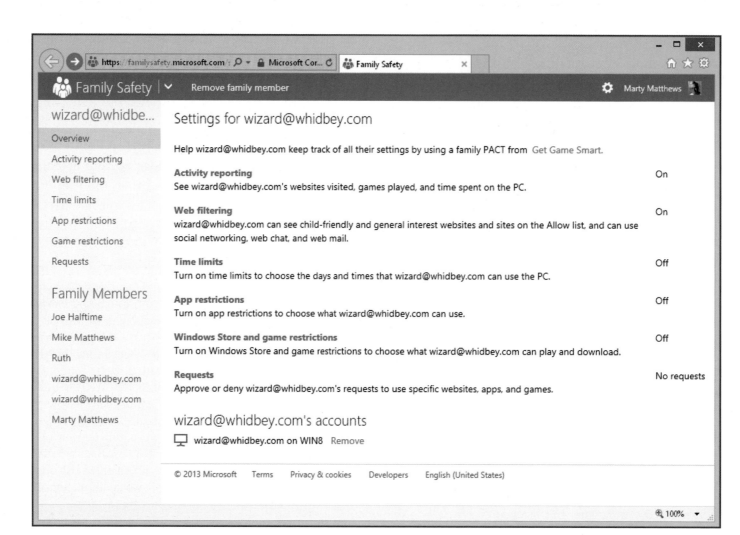

Figure 4-11: You can place a number of controls on what a particular user can do on a computer using the Family Safety feature.

CAUTION! Material you copy from the Internet is normally protected by copyright; therefore, what you can do with it is limited. Basically, you can store it on your computer and refer to it. You cannot put it on your own website, sell it, copy it for distribution, or use it for a commercial purpose without the permission of the owner.

Copy a Picture from the Internet

To copy a picture from an Internet webpage to a folder on your hard disk:

1. Open either version of Internet Explorer and locate the webpage containing the picture you want.

2. Open the context menu for the picture. In Start screen IE, select **Save To Pictures Folder**. In desktop IE, select **Save Picture As**, locate the folder in which you want to save the picture, enter the filename you want to use and the file type if it is something other than what is already assigned to the picture, and select **Save**.

Copy Text from the Internet to a Document or Email

To copy text from a webpage to a Microsoft Word document or email message:

1. Open either version of Internet Explorer and locate the webpage containing the text you want.

2. Move across the text to highlight it, open the context menu for the selection, and select **Copy**.

 TIP To highlight and copy text using touch, slowly double-tap a word in the text to be copied. Two circles will be displayed under the selection. Move each circle in opposite directions to highlight more text. Touch and momentarily hold the selection to open the context menu. Tap **Copy** to complete the operation.

3. Open a document—for example, in Microsoft Word—or an email message in which you want to paste the text. Open the context menu for where you want the text, and select **Paste Options**.

4. Save the Word document and close Microsoft Word or your email program if you are done with them.

Copy a Webpage from the Internet

To make a copy of a webpage in desktop IE and store it on your hard disk:

1. Open desktop IE and locate the webpage you want to copy.

2. In desktop IE, select the **Tools** icon and then select **File | Save As**.

3. In the Save Webpage dialog box, select the folder in which to save the page, enter the filename you want to use, and select **Save**.

4. Close Internet Explorer if you are done.

TIP To search for information on an open webpage in desktop IE, press **CTRL+F;** in Start screen IE, select **Page Tools | Find On Page**.

Play Internet Audio and Video Files

You can play audio and video files on the Internet with Internet Explorer directly from a link on a webpage. Many webpages have links to audio and video files, such as the one shown in Figure 4-12. To play these files, simply select the links. If you have several audio players installed (for example, Windows Media Player and iTunes Player), you will be asked which one you want to use. Make that choice, and the player will open to play the requested piece. Chapter 7 discusses working with audio and video files in depth, including how to play these files in various ways.

USE THE INTERNET

The Internet is a major way in which you can connect with the world that provides information, shopping, contact with government agencies, getting directions and maps, and planning and purchasing travel, to name only a fraction of what you can do. In later chapters of this book we'll look at using the Internet for email, social networking, digital photography, music and video, personal finance, and genealogy. For the rest of this chapter we'll look at using the Internet in a number of other, more general, ways.

Figure 4-12: Play an audio or video file on a webpage by selecting the link.

Get Information

The start of many things you do on the Internet is through a search. As you have seen earlier in this chapter, searching the Internet is easy through either the Internet Explorer's Search box, which by default is the Microsoft Bing search engine, or a search website like Google.com. While there are a number of other search sites—for example, Yahoo.com—I've found that Google and Bing are as good as any and handle all that I want to do.

TIP Search sites such as Google and Bing provide the ability to search the entire Internet. Search boxes on other sites, such as CNN and Amazon, are used to search those sites, not the Internet.

You can search for almost anything and, in most cases, find it. Sometimes you need to be more diligent than at other times, but often you can find what you are looking for. Several examples of searches follow. These searches can be done in either desktop IE or Start screen IE.

Mary Tudor vs. Mary Queen of Scots

In the last several years there have been movies and television programs on England's King Henry VIII and Queen Elizabeth I, his daughter. In these, two historical figures named Mary come up: Mary Tudor and Mary Queen of Scots. Let's say you are curious and want to know more about these two people and how they are related.

1. In Internet Explorer's address box, highlight the current contents and type google.com.

2. In Google's text box, type Mary Tudor and Mary Queen of Scots and press ENTER. The Google page similar to that shown in Figure 4-13 will open.

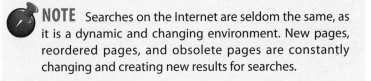

NOTE Searches on the Internet are seldom the same, as it is a dynamic and changing environment. New pages, reordered pages, and obsolete pages are constantly changing and creating new results for searches.

3. Review the first several entries, and select the first one you want to see. A page of detail about your subject will open.

4. If the results of the first entry do not satisfy your curiosity, select **Previous** in Internet Explorer's title bar to return to the list of search results and select another entry.

White Bean Soup

The Internet is a tremendous resource for recipes. All you have to do is search. Here is an example with white bean soup.

Figure 4-13: A search can be a question, a statement, a word, or a phrase. Often, a question can be truncated, as it is here, where "who were" has been left off.

In Internet Explorer's address box, type white bean soup. As you are typing, you will get suggestions, which you can select, or you can select **Go** or press ENTER. A list of sites with a recipe for this dish appears, similar to what you see in Figure 4-14.

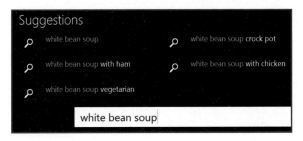

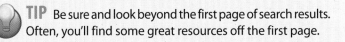

TIP Be sure and look beyond the first page of search results. Often, you'll find some great resources off the first page.

Figure 4-14: If you like to cook, the Internet is a great resource for you.

 NOTE When you do a Google search, the first several sites may be highlighted with a color background to tell you that those sites have paid to be at the top of the list. It is important to check several sites in both the paid and unpaid areas and compare prices of the items being sold. In my experience, I've found a lot of variability in price of the same item.

Get the News

With the Internet's almost-immediate communication, it is a great vehicle for getting news of all types, including local and national newspapers, general and specialized magazines, and newsletters of all types. Several examples follow.

Read Online Newspapers

Most newspapers have been online for some time. Generally, you can go right to their site by putting their name directly into the address bar followed by ".com" without searching for them. For example, the following URLs all work:

- ajc.com (*Atlanta Journal Constitution*)
- bostonherald.com
- chicagotribune.com
- denverpost.com
- kcstar.com (*Kansas City Star*)
- latimes.com (*Los Angeles Times*)
- miamiherald.com
- times.com (*New York Times*)
- inquirer.com (*Philadelphia Inquirer*)
- seattletimes.com
- wsj.com (*Wall Street Journal*)
- washingtonpost.com

 TIP Some online newspapers are still free, but many, like the *Wall Street Journal*, have or are beginning to implement a charging scheme for their current edition and archives, especially in electronic readers such as the iPad.

Read Online Magazines

Many magazines that once had paper editions are now only online, while other magazines are now charging for their online editions. For example, *Consumer Reports* (consumerreports.org or consumerreports.com) and *Cook's Illustrated* (cooksillustrated .com), which give you their home page for free, ask you to pay when you want to see the detail, as you can see in Figure 4-15.

Figure 4-15: While much of Internet news and information content is free, an increasing number of sites are beginning to charge for it.

For the most part, you can directly use the magazine title with ".com" in Internet Explorer's address bar.

▷▷ Contact Government Agencies

Most government agencies, from the local to the federal level, have an online presence that can be very useful for finding out about government programs, learning about public officials, and getting the results of elections. A couple of examples are the Social Security Administration and researching the position of a congressperson.

Social Security Administration

Probably the fastest way of locating a website is to search the name of the entity; similarly, the fastest way to find what you want in a site is to do an intrasite search. Let's say you want to find the current eligibility requirements for Social Security.

1. In the Internet Explorer's address box, type <u>social security</u> and press **ENTER**. One of the entries that appears is titled "Social Security Administration - Official Site." Select that site.

2. In the site's search box, type <u>eligibility requirements</u> and press **ENTER**.

3. Review the search results and select the entry that is most likely to give you the information you need.

4. Follow any additional links that you need to get your information.

Research a Congressperson

If you would like to determine the views of your congressperson and you don't remember his or her name or the district number he or she represents, you can find all that online.

1. In the Internet Explorer address box, type google.com.

2. In the Google search box, type your state name and "congressional districts," and press ENTER. Your results should be similar to the illustration.

3. Select the entry with "Congressional District Map" in its title with the address govtrack.us. The result should look similar to Figure 4-16, except for your state.

4. Note your district, scroll down to locate your congressperson, and select his or her name. A page about your congressperson should open with links to further information.

5. Follow any of the links that interest you.

▷▷ Get Maps and Directions

Google and Microsoft, as well as other sites, have excellent and very detailed maps and driving directions. Here's how Microsoft Maps works.

Use Microsoft Maps

1. In Internet Explorer's address box, type an address or location you want to see on a map, and press ENTER. Among the search results is a small map.

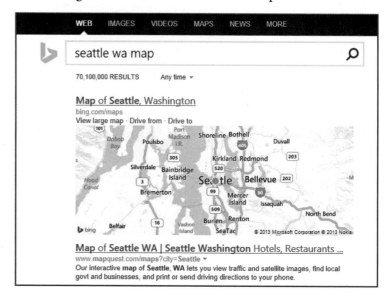

2. Select **View Large Map** to see a full-sized map of the location or address you entered, as shown in Figure 4-17.

3. On this map, you can:

- Zoom in for more detail or zoom out for area references by selecting the plus or minus symbols, dragging in the scale (both of these are in the upper right of the map), double-tapping, or pinching or expanding your fingers.

- Drag the map around to see areas not currently in view by moving either your finger or the mouse onto the map and dragging it in the direction you want it moved.

- View the map as a road map or as an aerial photograph in either straight-down Aerial view or the slightly angled Bird's Eye view using the option on the top-left corner.

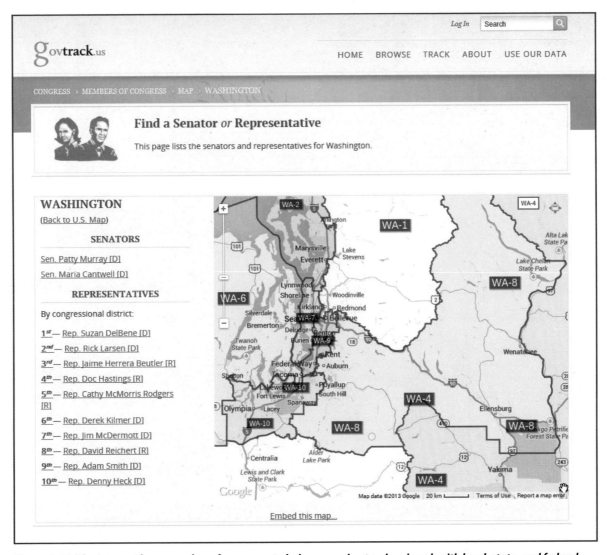

Figure 4-16: The Internet has a number of resources to help you understand and work with local, state, and federal governments.

- Get driving directions from another location by selecting **Directions** under the address.

- Locate restaurants, businesses, malls, and hotels by selecting **Nearby** on the upper-left corner.

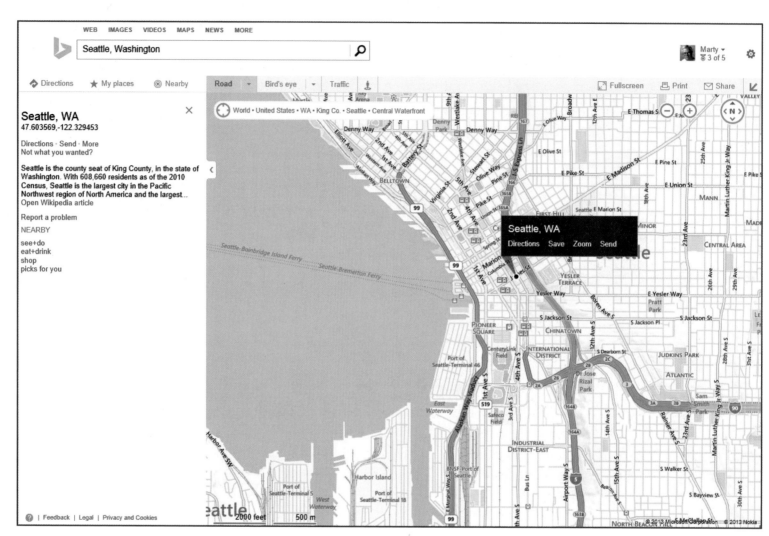

Figure 4-17: Excellent maps are available online with many features not available any other way.

⮞⮞ Shop on the Internet

Shopping is one of the great benefits of having access to the Internet. You don't have to leave your home, you have access to far more outlets than are available in most places, prices are generally modest, and you have the ability to do comparison shopping to find the best products at the best prices. Look at two examples of online shopping for a digital camera and airline tickets.

Digital Camera

You may be aware that digital cameras are improving quickly and getting cheaper at the same time. If you are interested in getting a new one, you may be in a quandary as which one to buy. Start by searching for camera reviews and then do some comparison shopping before finally buying a camera (you can't do this with all products, but electronics in particular can be handled in this way).

1. In either the Google or Bing search box, type <u>digital camera reviews</u> and press **ENTER**. A page of sites that review digital cameras will appear.

2. Open several of the sites and look at what they say. Some may be more comparison shopping than reviews of cameras. Select a site that looks interesting to you and open it.

Digital cameras: compare **digital camera reviews** - CNET Reviews
reviews.cnet.com/**digital-cameras**/ ▾
Digital camera reviews and ratings, video reviews, user opinions, most popular digital cameras, camera buying guides, prices, and comparisons.
Best digital cameras - Sony Cyber-shot DSC-RX100 - Nikon D5200 - Nikon D7000

---

3. Open several sites. One of my favorite is CNET, which is shown in Figure 4-18.

4. Pick the camera you want to investigate further, and select the title of the camera to open a page devoted to it. Read the review and other information on the page.

Airline Tickets

Airlines now prefer and reward buying tickets online. You often save money, sometimes a lot, may also be entitled to fast electronic check-in at the airport, and sometimes get bonus miles. There are many sources of airline tickets on the Internet, including the airlines themselves and numerous travel sites. Sometimes the sites can save you money, but often, the cheapest fares are from the airlines; however, some airlines, such as Southwest, do not allow sales through the travel sites, so you need to look at both the airlines and the travel sites. Also, some travel sites, such as Fly.com will compare the fares on several other travel sites. What I recommend is that you start by comparing travel sites with Fly.com, then go to the site that looks best, and finally go to the airline that looks best. Also, if you are going along a Southwest route, you want check them (Southwest does not charge for up to two pieces of checked luggage, which on other airlines can be $25 to $35 a bag).

1. In Internet Explorer's address bar, type <u>fly.com</u> and press **ENTER**. Type the from and to cities, select the departure and return dates and times and the number of travelers, and select the travel sites you want to compare, as shown in the illustration.

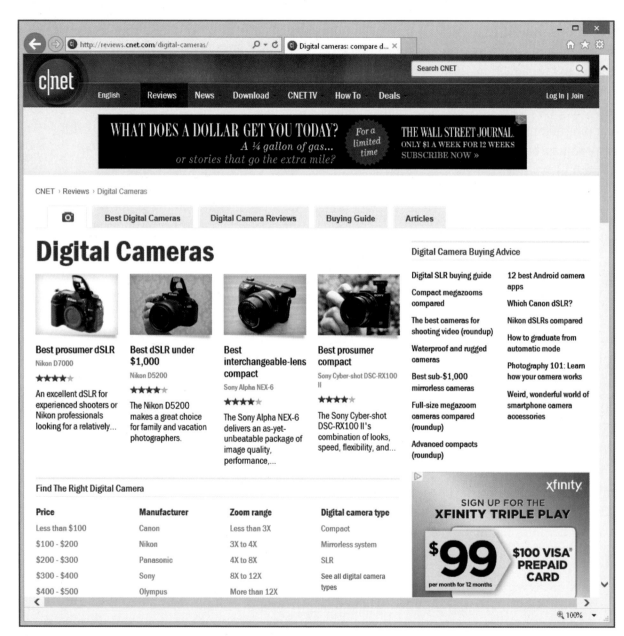

Figure 4-18: When shopping for electronics, there is a wealth of information that allows you to find what you want, compare alternatives, and shop for the best price and terms.

2. Select **Search**. Your screen becomes very busy, and you may see a message that a pop-up window has been blocked. Select to allow the pop-up. You see a Fly.com summary, shown at the right, and then, if you select **Allow Once** to allow pop-up windows, several additional windows will open, one for each of the travel sites you selected, as you can see in Figure 4-19.

3. Expand (select **Maximize** on the right of the title bar) and review

each of the travel sites (be sure to get the total price with both taxes and fees included, not just the advertised price).

4. Pick an airline and enter its name in the Internet Explorer address box (don't select its name in Fly.com or another travel site because you want the best fare the airline itself will offer). Re-enter the from and to cities and dates and times. Select **Search** or the equivalent button (Alaska Airlines uses "Find Flights"). The results for that airline will be displayed. It may surprise you.

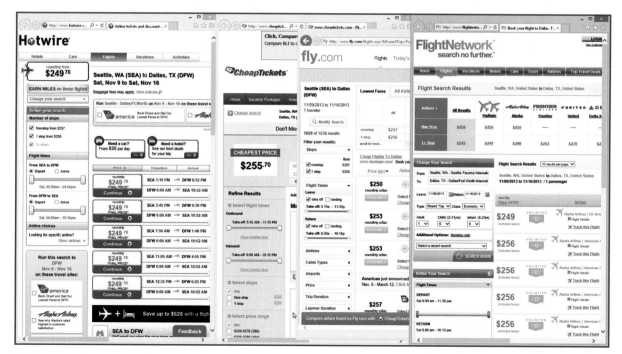

Figure 4-19: Fly.com provides a comparison of the fares on several travel sites.

5. If Southwest flies the route you want to fly (type <u>southwest. com</u> in the address box and enter your from and to cities), check their fares. Make sure taxes and fees are included.

It may take some work and perseverance to find the lowest fare.

Chapter 5

Sending and Receiving Email

For many seniors, having access to the Internet and email are the primary reasons for having a computer. The Internet provides a major means for worldwide communication between both individuals and organizations, allowing you to send and receive email, as well as communicate using blogs, forums, and text messages. In this chapter we'll talk about how to set up and use Windows 8.1's Mail app, including creating, sending, and receiving messages; handling spam; adding attachments and signatures; and applying formatting. We'll also briefly look at web-based alternatives for email, as well as how to use the Calendar.

USE INTERNET EMAIL

Windows 8 included a new Windows 8–style mail app, which allows you to send and receive email. You can also send and receive email through a web mail account using Internet Explorer, but this chapter will primarily describe using Mail. See "Use Web Mail" later in this chapter for a discussion of that subject.

Set Up Windows Mail

For email with Windows 8.1, this book describes the use of the Windows Mail app because it works well, comes free with Windows 8.1, and is designed for it. There are a number of other alternatives that you can buy or get for free, including Outlook from Microsoft, Google's Gmail, Eudora, Mozilla

Thunderbird, and Opera. If you wish to explore the alternatives, do an Internet search on any of these.

To begin the use of Windows Mail, you must establish an email account with one of the email providers recognized by Mail and then convey that information to the app.

Establish an Email Account

To send and receive email with Mail, you must have an Internet connection and an email account established with a recognized email provider.

For an email account, you need:

- Your email address, for example: mike@anisp.com
- The password for your mail account
- You may also need to know the type of mail server you are using, IMAP or POP (if you have a choice, IMAP is the more flexible of the two)

Mail recognizes accounts with Outlook.com (the new Microsoft Internet mail service replacement for Hotmail), AOL, Google, Yahoo!, and Exchange and Office 365 servers, as well as many smaller Internet service providers (ISPs). Since you had to have a Microsoft account to use Windows 8.1, you can generally use that for your Mail account. You can also open Internet Explorer from either the Start screen or the desktop and go to Outlook .com (not the Office product, but the replacement for Hotmail) and create a new account.

Initiate Windows Mail

With your account information, you can set up an account in Mail.

1. In the Start screen, select the **Mail** tile. Mail will try to set up an account for you based on the email address in

your Microsoft account. If your account is not in Hotmail, Outlook.com, or Google, you will be asked what kind of account you have: Exchange (generally in larger enterprises) or IMAP (Internet Message Access Protocol). With either of the other choices, select **Connect.**

2. If you have an existing Hotmail, Google, or Outlook.com account that you have used to register with Microsoft, you will automatically be signed in and you can start using Mail.

3. If you do not have a Hotmail, Google, or Outlook.com account but you are still trying to use the mail account you used to register with Microsoft, you will be asked to enter your password and select **Connect**. As needed to connect to your ISP, you may be asked to enter additional information, such as your incoming and outgoing mail servers. If you don't know this, you'll need to ask your ISP. Enter this information and again select **Connect**. You should connect with your ISP and see your mail, as you can see in Figure 5-1.

4. If you do not want to use the email address that you used to register with Microsoft, or if you want to set up another email account and the list of email servers is on your screen, select one of the servers or select **View All In Settings**.

5. If the list of email servers is not on your screen but Mail is still displayed, open **Charms** and select **Settings | Accounts | Add An Account** in the Settings pane.

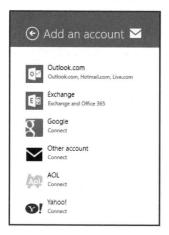

6. Select the type of email account you have—for example, **Google**—enter your email address, press **TAB**, enter your email password, and select **Sign in**. You are asked if is okay that Mail views and manages your Gmail account. If you want to use Mail with Gmail, you must select **Accept**. Finally, you are asked if you want Mail to remember your Gmail sign-in name and password so you don't have to enter it each time you get your mail. Select **Yes** or **Skip**. Your email account will open as you can see in Figure 5-2.

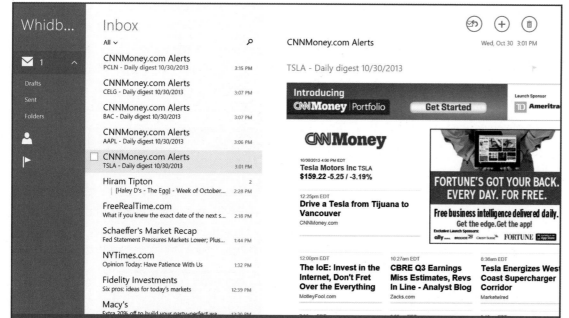

Figure 5-1: Windows Mail provides an easily readable layout for handling mail.

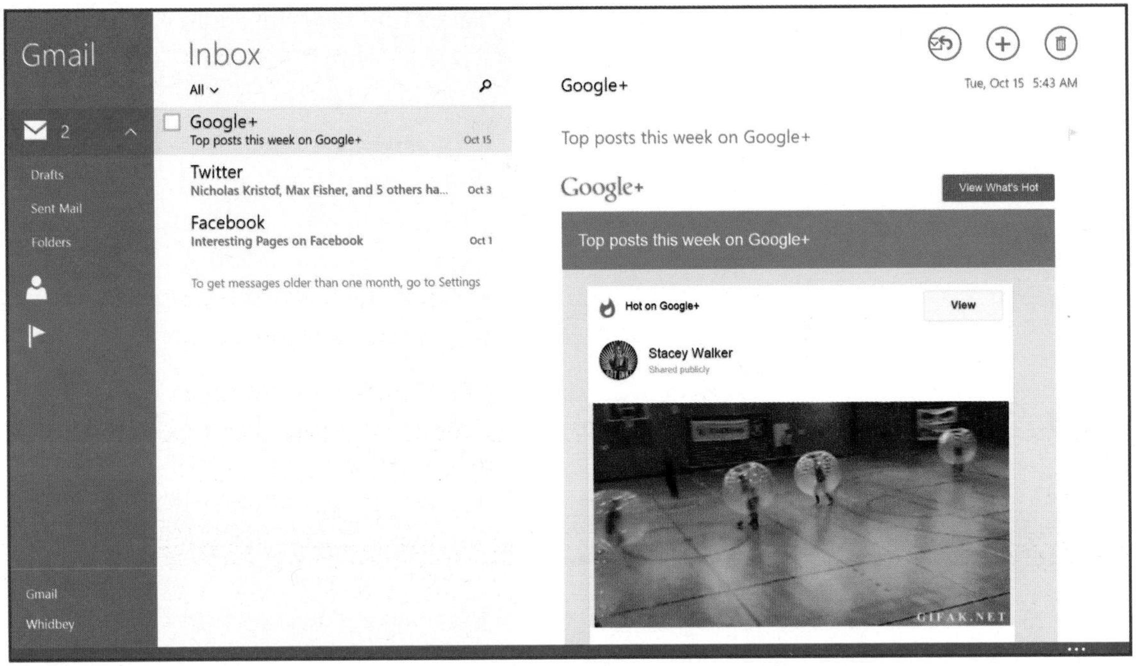

Figure 5-2: *A Gmail account can be used to get mail from any computer, not just your own.*

▷▷ Send, Receive, and Respond to Email

The purpose, of course, of email is to send messages to others, receive messages from them, and respond to the messages you receive. Windows Mail does this with simple elegance.

Create and Send Email

To create and send an email message:

1. Select the **Mail** tile and in the page that opens, select the **New** icon ⊕. The New Message window will open, similar to the one in Figure 5-3.

2. Start to enter a name in the To text box. If the name is in your People (see "Use People" in this chapter), it will be completed automatically and you can press **ENTER** or

tap to accept that name. If the name is not automatically completed, finish typing a full email address (such as mike@anisp.com) and then press **ENTER**.

3. If you want more than one addressee, after pressing **ENTER** as directed in step 2 where a space is automatically added (you can also press **;** in place of **ENTER**), simply begin typing a second one as in step 2.

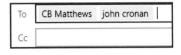

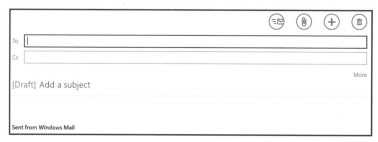

Figure 5-3: *Email messages are an easy and fast way to communicate.*

> **TIP** To look up a name in People, select **To** on the left of the address box to open People and select the name | **Add**.

4. If you want to differentiate the addressees to whom the message is principally being sent from those for whom it is just information, select the **Cc** text box, and enter the desired addressees there as you did in the To text box.

5. If you want to send the message to a recipient and not have other recipients see to whom it is sent, select **More** on the right of the addresses, and type the address(es) to be hidden in Bcc. (Bcc stands for "blind carbon copy.")

6. Select **Add A Subject** and type a subject for the message.

7. Select the area beneath the line on the right and type your message.

8. When you have completed your message, select the **Send** icon (≡) at the top. For a brief time, you may see a message in your Outbox and then, if you look, you will see the message in your Sent folder (both the Outbox and Sent folders are in the Folders link on the sidebar). If you are done, close Mail.

> **NOTE** If you want to copy, edit, or remove an email addressee, open the context menu (right-click or touch and briefly hold) for the addressee and select the option you want.

Receive Email

Mail will automatically receive any messages sent to the accounts you have established in it. To open and read your mail:

1. Open **Mail** and select the Inbox icon , which contains all of the messages you have received and haven't deleted. (The number beside the word "Inbox" is the number of unread messages.)

> **TIP** Have a friend send you an email message so you know whether you are receiving messages. Then send the friend a message back and ask them to let you know when they get it so you know you are sending messages.

2. Select a message in the inbox message list to have it displayed and then read it in the reading pane on the right of the Mail window, as shown in Figure 5-4.

3. If you wish, you can delete a message while it is selected by selecting the **Delete** icon (🗑) on the upper right.

Respond to Email

You can respond to messages you receive.

- Select the message in the message list and then select **Respond** (↩) on the right of the screen. From the menu that appears, select:
  - **Reply** to return a message to just the person who sent the original message.

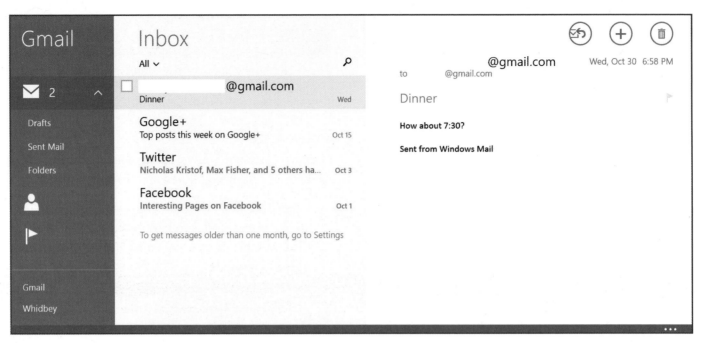

Figure 5-4: *Email messages can be very simple.*

- **Reply All** to return a message to all the people who were addressees (both To and Cc) in the original message.

- **Forward** to relay a message to people not shown as addressees on the original message.

In all three cases, a window similar to the New Message window opens and allows you to add or change addressees and the subject and add a new message.

▷▷ Apply Formatting

Windows Mail messages are sent with formatting, which you can set and change in several ways.

Format an Email Message

To use particular formatting on an email message:

1. Open an email message you want to create or that is in response to a message you received, as described in the previous sections of this chapter.

2. Type the text you want in the message, and then select the text you want specially formatted. When the text is selected, a formatting bar will open, as you see in Figure 5-5.

   –Or–

   You may apply formatting before you enter text by right-selecting the text line where you are about to enter it. The formatting bar will open.

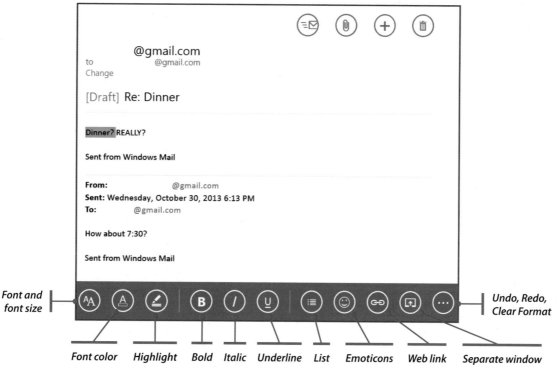

Font and font size

Undo, Redo, Clear Format

Font color   Highlight   Bold   Italic   Underline   List   Emoticons   Web link   Separate window

Figure 5-5: Mail allows you to change the fonts, weighting, color, and other formatting.

3. Select the font, size, style, or color; add bulleted or numbered lists and other formatting that you want to use; or select **More** to undo, redo, and clear the formatting you have just applied.

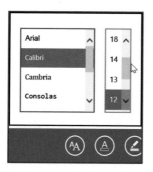

TIP If you are applying formatting as you type, instead of selecting it after the text is typed, you will probably want to turn off the formatting at some point. Do that by right-selecting where you want it turned off and selecting the formatting attributes that you want to turn off; they should be highlighted.

Change the Default Formatting

Mail allows you to set the default font, font size, and color that are automatically applied to a new message you are preparing to send. You can, of course, change this, as described in the preceding section, but you may want to have the default better reflect you than the way it is initially set. To change the default email formatting, as well as several options of handling mail:

1. With Mail open on your screen, open **Charms** and select **Settings**.

2. Select **Options**. At the top of the pane are three nonformatting options, all on by default, that group your incoming messages by their subject, add your outgoing messages to those groupings, and automatically mark an incoming message as read if it is selected. Select any of these options to change them from on to off.

3. In the lower part of the Options pane, select the down arrow for the font and the down arrow for the font size to change the defaults, and select the font color you want to use as a default. Notice that the words "Sample text" will change to reflect your selections.

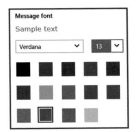

Attach a Signature

You may have noticed that the emails you send from Mail all say "Sent from Windows Mail" at the bottom of the message. This is a closing, or "signature," that you can either change or turn off altogether. To change this signature on all of your email messages:

1. With Mail open on your screen, open **Charms** and select **Settings**.

2. Select **Accounts** and then select the account whose signature you want to change. Scroll down until you see "Use An Email Signature."

3. If you do not want to use a signature, select the on/off switch to turn it off (it should be on by default).

4. If you want a default closing on your email that is different from "Sent from Windows Mail," select those words and type the words you want to use. Here is one I use:

5. Review the other options in this pane. In most circumstances, the default settings are the ones to keep.

 NOTE If you have several email accounts, you will need to open each one and change the signature block.

▷▷ Attach Files to Email

You can attach and send files, such as documents or images, with email messages.

1. Open an email message you want to create or that is in response to a message you received, as described in the previous sections of this chapter.

2. Select **Attachments** (📎) on the mid-right of the command bar at the top of the message window. Your most recently opened Library folder will be displayed as shown in Figure 5-6.

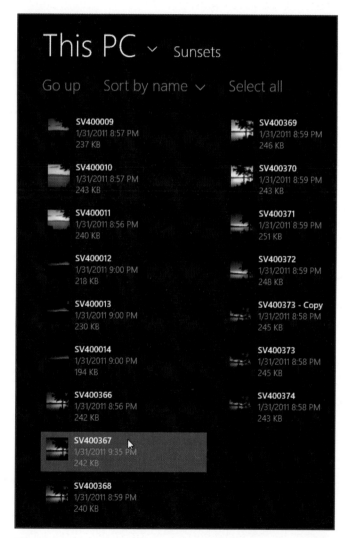

Figure 5-6: *You can attach any file on your computer to an email message.*

3. If what you want is shown in that folder, select as many objects as you want and select **Attach**. The attachment(s) will appear in your email message.

4. If what you want is in another folder, select **Go Up** at the top, select the parent and successive folders necessary to display the file you want, and then perform step 3.

   –Or–

   Repeatedly select **Go Up** until you reach the parent folder you want, and then select successive subordinate folders as needed to reach the document you want and then perform step 3.

5. Repeat steps 3 and 4 as needed. When you are ready, address the email, enter text, and send the message as you would normally.

▷▷ Use Web Mail

Web mail involves sending and receiving email over the Internet using a browser, such as Internet Explorer, instead of an email app, such as Mail. There are a number of web mail apps, such as Windows Outlook (outlook.com), Yahoo! Mail (mail.yahoo.com), and Google's Gmail (gmail.com). So long as you have access to the Internet, you can sign up for one or more of these services, or you may already be signed up for

✔ QuickFacts

Handle Unsolicited Email

Unsolicited email, or **spam**, often trying to sell something, from Viagra to cheap designer watches, can be harmful as well as irritating. Spam can contain viruses or malware buried inside a harmless-looking link or sales offer. If you do not handle spam, it can overwhelm your Inbox. There are essentially three ways to deal with it:

- **Your ISP often can filter email for their clients if the clients choose.** If you are suffering from too much spam, your first step is to ask your ISP to increase the filtering level for your account. They capture email that is suspicious and present it to you in a list for you to check. If you see valid email, you can rescue it. If your ISP cannot do this, or doesn't guide you through finding a way to do it, you might look for a different ISP. This can be a serious problem.

- **Your email app, such as Google's Gmail, will usually have a filtering mechanism.** Gmail automatically filters your incoming mail and places what it thinks is spam in a spam folder. You can look at this by opening your Gmail account in Mail and selecting **Folders | Spam**. You can see what Gmail

considers spam and, by looking at the email you are receiving, what Gmail doesn't consider spam.

- You can find third-party software that specializes in filtering email and providing a way for you to safely sift through your email without a lot of hassle. I have used MailWasher for this with good results (see mailwasher.net for a free download). You can get a list of products and reviews from Google. Type <u>Google.com</u> into your browser address text box, type <u>anti spam software</u> into the search text box, and press ENTER or click Search (the magnifying glass). You'll find a list of antispam software sites as well as sites reviewing antispam software. (A review site I find interesting—not sure it is totally unbiased—is TopTenREVIEWS, but look at the review date and make sure it is a current.)

one. The basic features (simple sending and receiving of email) are generally free. For example, to use Outlook.com:

1. Open either version of Internet Explorer. In the address box, type <u>outlook.com</u> and press **ENTER**.

2. Since you already have a Microsoft account, you will automatically be signed in.

3. The Outlook.com page will open and display your mail, as shown in Figure 5-7.

4. Select a message to open and read it.

5. Select **New** on the toolbar to write an email message. Enter the address, a subject, and the message. When you are done, select **Send**.

6. When you are finished with Outlook.com, close Internet Explorer.

 NOTE Many malware protection packages labeled "Internet Security" include antispam capability. Examples of two highly rated apps include Norton Internet Security 360 Protection and Kaspersky Internet Security.

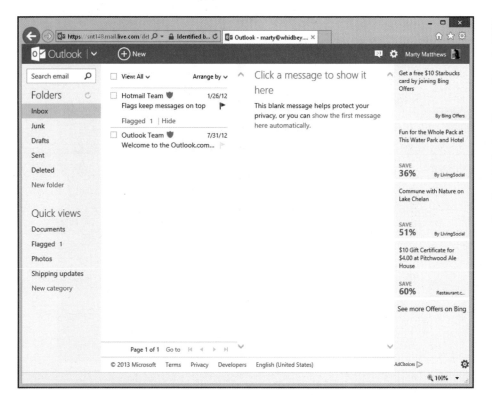

Figure 5-7: *Web mail accounts are a quick and free way to get one or more email accounts.*

TIP A way to quickly open Outlook.com is to add it to your Favorites list or Favorites bar. See the earlier discussion in Chapter 4 to do this.

USE PEOPLE

People, shown in Figure 5-8, allows you to collect email addresses and other information about the people with whom you correspond or otherwise interact. It starts out by asking you if it can look at the lists of people you have, such as Facebook, Twitter, and Google, and if you are on an Exchange Server, it would like to look at that too.

Add New People

You can add people by including more accounts to be searched and by adding individuals.

Add People in Accounts

People will connect to and gather people you correspond with from your accounts on Facebook, Hotmail, Twitter, LinkedIn, and Google, and from an Exchange Server if you are connected to one.

1. Select the **People** tile on the Start screen to open the People window. You may or may not have anyone in your People window.

2. If you have existing accounts in the services shown on the left of Figure 5-8, select the service to open its page, where you need to select **Connect** again. When it is done, you are returned to People.

3. To add more accounts, select **Connected To** in the bottom-right corner. The Accounts list will appear on the right of the screen. Select **Add An Account** to see a list of additional accounts from which you can add people.

4. Select an account. A page will open explaining what will transpire

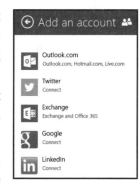

between the other account and your Microsoft account. Select **Connect** and follow the instructions on the page. Select **Done** when you are finished.

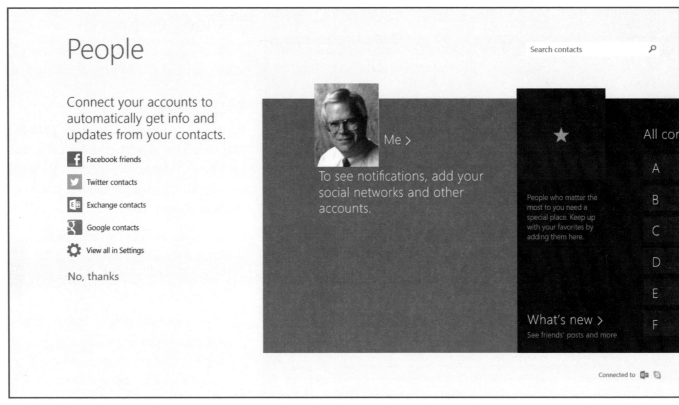

*Figure 5-8: **People provides a way to collect the people you correspond with across various accounts.***

Add People Individually

You can add individuals to People one at a time.

1. Open the command bar at the top and bottom of the People screen (right-click or swipe up or swipe down from the bottom or top of the screen) and select **New Contact** in the bottom-right corner. The New Contact window opens as shown in Figure 5-9.

2. Enter as much of the information as you have or want. For email, you need at least an email address and a name. If you have additional information, such as a nickname, several email addresses, several phone numbers, or a home address for the contact, select the plus sign next to those items and fill in the desired information.

3. When you are done, select **Save This Contact** ⓡ to save the contact and close the New Contact window.

> 💡 **TIP** When you have several email addresses in a single contact's record, they are all displayed when you go to enter the contact in an email message so you can select the address you want.

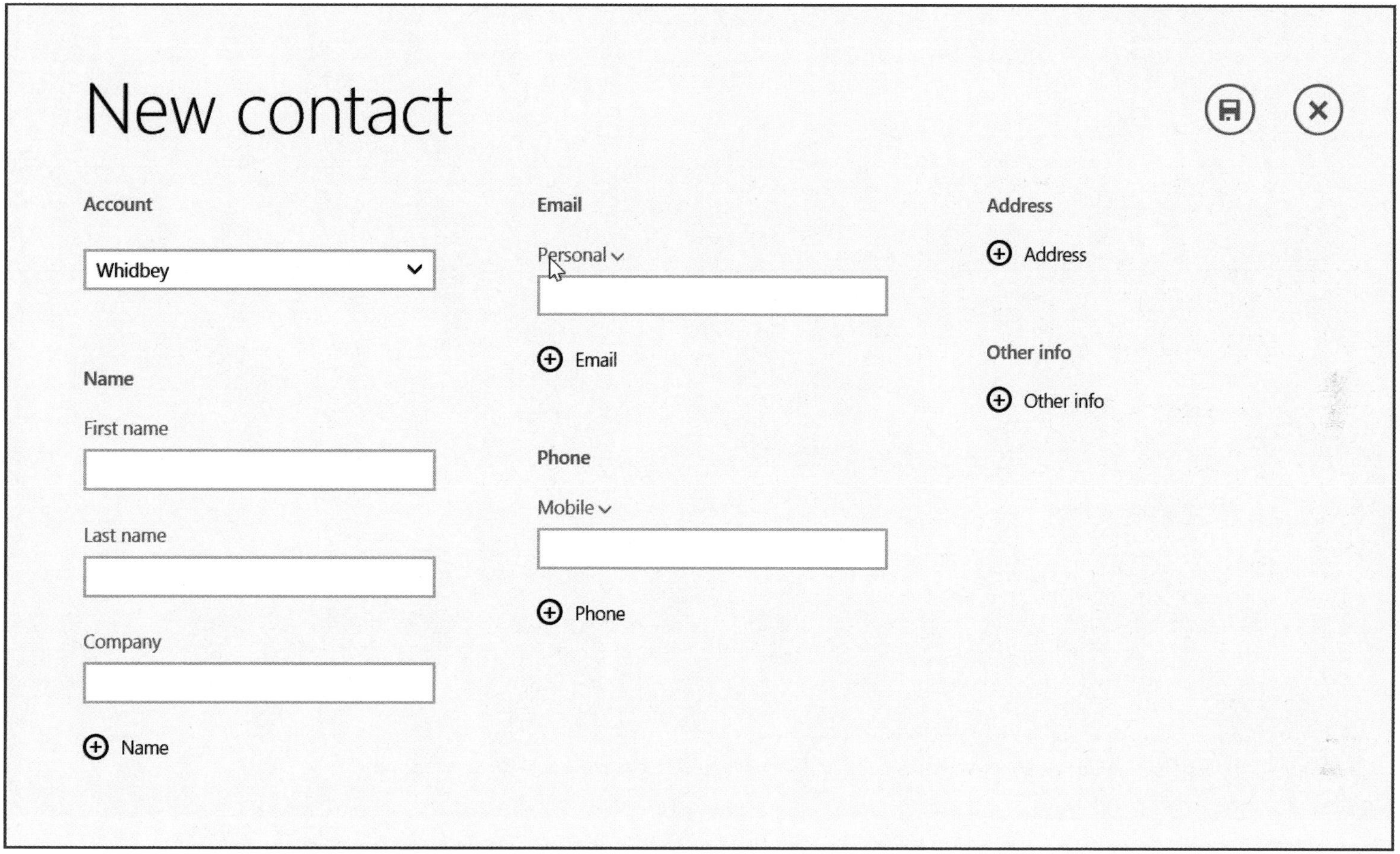

New contact

🖫 ⊗

Account

| Whidbey ▾ |

Name

First name

Last name

Company

⊕ Name

Email

Personal ▾

⊕ Email

Phone

Mobile ▾

⊕ Phone

Address

⊕ Address

Other info

⊕ Other info

*Figure 5-9: **People allows you to store a lot of information about an individual.***

USE CALENDAR

Calendar, which you can use to keep track of scheduled events, is an app on the Start screen. To open and use Calendar:

- From the Start screen, select the **Calendar** tile. The Calendar will open in one of its five views, the last one

you used. The default, if you haven't used Calendar before, is the What's Next view shown in Figure 5-10.

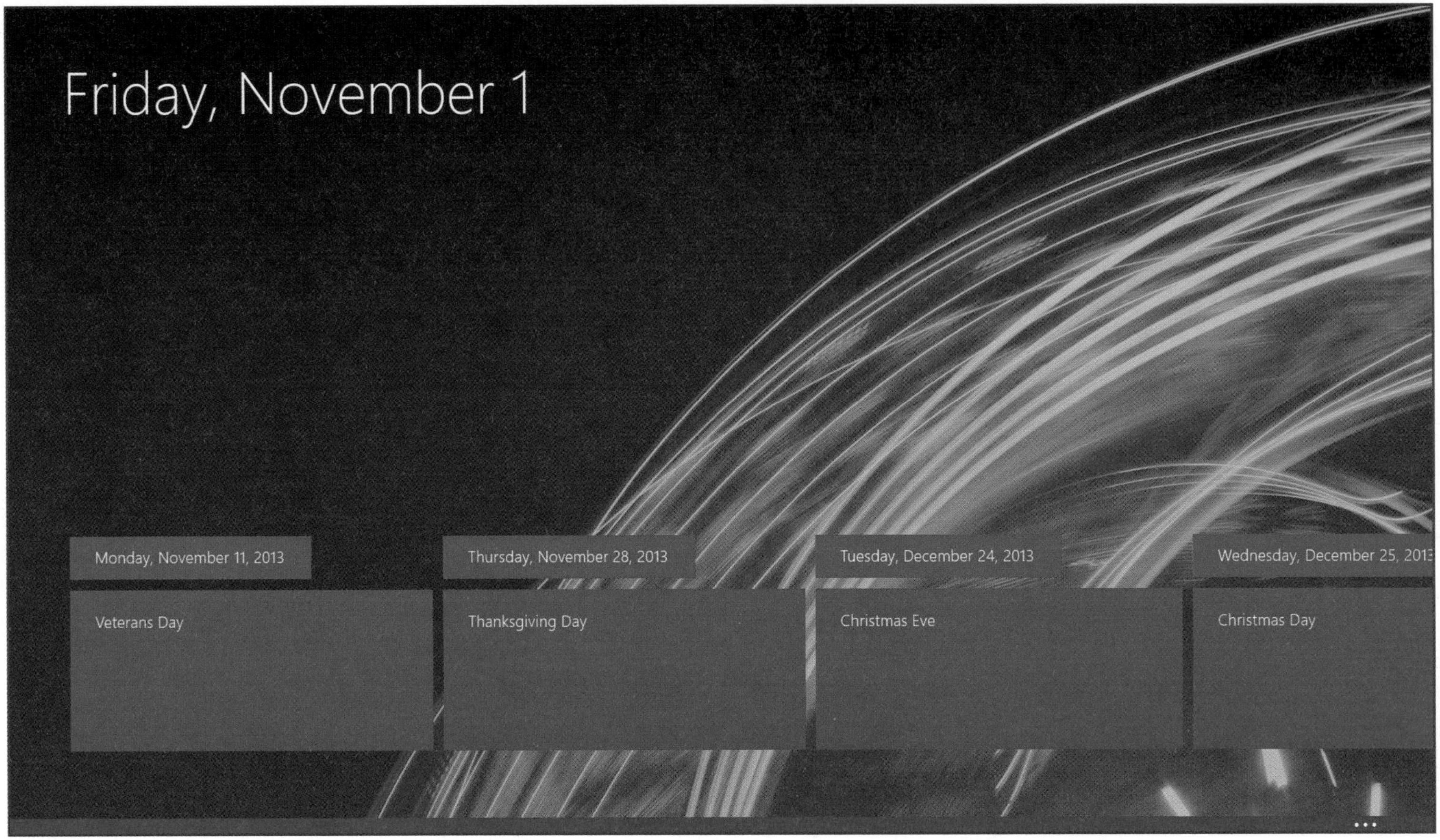

Friday, November 1

| Monday, November 11, 2013 | Thursday, November 28, 2013 | Tuesday, December 24, 2013 | Wednesday, December 25, 2013 |
| Veterans Day | Thanksgiving Day | Christmas Eve | Christmas Day |

Figure 5-10: **The Calendar provides a handy way of keeping track of scheduled events, especially those scheduled through email.**

▷▷ Add Events to Calendar

To add an event to Calendar:

1. With Calendar open on your screen, open the App bar at the top and bottom of the screen and select **New** in the bottom-right corner.

   –Or–

Open a calendar view with individual dates from the top App bar, as shown in Figure 5-11, and select the date on which you want to add the event. If it is in a different month, use the right or left arrows on the edges near the top, or swipe left/right using touch to select the desired month, select the day, and then select the down arrow on the right of the event and select **Add Details**. In either case, the new event window will open.

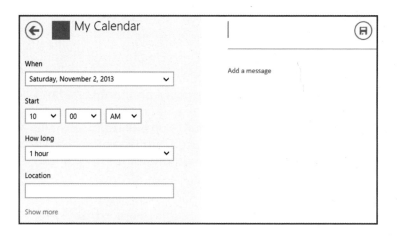

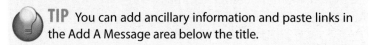

2. Enter the title on the upper-right area, then, on the left, enter when it will start, how long it will run, and where it will be held.

TIP You can add ancillary information and paste links in the Add A Message area below the title.

3. If the event will happen on a recurring basis, select the **Show More | How Often** down arrow and select the period for this event.

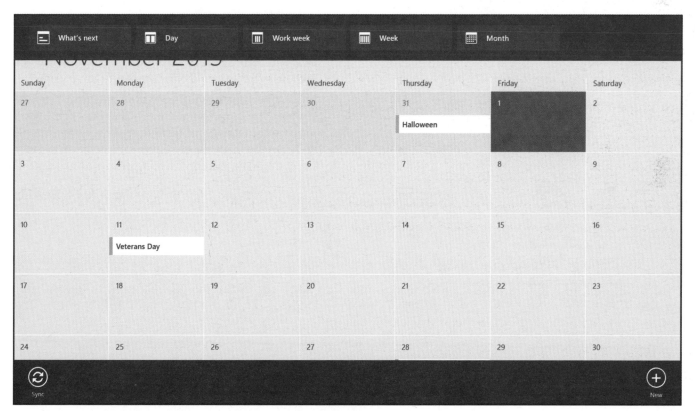

Figure 5-11: Each of the five calendar views look at the same calendar.

4. If you have selected **Show More**, you can select how long before the event you want to be reminded of it, and you can have the calendar reflect your status during the event.

5. When you have completed the event, select the **Save This Event** icon in the upper-right corner to store the event on your calendar.

TIP You can control several calendar options by opening **Charms** and selecting **Settings | Options** to see a list of your calendars with controls to turn them on or off and select the colors with which they are displayed.

Chapter 6

Working with Documents and Pictures

Much of what we think of in classic computing is working with documents and pictures. Today this has been at least equaled, if not surpassed, by working on the Internet. Nevertheless, creating and working with documents and photos can be very important to many people. In this chapter you will discover many aspects of creating documents and pictures, installing and using digital cameras and scanners, and installing and using printers and their fonts with documents and pictures.

CREATE DOCUMENTS AND PICTURES

Creating documents and pictures is primarily done with apps outside of Windows 8.1, although Windows also has simple apps to do this. Windows 8.1 also has facilities to bring documents and pictures in from other computers, from the Internet, and from scanners and cameras.

▷▷ Acquire a Document

The documents in your computer got there because they were created with an app on your computer, or they were brought to the computer on a disk, transferred over a local area network (LAN), or downloaded from the Internet.

Create a Document with an App

To create a document with an app:

1. Start the app. For example, start Microsoft Word from the Start screen by selecting the **Word** tile if it is there or by typing Word on the Start screen to search for it and then selecting the app that you want to use.

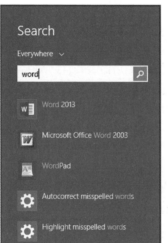

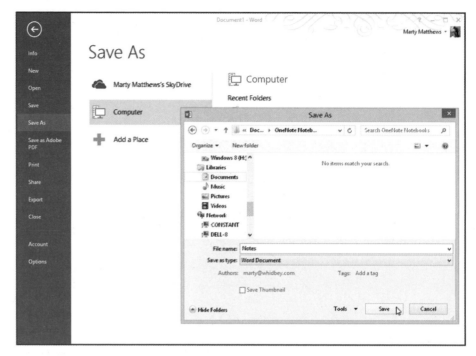

Figure 6-1: **Most document-creation apps let you choose where you want to save the files you create.**

3. In Word, save the document by selecting the **File** tab. Then select **Save As | Computer**, if needed; select **Browse**; and select the disk drive and folder in which to store the document. Enter a filename and select **Save**, as shown in Figure 6-1.

4. Close the app used to create the file.

Locate a Document on Your Computer

Use File Explorer to locate a document on your computer.

1. Open File Explorer from the desktop taskbar. In the navigation pane on the left, select **Libraries** and then either **Documents** or **Pictures** depending on what you want to work with.

 TIP If you don't have Microsoft Word, you can use WordPad, which is included with Windows (from the Start screen type <u>wordpad</u> to locate it), or you can use the free Cloud version of Word by opening Internet Explorer and typing <u>office.microsoft.com/web-apps</u>, as described in Chapter 8.

2. Create the document using the facilities in the app. In Word, for example, type the document and format it using Word's formatting tools.

2. Open the folder from which you want to retrieve a file. This may require that you open one or more intermediate folders to locate the file and so you can see it in the subject (middle) pane (assuming your File Explorer window displays a three-pane view: navigation, subject, and preview—see the discussion in Chapter 3).

3. Select the document you want so you can see it in the preview pane, as shown in Figure 6-2.

Download a Document from a Flash Drive

Use File Explorer to bring in a document from a universal serial bus (USB) flash drive or other memory device plugged into your computer.

1. Open **File Explorer** from the desktop taskbar. In the navigation pane on the left, select the removable disk that you inserted, although, technically it is not a "disk," but rather a USB flash drive or a memory card from a camera. Generally, it will be your only removable disk.

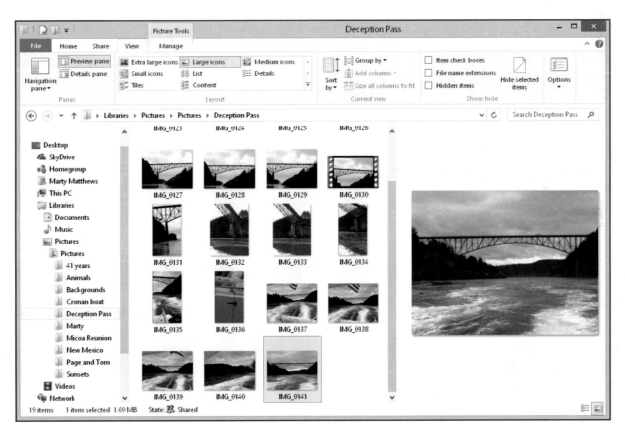

Figure 6-2: *To use a document on your computer, you must first locate it.*

2. Open the folders and subfolders needed to locate and open in the subject pane the document file.

3. In the navigation pane, display (but do not select or open) the drive and folder(s) to which you want to copy the file by selecting their respective triangles on the left.

4. Drag the document file from the removable device to the folder on your computer as you can see in Figure 6-3. When you are done, close File Explorer.

Download a Document from the Internet

Use Internet Explorer to bring in a document from a site on the Internet.

1. Select the **Internet Explorer** icon on the desktop's taskbar.

2. Type an address, search, or browse to a site and page from which you can download the document file.

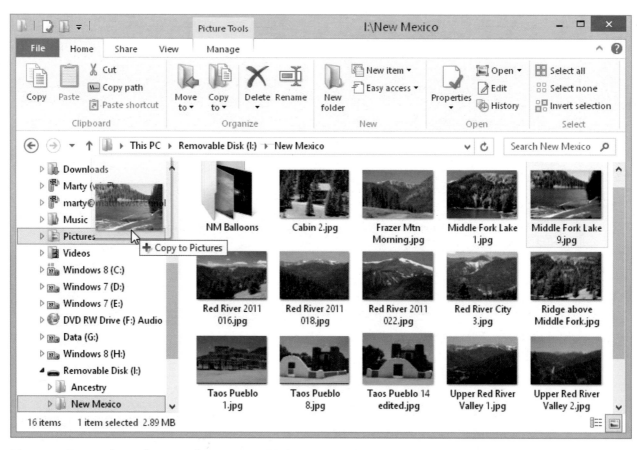

Figure 6-3: **You can drag a document from a removable device to a disk and folder on your computer.**

3. Use the links and tools on the website to select and begin the file download. For example, open the context menu for a picture and select **Save Picture As**. Some sites have download links for transferring the image or document to your computer.

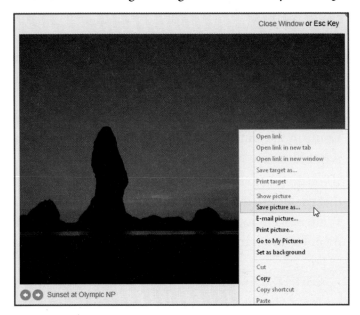

4. In the Save Picture As dialog box, select the disk and open the folder(s) in which you want to store the file on your computer.

5. Type or edit the filename, and press ENTER to complete the download. When you are done, close your browser.

 NOTE If you use Start screen IE, you only have the option of saving a picture from a website to the Pictures folder.

▷▷ Create a Picture

As you have seen by the preceding document examples, pictures are really just documents that contain an image. They can be created or brought into your computer in the same way as any other document. For example, to create and save a picture in Windows Paint:

1. From the Start screen, type <u>paint</u> and select the Paint app.

2. Create a picture using the tools in Paint. For example, select the **Pencil** tool, choose a color, and create the drawing.

3. Save the document by selecting **File | Save As**, and then select the disk drive and folder in which to store the document, enter a filename, select a Save As type, and select **Save**. Close Paint.

 NOTE In choosing a picture type or format to use, you may want to consider how you are going to use the image and the quality that you want. If you are going to display the image on a website or include it in an email, you may be more concerned with the size of the image then with the quality. If so, the .gif format is often the smallest. If you want a little better quality, then the .jpg format is a good choice because it also keeps the size relatively small. If quality is a top priority, then the .tif format may be the way you want to go.

▷▷ Install Cameras and Scanners

Installing cameras and scanners depends a lot on the device—whether it is Plug and Play (you plug it in and it starts to function), what type of connection it has, and so on. Most recent cameras and scanners are Plug and Play devices. To use them:

1. Plug the device into the computer, and turn it on. If it is Plug and Play, the first time you plug it in, you will see a message indicating that a device driver is being installed and then a message asking if you want to choose what happens with the device.

2. Select the message to choose what happens. This opens a device-specific dialog box and allows you to choose what you want to do. If you plugged in a scanner, skip to "Scan Documents" later in this chapter. If you plugged in a camera, skip to "Import Camera Images" later in this chapter. Otherwise, continue to step 3.

3. Open the **System** menu and select **Control Panel | Hardware And Sound | Devices And Printers**. If you see your device, installation is complete, and you can skip the remainder of these steps.

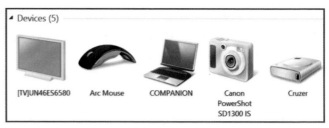

4. Select **Add A Device**. The Add A Device Wizard starts. Select the device you want to install and then select **Next**. Scroll through the manufacturer and model lists, and see if your device is there. If so, select it and select **Next**. Confirm the name you want to use, select **Next**, and then select **Finish** to complete the installation.

5. If you don't see your device on the lists and you have a disk that came with it, select **Cancel** and close the Devices And Printers window, place the disk in the drive, and use the manufacturer's installation app on the disk.

Scan Documents

Scanners allow you to take printed images and convert them to digital images on your computer. The scanner must first be installed, as described in "Install Cameras and Scanners" earlier in this chapter. If you ended up using the manufacturer's software to install the scanner, you might need to use it to scan images, too. If you used Windows to install the scanner, use the following steps to scan an image.

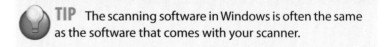

TIP The scanning software in Windows is often the same as the software that comes with your scanner.

1. Turn on your scanner and place what you want to scan onto the scanning surface.

2. On the Start screen, begin to type <u>fax and scan</u> and then select the **Windows Fax And Scan** app when it appears. The Windows Fax And Scan window opens.

3. Select **New Scan** on the toolbar. If needed, select the device to use and select **OK.** The New Scan dialog box appears. The scanner you installed should be displayed in the upper-left area. Change the scanner if you wish.

4. Choose the color, file type, and resolution you want to use and select **Preview**. The image in the scanner will appear in the dialog box.

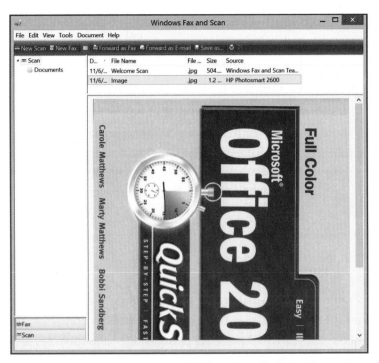

Figure 6-5: **Images that you scan can be faxed, emailed, saved, and printed.**

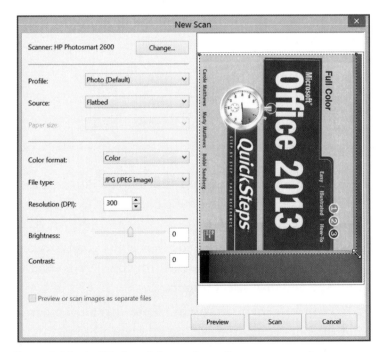

Figure 6-4: **In the Windows 8.1 scanning software, you can change several of the parameters, including the margins of what to include, and see the results in the preview pane.**

5. Adjust the margins around the page by dragging the dashed lines on the four sides, as shown in Figure 6-4. When you are ready, select **Scan**.

6. The scanned image will appear in the Windows Fax And Scan window (see Figure 6-5). If it isn't already selected, select the image in the list at the top of the window, and, using the toolbar, choose to:

   • **Forward As Fax** using the Windows fax capability

   • **Forward As E-mail** using your default email app

- **Save As** using File Explorer to save the image as a file on one of the storage devices available to you
- **Print** using a printer available to you
- **Delete** the image

7. Work through the related dialog box(es) that appear to complete the scanning process. When you are ready, close the Windows Fax And Scan window.

 TIP Documents that you scan into your computer are automatically saved in Libraries\Documents\Scanned Documents.

Import Camera Images

When most digital cameras or their memory cards are plugged into the computer (see "Install Cameras and Scanners" earlier in this chapter), the device-specific dialog box (shown earlier) appears and asks if you want to:

- **Import Media Files** in your camera using the PlayMemories app.
- **Open Device To View Files** in your camera using File Explorer, where you can select just the pictures you want and place them in the drive and folder where you want them. This gives you the most flexibility.
- **Import Pictures And Videos** in your camera using the Photos app.
- **Take No Action** to ignore the camera or memory card that was plugged in.

 NOTE If the Devices dialog box didn't appear, open the File Explorer from the taskbar to display the This PC window. In the navigation column on the left or the subject pane on the right, look for the device or an extra removable disk (if you have more than one of them, it would be the most recently accessed one), and open the necessary folders to see images of the pictures in your camera.

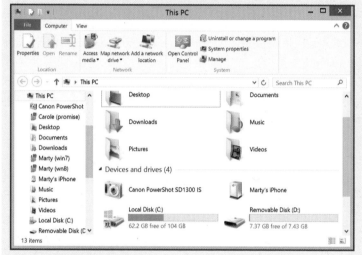

1. Select **Import Pictures And Videos**. The Photos screen should appear displaying the pictures on the camera, as you can see in Figure 6-6.

2. Select to check any photos you want that are not checked, and select to uncheck any pictures you do *not* want to import, and then select **Import**.

3. You will see a thermometer bar showing you the progress of the importing. You will be told when the process is completed. Select **Open Album**; the Photos app will open and display the pictures that were imported.

Figure 6-6: **The Windows 8.1 Photos app gives you a quick way to organize and view your pictures.**

Work with Pictures

Once you have brought pictures into your computer from a camera, a scanner, an Internet download, or a removable disk, you can look at and work with them on your computer screen. The Windows 8.1 Photos app, as discussed in "Import Camera Images," provides a quick way to view your pictures.

1. From the Start screen, select **Photos**. The Photos app will open.

2. Open one or more folders until you are displaying the pictures you want to view.

3. To see a larger image, select the picture, then, with touch, repeatedly spread two fingers; or with the mouse, repeatedly click the plus sign in the bottom-right corner of the screen.

4. If you have several pictures you want to view, select the right and left arrows in the middle of the left and right edges of the screen to go through them sequentially.

View Other Pictures

The Photos app will display photos that are in your Pictures library, your SkyDrive Photos folder, possibly in your Facebook page, and in devices (such as a camera) attached to your computer. If your pictures are not in Photos, you can locate and view them.

1. From the desktop, select File Explorer, and open the drive and folders necessary to locate your pictures.

2. Select the **View** tab and select **Extra Large Icons** so that you can adequately see the thumbnail images, as shown in Figure 6-7.

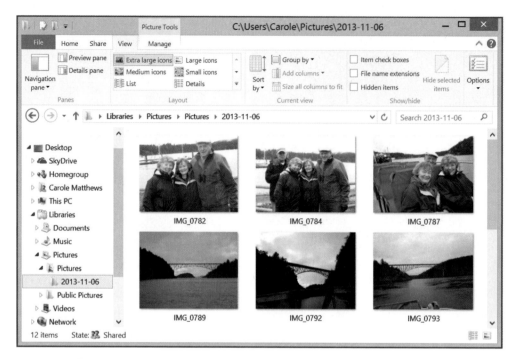

Figure 6-7: *The best way to locate the photo you want is with extra-large icons.*

3. Open the picture you want to view in a larger size. The Windows Photo Viewer will open and display the picture. Select **File**, **Print**, **E-mail**, or **Burn** to perform any of those functions. You can also select **Open** to open the picture in Photos or another program you may have on your computer.

Capture Snips

Windows 8.1 includes the Snipping Tool to capture images of the screen, called "screen shots" or "snips." This can capture four areas of the screen:

- **Full screen** captures the entire screen.
- **Window** captures a complete window.
- **Rectangular area** captures a rectangle you draw around objects.
- **Free-form area** captures any area you draw around objects.

Once you have captured an area, it is temporarily stored on the Clipboard and displayed in the mark-up window where you can write and draw on the snip to annotate it and, when you are ready, save the snip where you want it. To do all of that:

1. Display the windows or other objects on the screen whose images you want to capture (see the Note on capturing a menu).

2. On the Start screen, begin typing <u>Snipping Tool</u> and then select **Snipping Tool** when it is displayed. The Snipping Tool dialog box will appear.

3. If you want to capture a rectangular area, select **New** and drag the cross-hair from one corner of the rectangle to the opposite corner, as shown in Figure 6-8.

*Figure 6-8: **The Snipping Tool allows you to capture an image of an area of the screen for future reference or use.***

4. To capture a different type of area, select the **New** down arrow and select one of the other three types of areas. Then, with:

   - **Free-Form Snip**, drag the cross-hair around the area to be captured

   - **Window Snip**, select the window to be captured

   - **Full-Screen Snip**, the screen is automatically captured

5. In all cases, the mark-up window opens, showing you the area that was captured and allowing you to use the pen, highlighter, and eraser to annotate the snip.

6. From the mark-up window, you can also directly email the snip to someone by selecting **Send Snip** , which opens an email message with the snip in it (to send the snip as an email attachment, open the **Send Snip** down arrow). Save the snip by selecting **Save Snip**, selecting a folder, entering a name, selecting a file type, and selecting **Save**.

> **TIP** To capture a snip of a menu or one that includes a menu, open the Snipping Tool, press **ESC**, display the menu to be captured, press **CTRL+PRINT SCREEN**, select the **New** down arrow, select the type of area to be captured (Free-Form, Rectangle, and so forth), and delineate that area as you would otherwise.

Use Sticky Notes

Sticky Notes are exactly what the name implies: little notes to yourself that you can place anywhere on your screen. You can type messages on these notes; change their color; cut, copy, and paste the text on them with the Clipboard to and from other apps; create additional notes; and delete the note.

1. On the Start screen, start typing <u>Sticky Notes</u> and then select **Sticky Notes** when it appears. If you don't already have a note on your desktop, one will appear.

2. If you already have one or more notes on the desktop, the most recent one will be selected. If you want a new note, select **New Note** (the plus sign in the upper-left corner).

3. On the new note, type the message you want it to contain, or, having copied some text from another source, open the context menu for the note and select **Paste**. (You can resize a note like a window.)

4. Open the context menu for the note (right-select in the note outside the title bar), select the color you want it to be, and then drag the note by its title bar to where you want it.

5. When you no longer want the note on the desktop, select **Delete Note** (the X in the upper-right corner) and select **Yes**.

PRINT DOCUMENTS AND PICTURES

It is important to be able to install and fully use printers so that you can transfer your digital documents to paper.

Install a Printer

All printers are either automatically installed or done so using the Devices And Printers window. Because there are differences in how the installation is done, look at the sections in this chapter on installing local Plug and Play printers, installing other local printers, and selecting a default printer. Also, if you are installing a local printer, first consider the following checklist.

Printer Installation Checklist

A local printer is one that is attached to your computer with a cable or wireless connection. Make sure that your printer meets the following conditions *before* you begin the installation:

- It is plugged into the correct port on your computer (see manufacturer's instructions).
- It is plugged into an electrical outlet.
- It has fresh ink, toner, or ribbon, which, along with the print heads, is properly installed.
- It has adequate paper.
- It is turned on.

> **NOTE** Some computer-and-printer combinations are connected through a wireless connection. In this case, "plugging the printer into the computer" means to establish that wireless connection.

Install a Local Plug and Play Printer

Installing Plug and Play printers is supposed to be fairly automatic, and, for the most part, it is.

1. With your computer and printer turned off, connect the devices to each other. Then make sure the other points in the previous checklist are satisfied.

2. Turn on your computer, let it fully boot, and then turn on your printer. Your computer should find and automatically install the new printer and briefly give you messages to that effect.

3. Open the **System** menu and select **Control Panel | Hardware And Sound | Devices And Printers**. The Devices And Printers window will open, and you should see your new printer. Hover the mouse pointer over that printer, and you should see something like "Status: Letter, Portrait," as shown in Figure 6-9. (If you don't see your printer or the status says "Offline," it was not fully installed. Go to the next section.)

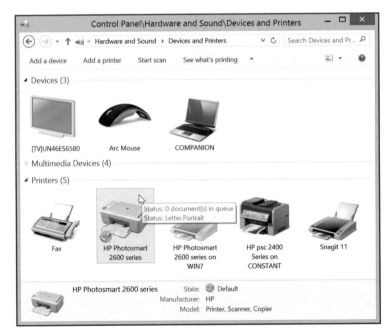

Figure 6-9: **When you connect a Plug and Play printer, it should be recognized by the computer and automatically installed.**

4. Open the context menu for the new printer, select **Printer Properties** (not "Properties"), and select **Print Test Page**. If the test page prints satisfactorily, select **Close**. Otherwise, select **Get Help With Printing**, follow the suggestions, and close the Help and printer windows when you are done. When you are ready, select **OK** to close the printer Properties dialog box.

5. If you want the new printer to be the default printer used by all apps on the computer, open the context menu for the printer and select **Set As Default Printer**.

6. Close the Devices And Printers window.

Install a Local Printer Manually

If a printer isn't automatically installed and verified in the process of using steps 1 through 3 in the previous section, you must install and verify it manually.

1. If a CD came with your printer, place that CD in the drive, and follow the on-screen instructions to install the printer. When this is complete, go to step 3 in "Install a Local Plug and Play Printer," and determine if the printer will print a test page. If so, skip to step 7.

2. If you don't have a manufacturer's CD or the CD didn't work with Windows 8.1, open the Devices And Printers window, as described in the previous section.

3. In the Devices And Printers window, select **Add A Printer** on the toolbar. If the printer you want to install is listed, select it and select **Next**.

4. If the printer wasn't listed, select **The Printer That I Want Isn't Listed | Add A Local Printer Or Network Printer With Manual Settings | Next**.

5. Select **Use An Existing Port**, open the drop-down list, and select the correct port (on newer printers, it is probably USB001; on the majority of older printers, it is LPT1), and select **Next**.

6. Select the manufacturer and model of the printer you want to install (see Figure 6-10). If you can't find your printer, select **Windows Update** to download the latest printer drivers. Then, once more, search for the manufacturer and model. When you find the correct printer, select **Next**.

7. Confirm or change the printer name, and select **Next**. Determine if you want to share this printer; if so, enter its share name, location, and comments. Select **Next**.

8. Choose whether you want this printer to be your default printer. Select **Print A Test Page**. If the test page prints

satisfactorily, select **Close**. Otherwise, select **Get Help With Printing**, follow the suggestions, and close the Help and Printer windows when you are done. When you are ready, select **Finish** to close the Add Printer dialog box, and close the Devices And Printers window.

 TIP If your printer was automatically installed but a CD came with your printer and you wonder if you should install using the CD, the general answer is no. Most printer drivers in Windows 8.1 originally came from the manufacturers and have been tested by Microsoft, so they should work well. Unless the printer came out after the release of Windows 8.1 (October 2013), the driver in Windows 8.1 should be newer, and in the installation dialog boxes, you can choose to update the drivers.

Change a Default Printer

If you have several printers available to you, one must be identified as your default printer—the one that will be used for printing whenever you don't select another one. To change your default printer:

1. Open the **System** menu and select **Control Panel | Hardware And Sound | Devices And Printers**. The Devices And Printers window will open.

2. Open the context menu for the printer you want to be the default, and select **Set As Default Printer**.

3. Close the Devices And Printers window when finished.

Share a Printer

If you have a printer attached to your computer and you want to let others use it, you can share the printer.

![Add Printer dialog box: Install the printer driver. Choose your printer from the list. Click Windows Update to see more models. To install the driver from an installation CD, click Have Disk.]

Manufacturer	Printers
Fuji Xerox	HP Color LaserJet 6030 MFP PS Class Driver
Generic	HP Color LaserJet 6040 MFP PS Class Driver
Gestetner	HP Color LaserJet 8500 PS
HP	HP Color LaserJet 8550 PCL
InfoPrint	

This driver is digitally signed.
Tell me why driver signing is important

Windows Update   Have Disk...

Next   Cancel

*Figure 6-10: **Manually installing a printer requires that you know some facts about it.***

1. In the Devices And Printers window, open the context menu for the printer you want to share, and select **Printer Properties**. The printer's Properties dialog box will appear.

2. Select the **Sharing** tab, select **Share This Printer**, enter a share name, and click **OK.**

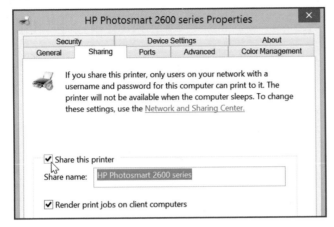

3. Close the printer Properties dialog box.

▶▶ Print

Most printing is done from an app. This section uses Microsoft Office Word 2013, whose Print window is shown in Figure 6-11, as an example.

Print Documents

To print the document currently open in Word:

Select **Quick Print** on Word's Quick Access toolbar to immediately print using the default settings.

TIP If Quick Print isn't on your Quick Access toolbar, select the **Customize** down arrow to the right of the Quick Access toolbar and select **Quick Print**.

Choose a Printer

To choose which printer you want to use:

Select the **File** tab and select **Print** to open Word's Print window shown in Figure 6-11. Select the **Printer** drop-down list, and choose the printer you want.

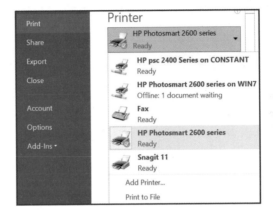

Determine Specific Pages to Print

In the first section of the Print window under Settings with the print range drop-down list, select the down arrow on the right and select:

Print All Pages to print the entire document.

Print Selection to print the text that has been selected.

Print Current Page to print only the currently viewed page.

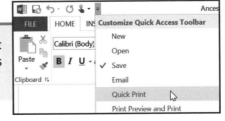

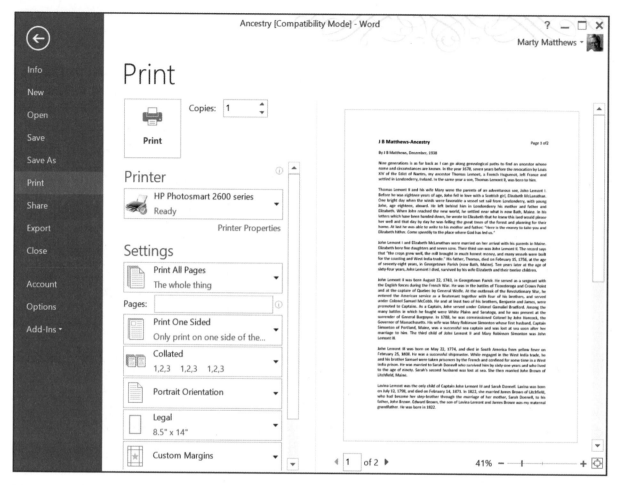

*Figure 6-11: **The Microsoft Office Word 2013 Print window has options similar to many other apps.***

Custom Print to print a series of individual pages and/or a range of pages by specifying the individual pages separated by commas and specifying the range with a hyphen. For example, typing <u>4,6,8-10,12</u> will cause pages 4, 6, 8, 9, 10, and 12 to be printed.

When you are finished printing, you can close Word.

NOTE You can print just the even or odd pages in a document by opening the print range drop-down list immediately under Settings in the Print window and making the relevant selection at the bottom of the list.

Print Pictures

Printing pictures from an app is exactly the same as described in "Print" in the preceding section. In addition, Windows has a Print Pictures dialog box used to print pictures from File Explorer.

1. From the desktop, open File Explorer.

2. Open the drives and folders needed to locate and select the picture(s) you want to print. You can select only one picture if you want. However, to select a contiguous set of pictures, select the first one, hold down **SHIFT**, and select the last picture. To select noncontiguous pictures, select the check boxes in the upper-left area of each icon, or hold down **CTRL** while selecting the pictures you want. (Both **SHIFT** and **CTRL** work with the mouse and with touch.)

3. Select the **Share** tab and select **Print** in the Send group to open the Print Pictures dialog box, as shown in Figure 6-12.

4. Select the printer, paper size, quality, paper type, number of photos on a page, number of copies, and whether to fit the picture to a frame. You can also select **Options** above the Cancel button to look at, and possibly change, several print settings. Select **OK** after looking at (and possibly selecting) the options.

5. When you are ready, select **Print**. The pictures will be printed. When you are done, close File Explorer.

Print Webpages

Printing webpages is little different from printing any other document.

1. On the desktop, select the **Internet Explorer** icon on the taskbar to open your browser (assumed to be Internet Explorer).

Figure 6-12: **If you use high-quality photo paper and a newer color printer, you can get almost professional-grade pictures.**

2. Browse to the page you want to print, open the context menu for the page, and select **Print**, as shown in Figure 6-13. The Print dialog box will open. Select the printer and other options, and select **Print** again.

3. Close your Internet browser.

Control Printing

To control printing means to control the process as it is taking place, whether with one print job or with several in line. If several print jobs are selected for printing at close to the same time, they form a ***print queue***, waiting for earlier jobs to finish. You may control printing in several ways, as described next. These tasks are handled in the printer's window, which is

Figure 6-13: **You can print from Internet Explorer, but many webpages also have a "Print" button for the same purpose, and often it is better at printing their material.**

similar to that shown in Figure 6-14, and is shown by opening a printer's context menu and selecting **See What's Printing** in the Devices And Printers window, or by opening the printer icon in the notification area of the taskbar  and then selecting **See What's Printing**.

Pause, Resume, and Restart Printing

While printing, a situation may occur (such as needing to add ink) where you want to pause and then resume printing, either for one or all documents:

- **Pause all documents** In the printer's window, select **Printer | Pause Printing**. "Paused" will appear in the title

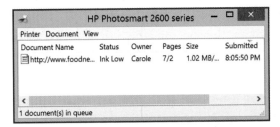

Figure 6-14: *Controlling printing takes place in the printer's window and allows you to pause, resume, restart, and cancel printing.*

bar, and, if you look in the Printer menu, you will see a check mark in front of Pause Printing.

- **Resume printing all documents**   In the printer's window, select **Printer** and select **Pause Printing**. "Paused" disappears from the title bar and the check mark disappears from the Pause Printing option in the Printer menu.

- **Pause a document**   In the printer's window, select the document or documents to pause and then select **Document | Pause**. "Paused" will appear in the Status column of the document(s) you selected.

- **Resume printing a paused document where it left off**   In the printer's window, select the document and then select **Document | Resume**. "Printing" will appear in the Status column of the document selected.

- **Restart printing at the beginning of a document**   In the printer's window, select the document and then select **Document | Restart**. "Restarting" and then "Printing" will appear in the Status column.

NOTE You cannot change the order in which documents are being printed by pausing the current document that is printing. You must either complete printing the current document or cancel it. You can, however, use Pause to get around intermediate documents that are not currently printing. For example, suppose you want to immediately print the third document in the queue, but the first document is currently printing. You must either let the first document finish printing or cancel it. You can then pause the second document before it starts printing, and the third document will begin printing when the first document is out of the way.

Cancel Printing

Canceling printing can be done either at the printer level for all the jobs in the printer queue or at the document level for selected documents. A canceled job is deleted from the print queue and must be restarted by the original app.

- **Cancel a job**   In the printer's window, select the job or jobs that you want canceled. Select **Document** and select **Cancel**. Select **Yes** to confirm the cancellation. The job or jobs will disappear from the window and the queue.

- **Cancel all the jobs in the queue**   In the printer's window, select **Printer** and select **Cancel All Documents**. You are asked whether you are sure you want to cancel all documents. Select **Yes**. All jobs will disappear from the queue and the printer window.

Change a Document's Properties

A document in a print queue has a Properties dialog box, shown in Figure 6-15, which is shown by opening the context menu

Figure 6-15: *Setting the properties of a document in the print queue can change its priority and when it prints.*

well as when a document has finished printing, put the name of another person (the individual's user name on a shared computer or network) in the Notify text box of the document's Properties dialog box.

- **Set print time** To change when a job is printed, open a document's Properties dialog box, select **Only From** at the bottom under Schedule, and then enter the time range within which you want the job printed. This allows you to print large jobs, which might otherwise clog the print queue, at a time when there is little or no load.

for the document and selecting **Properties**. The General tab allows you to change a number of things:

- **Priority** To change a document's default priority of 1, the lowest priority, so that the document can be printed before another that hasn't started printing yet, set the document's priority in the document's Properties dialog box to anything higher than the other document by dragging the **Priority** slider to the right.

- **Whom to notify** To change who is optionally notified of any special situations occurring during printing, as

▷▷ Handle Fonts

A *font* is a set of characters with the same design, size, weight, and style. A font is a member of a *typeface* family, all with the same design. The font 12-point Arial bold italic is a member of the Arial typeface with a 12-point size, bold weight, and italic style. Windows 8.1 comes with a large number of fonts, a few of which are shown in Figure 6-16.

Add Fonts

To add fonts to those that are installed by Windows 8.1:

1. Open the **System** menu and select **Control Panel | Appearance And Personalization | Fonts**. The Fonts window opens as shown in Figure 6-16.

2. Either use File Explorer to locate a font (or fonts) on your computer (this can be a flash drive, a CD/DVD, or a hard disk) or on your network, or use Internet Explorer

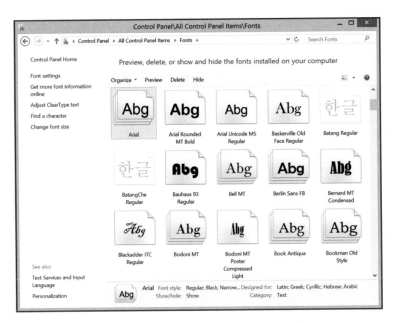

Figure 6-16: ***Although a number of fonts come with Windows, you can add others that come with other programs or that are available on the Internet.***

to download a font to your computer and then, with File Explorer, locate it so you can see and then select the new font(s) you want to install.

3. Open the context menu for the selected new font(s), and then select **Install**. A message will tell you the fonts are being installed. When you are done, the new fonts will appear in the Fonts window.

Delete Fonts

Remove fonts simply by selecting them in the Fonts window and pressing **DELETE** or by opening the context menu for the font(s) and selecting **Delete**. In either case, you are told that if

the font is deleted, some text might not appear as you intended and asked whether you are sure you want to do that. Select **Yes** if you are. The fonts will be deleted *permanently* and *cannot* be retrieved from the Recycle Bin.

Use Fonts

Fonts are used or specified from within an app. In Microsoft Word, for example, you can select a character, word, or line or more of text and then open the Font drop-down list in the Font group (in Office 2007 and later). Every app is a little different. One nice feature in recent versions of Word is that the list shows what the fonts look like.

99 QuickQuotes

Jim Finds Lots of Information

I use my computer for a lot of things, including email, banking, and working with my photos, which included organizing them, putting them on CDs, and printing them. Probably most valuable, though, is the access to the Internet, which I use quite often. Although I'm now retired, I often go on Web MD to look up drug interactions and other information. I also find the Internet very useful in looking up random information. For example, we had a house guest from France and got to talking about bridges. I mentioned a bridge in France I knew about that he did not. We looked it up on the Internet and, sure enough, found the bridge I had remembered. I think this capability is truly amazing to have in your home. Before the Internet, you might have been able to go to a library and find it, but even there, it would have been much more difficult.

Jim T., DDS, 80, Missouri

Chapter 7

Enjoying Multimedia

Multimedia is the combination of audio and video, with the term *media* referring to either audio or video. As an operating system, Windows 8.1 has to handle audio and video files and accept their input from a number of different devices. It has three default apps—Music, Video, and Windows Media Player—that enable you to work with multimedia files and read and write them onto CDs, DVDs, flash drives, and music players, as well as **stream** them to other computers (streaming sends audio or video files to another computer in such a way that the other computer can play and/or display the files as they are being sent). We'll look first at sound by itself, then at video with sound.

WORK WITH AUDIO

Audio is sound. Windows 8.1 works with and uses sound in several ways, the simplest being to alert you of various events, like an incoming email message or closing down the system. Chapter 2 shows you how to customize the use of sounds for these purposes. The other use of sound is to entertain or inform you—be it listening to music or lectures from CDs, Internet radio, or another Internet site. It is this use of sound that is the subject of this section.

> **NOTE** The term "audio CD" in this context means it contains audio files specifically formatted for CD players and not a collection of mp3's burned to a disc.

▶▶ Play CDs

Playing a CD is as easy as inserting a disc in the drive. When you first do that, Windows asks you to choose what happens with audio CDs. If you select that message, you will be asked if you want Windows Media Player, or possibly another player, to play the disc. If you select **Play Audio CD Windows Media Player**, you are asked if you want Windows Media Player to be your default player. Select **Recommended Settings | Finish**. Media Player will open and begin playing the disc. Initially, the on-screen view, called "Now Playing," is a small window, as shown in Figure 7-1. If you select **Switch To Library** in the upper-right corner under the Close button ▦, a larger, more comprehensive window will open, as you can see in Figure 7-2 (depending on the size of the window, there are some differences in what is displayed). The Media Player library window has a variety of controls that enable you to determine how it functions and looks. These controls are located either in the functional controls and option menus at the top of the window or in the playback controls at the bottom.

DVD RW Drive (F:) Audio CD
Tap to choose what happens with audio CDs.

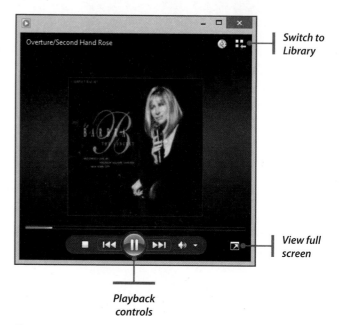

Switch to Library

View full screen

Playback controls

Figure 7-1: **Windows Media Player Now Playing view shows you its controls when you move the mouse over it.**

- **Menu options** include facilities to:
  - **Organize** the Media Player window.
  - **Stream** media from your computer.
  - **Create a playlist** of selected tracks.
- **Functional controls** allow selection of the primary Media Player functions:
  - **Rip CD** copies audio CDs to the Media Library.
  - **Rip settings** determines how audio is copied from a CD.
  - **Play** plays selected tracks and creates a playlist.
  - **Burn** copies playlists from the library to writable CDs and DVDs.
  - **Sync** synchronizes content between portable music devices and your PC.

Menu options

Functional controls

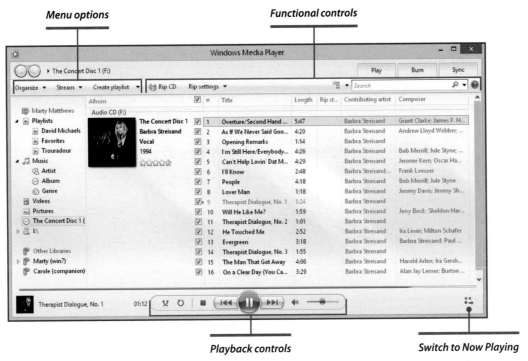

Playback controls

Switch to Now Playing

Figure 7-2: **Windows Media Player Library view gives you access to a wide range of audio and video entertainment.**

- **Playback controls** provide CD player–like controls to play/pause, stop, go to a previous track, go to the next track, and adjust volume/mute, as well as randomly play tracks (shuffle) and repeat a specific track.

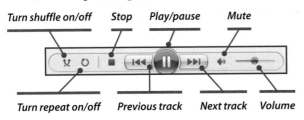

When you select any of the three tabs for the functional controls in the upper-right area, the list pane opens. The Play tab initially lists what is currently being played, but can be cleared and used to build your own playlist. The parts of the Media Player in Play mode are shown in Figure 7-3, and include the following:

- **List options** hide (close) the list pane and manipulate the list.

- **Play to** starts an audio or video stream to a media device.

- **Clear list** stops what is being played and prepares the pane for creating a playlist.

Figure 7-3: *The list pane shows what is currently playing and is where playlists are created.*

- **Save list** saves the current playlist to your Media Library.
- **Shop CD/DVD** enables you to buy the item you are listening to or watching.
- **Previous** and **Next** let you cycle through the playlists in your library.
- **Switch to Now Playing** collapses the window to just the small window shown in Figure 7-1.

⏩ Explore Music

If you have a broadband Internet connection (as described in Chapter 4) of at least 1 Mbps (more will improve your experience) and sound capability (speakers in or attached to your computer), you can find a large amount of media, including music, movies, and TV. Windows 8.1 facilitates that through the Xbox Music app, plus you can access online content directly through Internet Explorer.

Controlling the Volume

You can control your computer's audio volume from several places, including the physical volume control on your speakers or on your laptop computer, the volume control on the bottom-right of the playback controls of the Media Player, and the Volume icon 🔊 in the notification area on the right of the taskbar.

Selecting the **Speakers** or **Volume** icon in the notification area, which displays the percentage of full volume when pointed to, opens a small volume slider that you can drag for louder or softer sound, or you can select **Mute** (the blue speaker at the bottom of the slider) to do just that. The Mixer option at the bottom of the slider lets you individually control the volume level for different devices and apps such as Speakers, System Sounds, iTunes, and Media Player. Select anywhere on the desktop to close the volume slider.

Windows 8.1's Xbox Music app allows you to search for, preview, and purchase music online, as well as play music in your library. The first time you open Music, you will be given three options, as shown in Figure 7-4:

Collection accesses, organizes, and plays the music on your computer.

Radio streams music you select from the Internet to your computer.

Explore locates, previews, streams, and enables you to buy music on the Internet.

Collection assumes that you have music on your computer, so before discussing that we'll look at getting your own music from Music and other Internet sources, as well as copying CDs you may have onto your computer. Begin by opening Music and exploring it a bit.

1. On the Start screen, select the **Music** tile. Music will open as shown in Figure 7-4.

2. If you see Sign In in the upper-right corner, select it to add an Xbox membership to your Microsoft account. You then need to verify your Microsoft account user name and password. If you already have an Xbox profile, select that link, then review the Xbox Terms Of Use and Privacy Statement, and when you are ready, select **I Accept**.

3. When you are returned to Music's Home page, select either **Explore** on the left or **Browse Millions Of Songs** in the lower-right. Currently popular music will be displayed (see Figure 7-5).

4. Preview some of this music by selecting one of the albums and then selecting the right arrow next to the album cover to play the songs on the album, or select a particular song to play it.

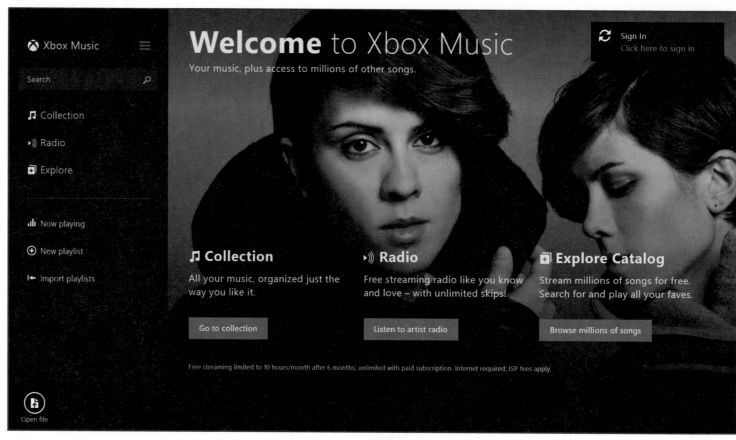

*Figure 7-4: **Music lets you work with music both on your computer as well as on the Internet.***

In the following sections we'll look at searching for and purchasing music both from the Music app as well as on the Internet in general.

▷▷ Find Your Music Online

Having spent my adolescent youth in the late 1950s, some of my favorite songs from that era are by The Platters and include *Unchained Melody, Smoke Gets in Your Eyes,* and *Twilight Time.* You can easily find and listen to your favorite music by searching both Music and the Internet.

Search Music

Music provides the ability to search the music industry and display the music related to your search. In my case, I want to search for The Platters.

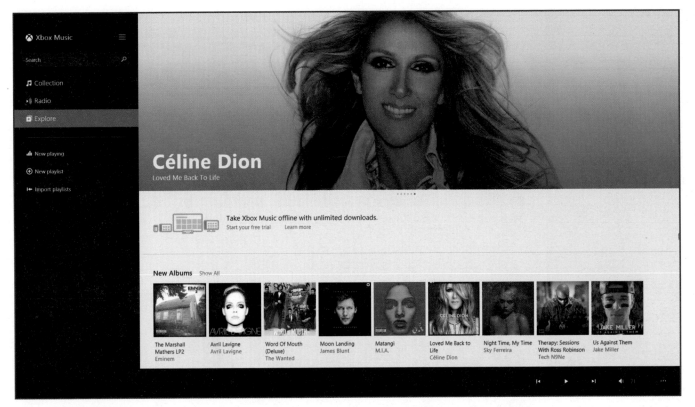

Figure 7-5: While Music dwells on currently popular music, music of many genres and periods is available.

1. With the Xbox Music app open on your computer (see "Explore Music" previously), select the Search text box in the upper-left corner; type the artist's name, album name, group name, or composer name; and press **ENTER** or select **Search** (the magnifying glass). The results will be displayed, as you see in Figure 7-6 for The Platters.

2. Select any of the albums, and then select the right arrow next to the album cover to play the songs on the album, or select a particular song to play it. We'll talk about purchasing music later in this chapter.

Search Google or Bing

You can find most other popular songs by simply typing a song's name into either the Google or Bing search text box. For example, I might type Platters – Unchained Melody. This produces a list of links to sites where you can listen to the song, read the lyrics, or watch a performance, as you can see on the left of Figure 7-7. Many of the links that are found are on YouTube. Selecting one of these links opens YouTube and begins playing the song. On the page that opens there are links to either other songs by the same artist or other artists performing the same song, as you can see on the right of Figure 7-7.

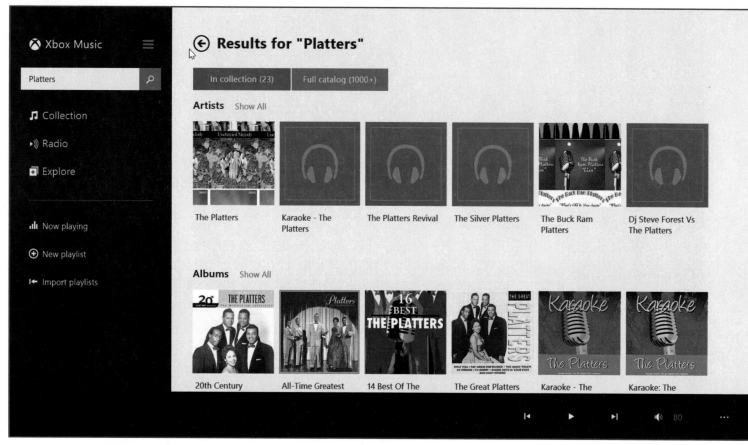

Figure 7-6: *Music provides a full collection of many genres, artists, and eras.*

▷▷ Buy Media Online

There are many sources of media on the Internet. Windows 8.1's Music app is one such source.

1. Select the album you want to buy, either in total or a single song. The album list of songs will open, as you saw earlier for the Celine Dion album.

2. To buy a single song, right-click or swipe from right to left the song and then select **Buy Song** in the bottom of the screen, as shown in Figure 7-8. To buy the entire album, select the shopping cart opposite the album cover.

3. Enter your Microsoft account password. The confirmation information will appear.

Figure 7-7: Finding music online is simply a matter of typing the name of the performer and/or the song in a search text box and then selecting the one you want to hear.

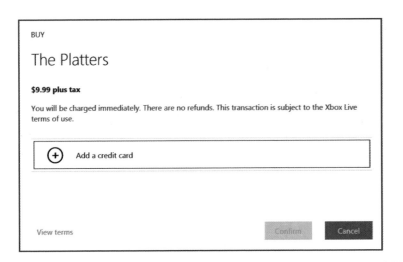

BUY

The Platters

$9.99 plus tax

You will be charged immediately. There are no refunds. This transaction is subject to the Xbox Live terms of use.

⊕   Add a credit card

View terms   Confirm   Cancel

4. If needed, select **Add Credit Card** and fill in the credit card information. Then select **Save Info | Confirm**, or if your credit card was already displayed, just select **Confirm**. You will get a message that your purchase is being automatically downloaded. If you return to the Music home screen, you should see the song/album under Collection.

3	Twilight Time	2:46	The Platters
4	The Great Pretender	2:39	The Platters
5	Only You	2:34	The Platters
6	Harbour Lights	3:10	The Platters
7	Unchained Melody	4:56	The Platters
8	I Love You 1000 Times	2:45	The Platters

*Figure 7-8: **It is almost too easy to buy media on the Internet.***

TIP You can get information about your payment options, billing history, and other information related to your purchases through Music by opening **Charms** and selecting **Settings | Account** while Music is open.

CAUTION! The Xbox Music app and many other online stores make it *very easy to buy from them,* and you can quickly run up a sizable bill. You need to create an account with the store and provide your name, address, email, and credit card info.

Copy (Rip) CDs to Your Computer

Media Player gives you the ability to copy (or "rip") CD tracks that you like to your hard disk so that you can build and manage a library of your favorite music and copy this material to a recordable CD or DVD, or to a music player. To copy from a CD (see Figure 7-9):

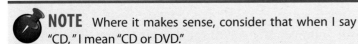

NOTE Where it makes sense, consider that when I say "CD," I mean "CD or DVD."

NOTE Copying a music track from a CD to a digital file on your hard disk is time-consuming, even on a relatively fast computer. It also produces large files. To see the copying progress, look at the Rip Status column of the Media Player window, as well as the message in the bottom-right corner (see Figure 7-9).

1. Insert the CD from which you want to copy tracks. If it doesn't automatically start playing, click **Play Audio CD Using Windows Media Player** to open Windows Media Player.

2. Select **Switch To Library** in the upper-right corner. In the details pane, select the tracks you want to copy to your hard disk by selecting the check boxes to the left of each track. Select **Play** in the playback controls to listen to the tracks and to make sure your choices are correct.

3. If you wish, select **Rip Settings** in the command bar at the top of the window (if you don't see Rip CD and Rip Settings, widen the window) and review the settings that are available

*Figure 7-9: **Media Player can be used to build a music library from your CDs.***

to you. For the most part, the default settings provide the best middle ground between high quality and file size.

4. When you are satisfied that you have selected the correct tracks and settings, select **Rip CD**. The selected tracks will be copied to your hard disk. When you are done, remove the CD and close Media Player.

 ## Organize Music

Once you have copied several CDs and have downloaded other music to your hard disk, you will likely want this material organized. When music and videos are copied to the library, the contents are automatically indexed alphabetically by album, artist, and genre. You may want to combine selected tracks into a *playlist* that allows you to play pieces from several albums.

You can work with music with both the Music app and with the Windows Media Player

Use Music

Music automatically goes through your computer and tries to gather all the music on it. When you open Music and select **Collection**, you are shown the music that you have collected and that has been found by the Music app. My collection is shown in Figure 7-10. If you believe that you have music not found by the Music app, select the **All Done!** message and then the plus sign to search for additional folders where you might have more music.

Once you have a number of albums where you probably have three or four favorite songs out of ten, you may want to build one or more playlists of just your favorites. To do that:

1. With Music open, select **New Playlist**, type a name for the playlist, and press **ENTER**. Your new playlist will appear in the column on the left.

2. To add songs to the playlist, select **Collection** | an album | a song | the plus sign | your new playlist. If you wish to add a complete album, select the plus sign opposite the album cover and then your new playlist.

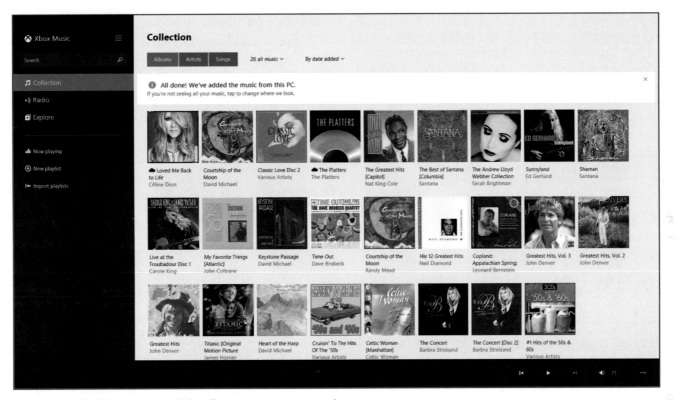

Figure 7-10: *Music lets you see all the albums on your computer in one screen.*

3. Repeat step 3 for all the songs or albums you want in the playlist.

4. You can see the music on your computer and select songs and albums for playlists in different ways. At the top of Collection, the default is to see your music organized by albums, but you can also see it organized by artist and by song. You can also select whether you see all your music, music you have on your computer, or on the cloud. Finally, you can sort albums and songs alphabetically, by date added (the default), by release year, by genre, and by artist.

 NOTE The little black cloud that you see next to albums and songs indicates that it is additionally stored on Microsoft's cloud service (meaning that it is stored on Microsoft computers and available to you over the Internet), as well as on your computer. If you buy a song or album from Microsoft's Xbox Music, it will automatically also be available on the cloud. When a piece is on the cloud, you can access it on other computers, tablets, game controllers, and smartphones that can run Xbox Music and use your Microsoft ID. See Chapter 8 for more information on using the cloud.

TIP You can add music to the Microsoft cloud that has been purchased elsewhere or that you have ripped from CDs by opening Charms with Music active and selecting **Settings | Preference** and then under Cloud Collection selecting **Automatically Add Matched Songs On This PC To My Music In The Cloud**. This allows you to play songs in your Music Collection on other devices via the cloud. The songs in your Collection must have a match to songs in Xbox Music.

Use Windows Media Player

The Windows Media Player that you saw in earlier sections and figures in this chapter provides the same organizational capabilities from the desktop as are available in Music. To build a new playlist:

NOTE You cannot add music to playlists directly from a CD in your drive even though it appears in Media Player. You must first add the music to your library and then select it from there.

1. On the Start screen begin typing <u>Media Player</u> and select **Windows Media Player** when it appears.

2. Select **Create Playlist** in the command bar at the top of the window. Type the name you want for the new playlist, and press **ENTER**. A new playlist will appear in the list of playlists in the navigation pane.

3. Open an album, artist, or genre; and select a piece or the pieces (hold down **CTRL** as you select multiple pieces that you want in the new playlist). Drag the piece(s) to the playlist title in the navigation pane.

4. Select other pieces you want to add, and drag them to the playlist title in the navigation pane. Select the playlist to display the contents in the details pane, or open the playlist to display it in the Play tab in the list pane and begin to play it.

–Or–

1. Open Media Player and select the **Play** tab to open it in the list pane. Select from the navigation pane and display in the details pane the music you want in the playlist. Drag the piece(s) you want to the list pane, as you can see in Figure 7-11.

2. When you have added all the pieces that you initially want (you can always add more later), select **Save List** in the command bar under Play, type a name, and press **ENTER**.

3. Listen to the playlist by selecting the **Play** button in the playback controls. When you are done, select **Clear List** and then select the **Play** tab to close the list pane, and close Media Player.

Figure 7-11: *Media Player provides a way to manage the media you store on your computer, including building playlists.*

 TIP When listening to a playlist, you can randomize the order in which the pieces will play by selecting **Turn Shuffle On** ⚡ in the playback controls, which is the first button on the left. Select it a second time to return to normal play.

Make (Burn) a Music CD

Once you have created a playlist (see "Organize Music" earlier in this chapter), you can write (or "burn") it to a writable CD using Media Player's Burn feature. This creates an "audio" CD that works in a portable or car CD player. This is not the

same as simply making a copy of the digital files as explained in step 4 of this procedure.

1. Put a blank recordable disc in the CD recording drive. A dialog box will appear and ask what you want to do. Select **Burn An Audio CD** to open Windows Media Player with the Burn functional area displayed.

TIP If the Burn tab isn't automatically opened when Media Player opens, select the Burn tab in the upper-right area of the Media Player.

2. Open your playlists in the navigation pane, and drag a playlist (or individual songs from an open playlist) that you want on the CD to the Burn List on the right. Do this in the order you want the songs played. You can see how much of the CD is being used and the amount of time remaining just above the Burn List, as shown in Figure 7-12.

3. You can make corrections to the Burn List by dragging additional songs there until you use up the remaining time, or by opening the context menu for a song on the Burn List and selecting **Remove From List** in the context menu that opens. You can also clear the Burn List and start over.

4. When you are sure you have the list of pieces you want to burn, select **Start Burn**. The digital files will first be converted to analog music files and then written to a CD or DVD. You can see the progress in the thermometer bar near the top of the list pane (it is not very fast!). When the burn is complete, and if no one has changed the default settings, the disc will be ejected from the drive. Write the title on the disc with a soft felt-tip marker, or use a LightScribe drive to burn a label on the special discs you use for that purpose.

The resulting CD should be playable in most CD players.

*Figure 7-12: **Burning a playlist to a writable CD allows you to create a disc that has just your favorite songs.***

▷▷ Copy to (Sync with) Music Players

Windows Media Player allows you to plug in a digital music device, such as an iPod or MP3 player, and transfer music to and from (sync with) the device.

1. Start Windows Media Player, and select **Sync** in the Windows Media Player functional controls. You will be told to connect your device.

2. Start your device and then plug it into your computer. The first time you do that, Windows will install a driver for it, and then the AutoPlay dialog box will appear.

3. If the Devices Setup dialog box appears, select **Finish** or **Cancel**, depending on your situation.

4. When your device appears in the Media Player, drag the playlists and/or songs you want on the device to the Sync List on the right. If you wish, you can play the Sync List by opening the first playlist or song.

5. When you are certain that you have all the music in the Sync List that you want on your device, select **Start Sync**, as shown in Figure 7-13. The music will be copied to the device.

6. When you see that the sync is complete, select **Click Here** to see the results on the player. When you are ready, disconnect your player.

Figure 7-13: ***A digital music device can mirror your Media Player library if it has enough room and that is what you want.***

▷▷ Listen to Internet Radio

A number of organizations are now offering "Internet Radio," which streams music to you based on the selection of an artist or genre that you like. You can set up "stations" based on a selection you have made, and you can have several of these. The service generally starts out free with some advertising and then offers you a subscription that may remove the ads. One of the earliest of these services was Pandora, which you can access with Internet Explorer by entering <u>Pandora.com</u> in the address box. The Music app in Windows 8.1 offers this service with the Radio option on the home page.

1. From the Music app's home page, select **Radio** and select **Start A Station**. You are given a prompt to enter an artist and shown a long list of currently popular artists. Unfortunately, none are from my generation.

2. Type a name of an artist that you want to build a station around that not only plays their music, but also includes similar artists from the same genre. For example I entered "Dave Brubeck."

3. Select the icon on the right of the name entry field. The artist picture will appear, and the music will start playing. You are also told some of the other artists that will be included.

4. Select **Start A Station** again if you want additional stations, and repeat steps 2 and 3.

After playing for a bit you will be given an offer for an Xbox Music Pass, which is initially free, but after a short while there will be a subscription fee. If you don't get the Music Pass, you will get other ads.

WORK WITH VIDEO

Windows 8.1 lets you watch videos downloaded from the Internet using the Xbox Video app, which works with videos in a similar way to how Music works with songs. Windows 8.1 also allows you to capture videos and still images from a digital camcorder, digital camera, tablets, or smartphones.

Import Video from a Camcorder

You can import or copy video directly from your camcorder to your hard drive, and then view the resulting file with the Windows 8.1 Video app or with Windows Media Player.

1. Using a cable connected to your camcorder, plug the other end of cable into a USB or FireWire (IEEE 1394) port on your computer, and turn the camera on. Alternatively, if your camera also has a removable memory card, you can remove it from the camera and plug it into the memory card slot on your computer.

2. In either case, Windows 8.1 will see the camcorder or the memory card as a removable disk, install any needed driver software, and open a message asking you to choose what to do.

3. Select the message to open a list of options. The options of interest here are:

a. **Play** opens Windows Media Player and the video files begin to play.

b. **Import Photos And Videos** opens the Photos app and displays the video segments on the screen (if you see a right arrow, click it to preview the segment). Uncheck

the segment if you don't want to import it, enter the folder where you want the files, and select **Import** to finish the process.

c. **Open Folder To View Files** opens the File Explorer displaying the video files on the camera, as shown in Figure 7-14. This allows you to move the files anywhere on your hard disk. It is recommended that you put the video files in a folder in the Library's My Videos folder so the programs on your computer can easily find them.

4. To view your video with the Video app, type <u>Video</u> on the Start screen and select **Video** to open the app. On the left side of the app (you may have to use the horizontal scroll bar to get there), you should see the videos you have added. Select a video to view it.

and double-select the file you want to play. Depending on the format of your videos, either Media Player or the Video app will open and play the file.

Figure 7-14: *Opening the folder to view the files gives you the greatest flexibility in storing your videos, but putting them in My Videos makes viewing them easier.*

5. To view your videos with Windows Media Player, in the Start screen, begin typing <u>Media Player</u> and select Windows Media Player when it appears. In the navigation pane, select **Videos** to display your files. Scroll down to find and select the one you want to play, as you can see in Figure 7-15. Double-select the file to play it in Media Player.

6. You can also use File Explorer to locate and play videos. On the desktop, select File Explorer; in the navigation pane, open the drive and folders needed to locate your files;

 NOTE The File Explorer has a Video Tools Play contextual ribbon for playing videos and building a playlist of them.

 TIP The discussion about buying, organizing, and burning CDs applies equally to DVDs.

Figure 7-15: *The Windows Media Player gives you a better understanding than the Video app of where your files are located.*

Gene Depends on His Computer

When there is a disaster, the Federal Emergency Management Agency (FEMA) may call me in to help communities recover from the event. I can be sent anywhere in the country, and I go with my own laptop computer and am issued another one by FEMA. I wouldn't and couldn't be without those computers. I use them many times a day to keep in contact with my colleagues at the agency, with the congressional staffs with which I'm working, and with my family and friends back home.

Gene L., "over 65," Washington

Chapter 8

Using the Cloud and Apps

The "cloud," as I have mentioned in earlier chapters, is a service facilitated by the Internet that allows you to remotely store files you have created and use apps that are not on your computer. When you store files on the cloud, it provides a backup for the same files stored on your computer, and it also allows you to access those files from any other computer that is connected to the Internet. Apps on the cloud are used through a browser and allow you to perform tasks without installing the app on your computer. In essence, the cloud gives you a very large extension to your computer, but it does require that you have a fast and stable connection to the Internet and have signed up with a cloud service. A number of major companies provide cloud services, including Microsoft, Amazon, Google, and Apple, as well as a number of new companies, including Copy, JustCloud, and Dropbox. Most of these companies (all the ones mentioned) provide an initial allotment of storage (2 to 15GB) for free and then offer (encourage might be a better word) additional storage for various prices. I've found you can do quite a lot in the free allotment, and Microsoft's service is one of the more generous and least expensive. Plus, Microsoft has integrated their cloud service into Windows 8.1 and their Office 2013 products.

In this chapter we will explore the use of the cloud both for storage and to use some cloud-based apps. In both cases we look at the Microsoft offerings in this area as implemented in Windows 8.1. We will also look at several useful Windows built-in apps, including Calculator, Character Map, Notepad, and Paint, and then we will finish with a commonly used third-party app, Adobe Reader.

EXPLORE THE CLOUD

Cloud computing is working with computer files and apps hosted on somebody else's (we'll primarily look at Microsoft's) remote servers over the Internet rather than on your own computer. This means that your files and apps are stored on an Internet server rather than on your own computer, and that the apps you use are accessed through a browser working on the Internet rather than from apps installed on your computer. This is a new world! Why this is even remotely a good idea really revolves around expanded ways of working with data files and other people and making them available any place, any time. The approach is much more about accessing and sharing data and collaboration than it is about an isolated person working alone. When you store data and have apps available from an Internet server (or "on the cloud"):

- You don't have to worry about losing your data if something happens to your computer or hard drive.

- You don't have to pay for a generous amount of storage until (or unless) you want to upgrade to higher-capacity storage.

- You don't have to worry about whether you have access to your computer at home, for instance, because you can access your files when traveling.

- You don't have to worry about whether you have the latest app updates.

- You don't have to worry about someone else being able to read your documents when they don't own the app or don't have the same version.

 NOTE There are several ways to use cloud computing: using the files and apps in the cloud, using files in the cloud with apps on your computer, and only using the cloud as a depository to share files.

Microsoft's cloud service, currently called SkyDrive (see Note), is built into Windows 8.1. By default, the photos you take on your computer, the documents you create, and your computer settings are automatically saved to SkyDrive, although you can change the automatic nature of this. As a result, using the default, you can access all of these items from any computer, whether or not you can access your originating computer. SkyDrive starts out with the first 7GB of storage for free. Then, if you need more, you can buy 20GB for $10.00 a year, 50GB for $25, and so on.

 NOTE At the time this book was written, a British court had ruled that the name SkyDrive infringes on British Sky Broadcasting's (BSkyB's) trademark and Microsoft must change it in the near future. For the lack of another name at the time, throughout the book we use SkyDrive, which Microsoft was able to use for a reasonable time. Just as this book was going to press, however, Microsoft announced that the new name for SkyDrive will be OneDrive.

EXPLORE SKYDRIVE

Windows 8.1 has made SkyDrive an integral part of the operating system and fully integrated it with the file system. It is available on the Start screen through the SkyDrive tile, on the desktop through the File Explorer, from apps, and from an Internet browser. We'll look at all of these in the following sections.

⏩ Use SkyDrive from the Start Screen

Begin by opening SkyDrive from the Start screen and go through Microsoft's SkyDrive Welcome message the first time you open it.

1. From the Start screen, select the **SkyDrive** tile. Select **Learn More Online** to open the Internet Explorer in a half pane, as you can see in Figure 8-1. Look at the video (it is a little over a minute long) and read down the remainder of the page. It is a good start that we'll build on here.

2. Close IE (drag its top border to the bottom of the screen) and double-select the three dots in the middle of the screen to re-enlarge SkyDrive. Finally, select **Close** in the "This is your cloud storage" message on the left.

3. By default, you should have in SkyDrive (on the screen) one or two folders, one named Documents, and possibly one named Pictures, as you saw in Figure 8-1. If you have no folders, shut down Windows and your computer so they are not running, and then restart your computer. In one instance, that got me a Documents folder when I had none. If you only have one folder, the next section will show you how to add folders to SkyDrive.

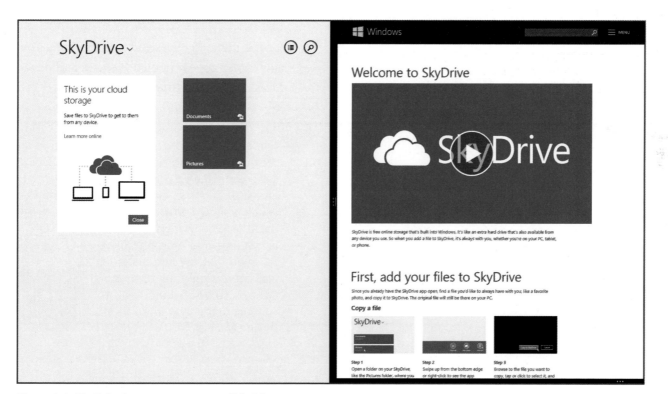

*Figure 8-1: **SkyDrive is as easy to use as a disk drive your computer.***

Add Folders to SkyDrive

SkyDrive usually starts out with one or two folders named Documents and Pictures to hold files you want to store there, as you saw in Figure 8-1. In the event SkyDrive doesn't show a Documents or Pictures folder, you can add them, as you'll see in a moment. You can also add folders as you wish, both at the same level as Documents and Pictures, and within those folders.

1. If SkyDrive is not already open, select the **SkyDrive** tile in the Start screen. Depending on whether you have a camera on your computer, you should see an image similar to one of these:

My experience is that a Documents folder is almost always created, so we'll assume that as our foundation.

NOTE The little cloud and computer icon in the lower-right corner of your folders in SkyDrive tells you that the information on this folder in SkyDrive is also available on your computer when you are not connected to the Internet, or "offline."

2. If you do have a Pictures folder, skip to step 4. Otherwise, create one by right-clicking a blank area of the screen or swiping up from the bottom to display the command bar and then selecting **New Folder**.

3. Type the name <u>Pictures</u> and select **Create**. You should see a new folder appear named Pictures and have at least two folders, Documents and Pictures.

TIP There two possible views of your SkyDrive folders that are controlled by the second icon from the right in the upper-right corner . Thumbnail view, with what I call boxy rectangles, is what has been shown in the figures and illustrations so far in this chapter; and Details view, which is shown next. In the Details view, the date is the date the folder was last modified, and the notation "Available Offline" tells you that the information is also stored on your computer. Otherwise you would have to connect to the Internet to access the information.

4. Create a folder within Documents by selecting that folder to open it, right-clicking a blank area of the screen or swiping up from the bottom to display the command bar, and then selecting **New Folder**.

5. Type a name for the folder—I'll use "Favorites"—and select **Create**. You should see a new folder appear. Repeat this if you want additional folders.

6. Create a new folder at the Documents and Pictures level that you can use for special projects or some other purpose. Select the left arrow in the upper-left corner of the SkyDrive screen to return to the Documents and Pictures level.

7. Right-click a blank area of the screen or swipe up from the bottom to display the command bar and then select **New Folder**.

8. Type a name for the folder—I'll use "Projects"—and select **Create**. You should see the new folder appear. Repeat this if you want additional folders.

Copy Files to SkyDrive

You can copy files to a SkyDrive folder in several ways, depending on where you are using SkyDrive from: the Start screen, another app, the desktop, or the Internet. You can do this by using the tools in SkyDrive, dragging files from their current folder, or saving them to a SkyDrive folder from an app you are using to create them. In this and the next several sections we'll look at all of those ways.

1. From the Start screen, open **SkyDrive** and select a folder you want to hold your new files by right-clicking the folder or swiping down on it to also open the command bar as you can see in Figure 8-2.

NOTE If you don't select a folder, the copied or moved file(s) will be placed in the "root," or outer, SkyDrive folder.

2. Select **Add Files** to open and display the folders in This PC. Open the folders necessary to locate the files you want to copy to the selected folder in SkyDrive.

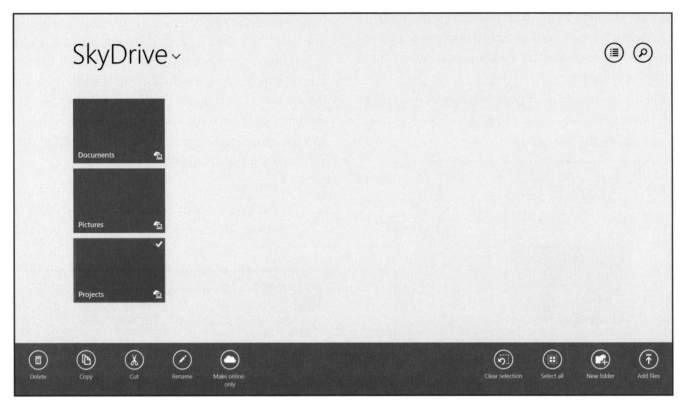

Figure 8-2: *The command bar provides the tools to use SkyDrive.*

3. Select the files you want to copy; they should have a check mark in the upper-right corner and be listed at the bottom of the screen.

4. Select **Copy To SkyDrive** to place a copy of the files in the selected SkyDrive folder while leaving a copy on your computer.

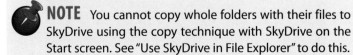 **NOTE** You cannot copy whole folders with their files to SkyDrive using the copy technique with SkyDrive on the Start screen. See "Use SkyDrive in File Explorer" to do this.

Move Files to SkyDrive

To move files to SkyDrive starting from the Start screen, where you remove the files from their folder on your computer:

1. From the Start screen, open **SkyDrive**.

2. At the top of the screen, select the down arrow on the right of SkyDrive and then select **This PC**.

Figure 8-3: *It is easy to see what files are being copied to SkyDrive when using the Start screen.*

3. Open (tap or click) the folder(s) necessary to locate the folder or files you want to move.

4. Select (right-click or swipe down) the folder or files you want to move. A check mark will appear in the upper-right corner, and the command bar will appear.

5. Select **Cut** on the left of the command bar. The paste option will appear in the command bar.

6. At the top of the screen, select the down arrow on the right of This PC (see Figure 8-3) and then select **SkyDrive**.

7. Open the folders necessary to locate where you want to move your file(s) or folder(s).

8. When you have open the final folder you want, right-click or swipe up from the bottom, and then select **Paste**. Your file(s) or folder(s) will appear in the SkyDrive folder and disappear in their original folder.

Save to SkyDrive from a Start Screen App

Since SkyDrive acts like another disk drive on your computer, other apps can see it as such and save files to it. Here, look at a Start screen app. In the following section, we'll look at desktop apps.

1. Open the app you want to use. For example, if I use Camera, it automatically saves my photos to the Camera Roll folder in Photos.

2. To move some of the photos I have taken to SkyDrive, I must select them in Camera Roll and select either **Cut** (to move) or **Copy**, and then select the down arrow on the right of the folder name at the top ("Pictures Library" in my example).

3. Select **SkyDrive**, open the necessary folders within SkyDrive, right-click a blank area of the screen or swipe up from the bottom of the screen, and select **Paste.**

▷▷ Use SkyDrive from the Desktop

While Microsoft would like us to think that the Start screen is the end-all of using our computers, most of us spend a lot of our time on the desktop and the Internet, but even in these locations SkyDrive has a dominant presence.

Use SkyDrive in File Explorer

So far in this chapter, all discussion of SkyDrive has been about using it from the Start screen. SkyDrive, though, is like an external disk drive and can be used just like one with File Explorer.

1. Open the desktop, select File Explorer from the taskbar, and open SkyDrive in the navigation pane so you can see the folder that will be the destination of what you want to do.

2. Also in File Explorer, open the folder(s) needed to display the folder(s) or files(s) in the subject pane want to copy or move to SkyDrive.

3. Select the file(s) or folder(s) that you want to move or copy and then:

   To move what you have selected, simply drag it to the SkyDrive folder you want, as you can see in Figure 8-4.

   To copy the selection, right-drag it holding the right mouse button, or hold **CTRL** while dragging it with your finger or the left mouse button. If you used right-drag, select **Copy Here** in the context menu that opens.

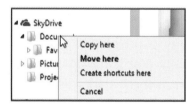

Use SkyDrive from a Desktop App

With SkyDrive's integration into the Windows 8.1 file system, it is easy to directly save a file to SkyDrive from a desktop app.

1. Open a desktop app—for example, Microsoft Word—and create whatever it is that you want to create.

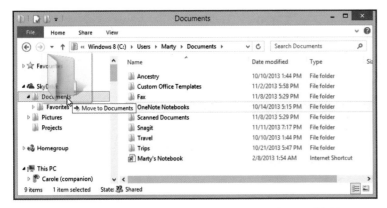

Figure 8-4: ***There is no difference between handling files and folders on your disks and on SkyDrive.***

2. When you are ready, begin to save the document as you normally would. In recent apps, especially Microsoft apps, you will see SkyDrive and be able to access it. It might be the default location for saving files if you just choose **Save** (see "Configure SkyDrive Settings" later in this chapter).

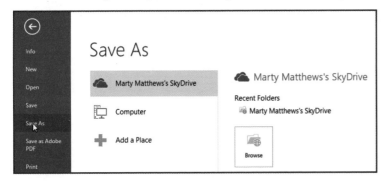

3. If you select **Save As** and then **Browse**, a Save As dialog box will open where you can select SkyDrive and then the

folders within it to get to the location where you want to store your file.

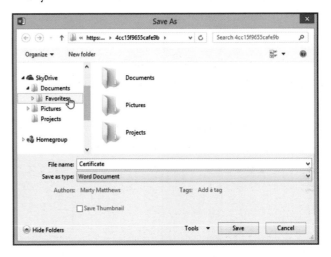

4. Complete the saving process as you normally would.

5. To open files that are on SkyDrive from an app you have open—for example, Microsoft Word—open your file system as you normally would and select **SkyDrive**.

6. In the Open dialog box, select the file you want to use as you normally would (see Figure 8-5).

Use SkyDrive on the Internet

Although SkyDrive exists on the Internet, the way Microsoft has built it, you don't directly see the Internet aspect of it. It looks and operates more like a disk drive on your computer, one that can follow you around as you go from computer to computer. Nevertheless, SkyDrive is on the Internet and you can access it from any browser. That is the way you can use it

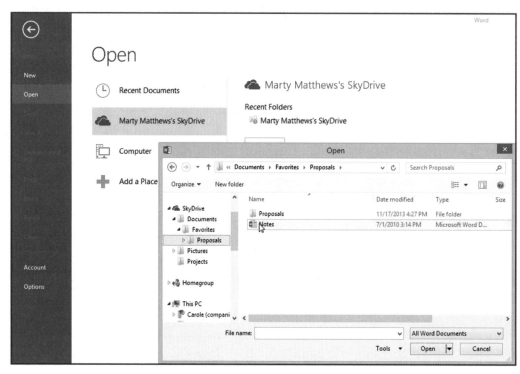

Figure 8-5: Your SkyDrive files are available to any app on any computer so long as you have your sign-in credentials.

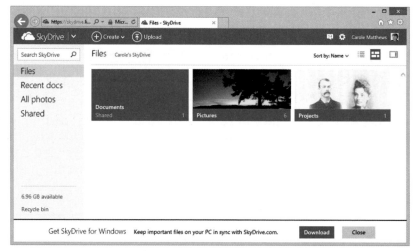

with any computer connected to the Internet and access your SkyDrive folders and files.

1. On the computer where you want to access your SkyDrive, on either the Start screen or desktop, open Internet Explorer and in the address box type skydrive.live.com. SkyDrive will open, displaying the files and settings belonging to the owner of the computer.

2. Select the owner's name in the upper-right corner and select **Sign Out**. The Sign In form appears.

3. Enter your email address and password, and select **Sign In**. SkyDrive will display your files and settings, as you see on your own computer.

4. Use SkyDrive as described in the earlier sections of this chapter.

⟫ Set Up SkyDrive

SkyDrive "out of the box" comes set up the way many people want to use it, but it is always worthwhile checking those settings to make sure they fit your needs. Also, you may want to share one or more of your files or folders in SkyDrive. Here we'll look at both of those situations.

Configure SkyDrive Settings

SkyDrive does not have a lot of settings, but you will probably want to consider the automatic saving to SkyDrive of your documents and photos and take a quick look at the other settings.

1. Open SkyDrive on the Start screen. Open **Charms** and select **Settings | Options**.

2. Consider if you want to force all files to be both on SkyDrive and on your computer, the latter meaning that they are available offline, when you are not connected to the Internet.

3. If you do want to force all files to also be on your computer, select the **On/Off** switch to turn it on.

4. Select the left arrow opposite Options to return to Settings, and select **Change PC Settings | SkyDrive**, where File Storage should be selected by default.

5. Observe how much of your SkyDrive storage allotment you are using and if you want to purchase more. By selecting **Buy More Storage** you can see what various amounts cost without actually buying any.

6. Here you can also choose to have the option to "Save to SkyDrive," the default, but you can select it to turn it off.

7. Select **Camera Roll** to review the settings for photos. By default, "good," or medium quality, photos are automatically stored on SkyDrive when they are added to your Camera

Roll folder in Pictures on your computer. You can choose to store the "best" quality photos on SkyDrive, but these take more storage space, or, alternatively, you can choose to not automatically store Camera Roll photos on SkyDrive. Finally, you can choose whether you want to automatically store your videos that go into the Camera Roll.

8. By selecting **Sync Settings**, you can choose what settings on your computer you want to use SkyDrive to sync with another computer that has your same Microsoft ID and password. By default, these are all on.

9. Finally, you are asked about using SkyDrive over metered connections, which are Internet connections where you pay by the minute, like on a smartphone. You can consider and turn on and off four settings.

Share SkyDrive Folders

The files and folders that you have stored on SkyDrive can be shared with others, both others on your computer, as well as others across the Internet. To do this, you must use the Internet access to SkyDrive.

1. Open Internet Explorer and open SkyDrive as you did earlier in this chapter.

2. Open the details pane on the right by selecting the icon on the far right of the second row of the SkyDrive Internet page 🖥.

3. Select the folder or file you want to share by opening any parent folders and then selecting the little white box in the upper-right corner of the folder or file you will share, as you can see in Figure 8-6.

4. Select **Share** to open the Share panel. Enter the email address of the person with whom you want to share with, enter any message you want, and select **Share**. This comes back and shows with whom you shared.

> ⓘ **CAUTION!** Before you see the Share panel, if you try to share a folder to which some apps automatically add files—for example, Pictures—you are warned that you might not want to have people share this folder.

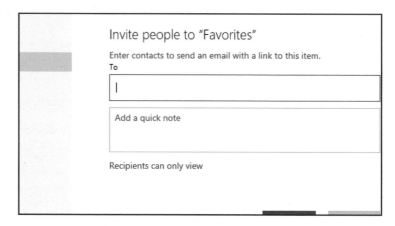

5. The recipient receives an email message with a link to the folder or file you have shared. They simply need to select the link to open your SkyDrive folders to see what you have

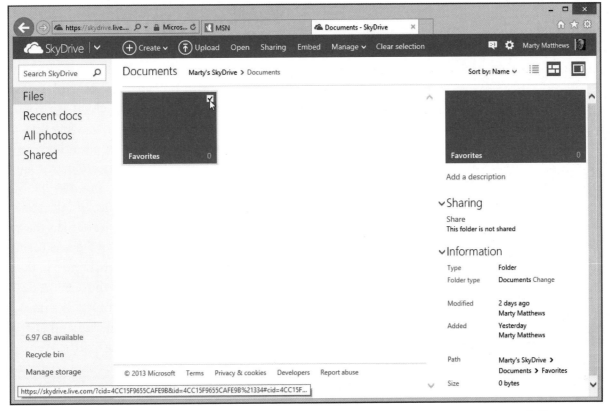

Figure 8-6: *The details pane available in SkyDrive viewed on the Internet gives you the ability to share a folder.*

shared. If you have given them permission to edit the folder, they can make any changes they see fit to the contents.

6. Back in the SkyDrive details pane in Internet Explorer on your computer, you will see who you have shared a particular folder or file with. If you again select **Share** to open the Share panel, select the person with whom you are sharing on the left, select **Can Only View** or **Can Edit**, and then select **Stop Editing** or **Stop Sharing**, you will discontinue either allowing editing or sharing with that person.

> **TIP** You can view and use your SkyDrive folder and files across a number of devices, not just Windows-based computers. Here is a screen shot of my iPhone looking at my SkyDrive folders.

CREATE AND EDIT DOCUMENTS WITH WEB APPS

Earlier in this chapter, we described how, with a SkyDrive account, you can upload files to Microsoft's SkyDrive site in order to store them in the "cloud" so you, or others with your permission, can access them at any time or place from a browser. Besides simply storing files there, using Microsoft's free Web Apps, you can also create new documents or view, edit, and download documents saved in the Microsoft Office file formats, without having Office installed on your computer. (Documents saved in the earlier Office file formats can be viewed and will be converted to the newer formats to be edited with Web Apps.) The editing capabilities in the free Web Apps are somewhat less capable than those in the desktop version of Office. However, if you are creating only a moderately complex document or primarily just editing and sharing documents with others, SkyDrive and the Office Web Apps provide a great opportunity to access and share your information from anywhere with only a browser and Internet connection.

▷▷ Create a Document with Web Apps

When you are signed on to SkyDrive, you have some of the Microsoft Office desktop apps available to you through the Office Web Apps. Simpler versions of Word, Excel, PowerPoint, and OneNote can be accessed online so that you don't need the desktop version of Office to work with these files. Here is how to create a new Word document with Web Apps:

1. In the SkyDrive toolbar on the top of the window, select the **Create** menu, and select the type of file you want to create; in this case, **Word Document**.

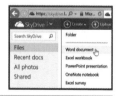

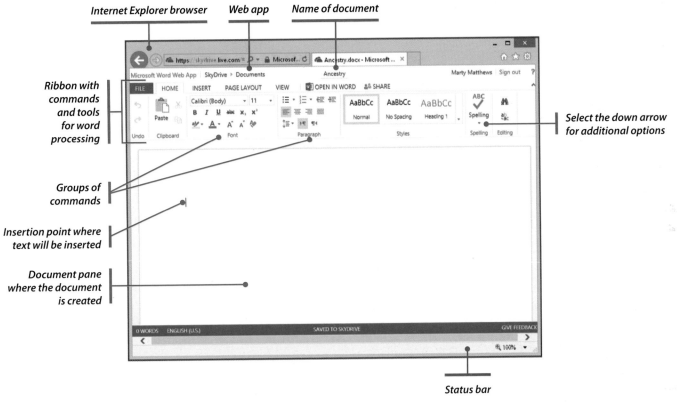

Internet Explorer browser   Web app   Name of document

Ribbon with commands and tools for word processing

Select the down arrow for additional options

Groups of commands

Insertion point where text will be inserted

Document pane where the document is created

Status bar

Figure 8-7: **The Word Web App is a simplified version of the desktop version of Word.**

2. Type the name of the document. Select **Create**. The Word window will open, as shown in Figure 8-7.

3. Type your document, formatting it as needed. See "Edit Documents in the Word Web App," later in this chapter. Figure 8-8 displays an overview of the ribbon functions.

4. When you are finished, just close the Word Web App. Your document has automatically been saved in your SkyDrive several times as you are working on it.

▷▷ Edit Documents in the Word Web App

To read and edit a document in the Word Web App:

1. Open SkyDrive in a browser and the folder that contains the document you want to view or edit.

2. Right-select (right-click or touch and hold for a moment) the file you want to edit. A context menu opens. The top five options are unique:

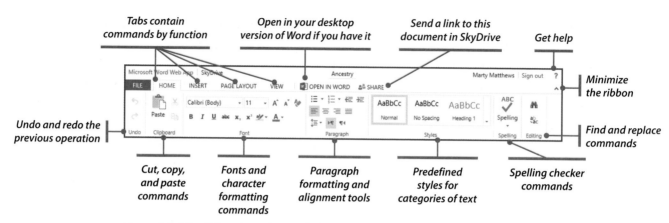

Figure 8-8: *The ribbon, here the Word ribbon, is the source of the tools and commands for the Web Apps.*

Open In Word opens the document in your desktop version of Word, assuming it is on your computer.

Open In Word Web App opens the document in the Word Web App.

Download brings the files from the cloud into your computer where you can edit or save it.

Share allows you to change your sharing options.

Embed allows you to embed the file in a blog or webpage

The remaining options, Rename, Delete, Move To, and so on, are self-explanatory.

3. Select **Open In Word Web App**. The document opens in a very limited Word Web App window. Select **Edit Document | Edit In Word Web App** to open the full Word Web App as displayed earlier in Figure 8-7. This window is similar to the desktop Word 2013 user interface, but if

you're used to the desktop version, you'll notice that several features, including the tools located on missing ribbon tabs (such as Design, References, and Review) and many of the options found on the desktop File tab are not included in the web app.

4. After editing the document using the tools on the available ribbon tabs, select **File | Save As**. You are told that you don't need to save because the document is automatically saved to SkyDrive. You can, though, choose to download the file

to your computer and then save it there. You can also print your file, share it with others, or get help.

5. When you are ready, choose **Exit** from the File tab to close the file and return to your SkyDrive folders to work with other Web App documents in the same manner, navigate to other webpages, or simply close your browser.

 TIP For information on how to use the desktop versions of Office apps, please look for *Microsoft Word 2013 QuickSteps, Microsoft Excel 2013 QuickSteps,* and *Microsoft Office 2013 QuickSteps,* all published by McGraw-Hill Education.

⟫ Edit Workbooks in the Excel Web App

As with Word, you can upload Excel files to Microsoft's SkyDrive to store them in the cloud so you, or others, can access them at any time or place from a browser. Besides simply storing files there, using the Excel Web App, you can also create, view, edit, and download workbooks saved in the Excel 2007 through Excel 2013 default .xlsx file format without necessarily having a version of Excel installed on your computer. (The Excel Web App will try to convert files in the earlier .xls format, but they may prove problematic and, if you have a desktop version of a recent Excel version, you should try to convert them there.) The editing capabilities in the Excel Web App are limited to the more basic features of Excel, as well as formatting actions and working with tables. However, for those cases where your edits are predominately data-centric, SkyDrive and the Excel Web App provide you a great opportunity to access your information from anywhere with only a browser and Internet connection.

Understand an Excel Worksheet

An Excel worksheet, which is contained in a workbook, is a matrix, or grid, of lettered **column headings** across the top and numbered **row headings** down the side. The first row of a typical worksheet is used for column **headers**. The column headers represent categories of similar data. The rows beneath a column header contain data that is either further categorized by a row header down the leftmost column or listed below the column header. Figure 8-9 shows an example of a common worksheet arrangement. Worksheets can also be used to set up **tables** of data, where columns are sometimes referred to as **fields** and each row represents a unique **record** of data. To understand Excel in all its capacity, refer to *Microsoft Excel 2013 QuickSteps*, published by McGraw-Hill Education.

Each intersection of a row and column is called a **cell**, and is referenced first by the column location and then by the row location. The combination of a column letter and row number assigns each cell an **address**. For example, the cell at the intersection of column D and row 8 is called D8. A cell is considered **active** when it is clicked or otherwise selected as the place in which to place new data.

Figure 8-10 shows the ribbon for the Excel Web App.

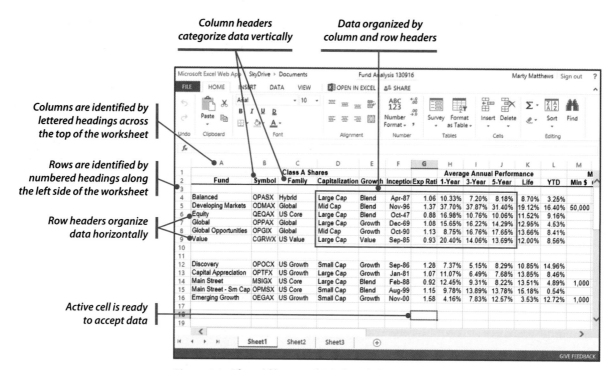

Column headers
categorize data vertically

Data organized by
column and row headers

Columns are identified by
lettered headings across
the top of the worksheet

Rows are identified by
numbered headings along
the left side of the worksheet

Row headers organize
data horizontally

Active cell is ready
to accept data

Figure 8-9: *The grid layout of Excel worksheets is defined by several components.*

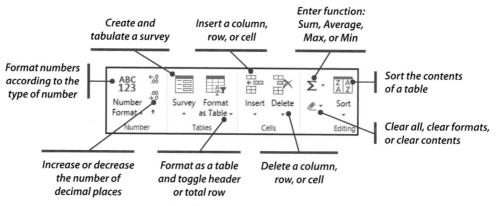

Create and
tabulate a survey

Insert a column,
row, or cell

Enter function:
Sum, Average,
Max, or Min

Format numbers
according to the
type of number

Sort the contents
of a table

Increase or decrease
the number of
decimal places

Format as a table
and toggle header
or total row

Delete a column,
row, or cell

Clear all, clear formats,
or clear contents

Figure 8-10: *The Excel ribbon offers specialized
commands and tools for working with numeric data.*

Edit in the Excel Web App

To edit a workbook in the Excel Web App:

1. Open the SkyDrive folder that contains the workbook you want to view or edit.

2. Right-select the file you want, and in the context menu, select **Open in Excel Web App | Edit Workbook | Edit In Excel Web App**. The workbook opens in a screen that appears similar to the Excel 2013 user interface (see Figure 8-9) but lacks certain features, including the tools located on missing ribbon tabs and some of the options found on a standard File menu.

3. After performing editing using the tools on the available ribbon tabs, select the **File** tab and select whether you want to open the file in your device's version of Excel, save it under a different filename (you don't need to save the workbook, as Excel Web App does that automatically), download it to your device as a standard workbook, print it, share it with others, or exit the Excel Web App.

4. When finished, in addition to using Exit, you can select SkyDrive or a listed folder in the top line of the SkyDrive page to return to your SkyDrive folders to work with other Office documents in the same manner, navigate to other webpages, or simply close your browser.

USE OTHER COMMON APPS

Windows 8.1 comes equipped with several useful accessory apps. Among these are Notepad, a simple text editor; Paint, for drawing and modifying pictures; Character Map for selecting special characters; and Calculator. Here is a brief overview of them.

In addition, Adobe Reader is a free third-party app commonly used to read PDF (Portable Document Format) documents.

▷▷ Run Accessory Apps

You can open the accessory apps by opening the Start screen and selecting the down arrow in the lower-left corner to open Apps view. You can find some of the accessory apps in the alphabetical list on the left. All the accessory apps are listed under Windows Accessories on the right, where you'll see Calculator, Character Map, Notepad, and Paint.

Use Calculator

In Windows 8.1 there are two completely different calculators you can choose from: a Start screen version, shown on the left in Figure 8-11, and a desktop version shown on the right. Both calculators are selected in Apps view on either the left (Start Screen version) or the right under Windows Accessories (desktop version). Both have several alternative calculators within them. The Start screen version has three alternatives: Standard, Scientific, and a converter. The Desktop version has four alternative calculators, each with its own view:

- Standard desktop calculator
- Scientific calculator
- Programmer calculator
- Statistics calculator

Figure 8-11: *Windows 8.1 has both a Start screen calculator (on the left) and a desktop one (on the right).*

In addition, the desktop calculator has a unit converter; a date calculator; and four worksheets for calculating a mortgage, a vehicle lease, and fuel economy in both mpg and L/100 km that are extensions to the current view. To switch from one view to the other, select **View** and select the other view. To use a calculator, select the numbers and arithmetic functions on the screen or type them on the keyboard.

Use Character Map

The Character Map, selected in Apps view under Windows Accessories on the right, allows the selection of special characters that are not available on a standard keyboard.

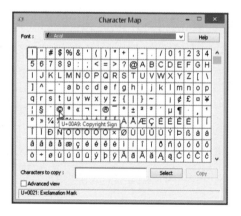

1. Select the **Font** down arrow, and select the font you want for the special character.
2. Scroll until you find the character, and then double-select it; or select it and select **Select** to copy it to the Clipboard.
3. In the app where you want the character, right-select an open area, and select **Paste** or press CTRL+V.

Use Notepad

Notepad, selected in Apps view under Windows Accessories on the right, can be used to view and create unformatted text (.txt) files. If you double-select a text file in File Explorer, Notepad will likely open and display the file. If a line of text is too long to display without scrolling, select **Format** and select **Word Wrap**. To create a file, simply start typing in the Notepad window, select the **File** menu, and select **Save**. Before printing a file, select **File**; select **Page Setup**; and select the paper orientation, margins, header, and footer.

Use Paint

Paint, selected in Apps view under Windows Accessories on the right, lets you view, create, and edit bitmap image files in .bmp, .dib, .gif, .jpg, .png, and .tif formats. Several drawing tools and many colors are available to create simple drawings and illustrations. You can also open many photographs and touch up and add embellishments to them (see Figure 8-12).

Figure 8-12: ***Paint allows you to make simple line drawings or touch up other images.***

QuickFacts

Using Adobe Reader

Adobe Reader is an app most computer users find essential. It enables you to read documents created in PDF format. This format is often used so that readers don't need to have a particular app, such as Word, to read it. Adobe also offers a more sophisticated package that allows you to create and edit PDF documents. However, the simple reader is what we're sure you will someday need, and it is free.

1. In your browser, type <u>adobe.com/reader</u> in the address bar, and press **ENTER**. The Adobe Reader page will display.

2. For simplicity, I uncheck the optional offer for Google Chrome, and then select **Install Now**.

3. Select **Run** and then select **Yes** to allow Adobe to continue to download the app onto your computer. Then, select **Next** and finally select **Finish** to complete the installation. You will see a display of the progress. Ignore any free offers and close your browser.

4. You should see a shortcut to Adobe Reader on your desktop and on the left side of Apps view.

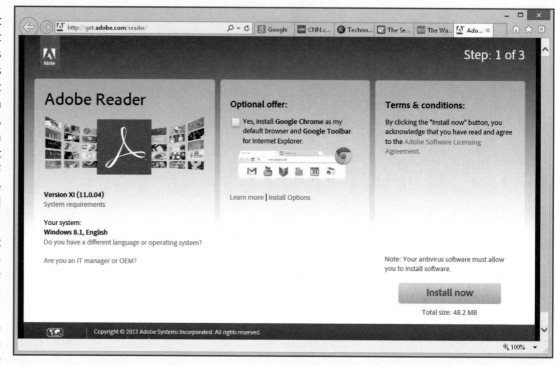

5. To open a PDF file, either select the Adobe Reader shortcut in Apps view and open the PDF file or double-select the PDF file. When you first bring Adobe Reader up, you'll have to accept the reader's license agreement. Select **Accept**. A computer restart is required to finalize the installation.

6. Point your cursor at the icons on the toolbar. You'll see how you can navigate through the document, share it with others, change the magnification, change the display of the page, or use the search feature to find specific words or phrases. Figure 8-13 shows how the reader displays a PDF file.

Toolbar provides common tools for working with PDF files

Expand or collapse bookmarks

Reading pane

Show tools pane

Sign document

Display page thumbnails

Display bookmark links

View file attachments

Add or review comments (opened)

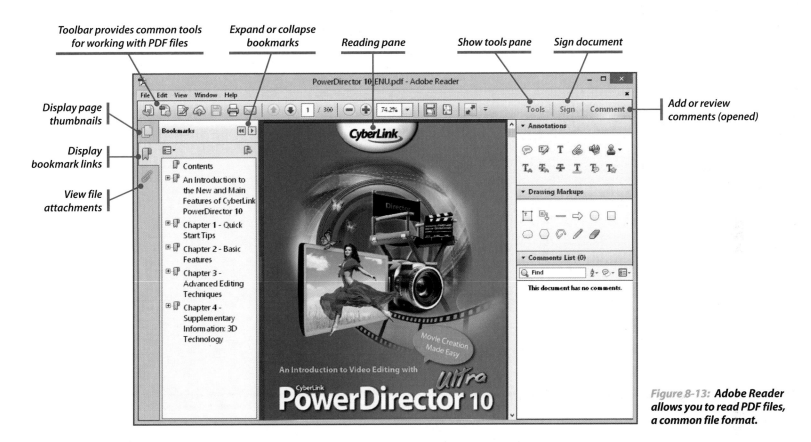

Figure 8-13: *Adobe Reader allows you to read PDF files, a common file format.*

Bob Finds Simple Is Easier

After being president of a succession of banks, I came into my retirement with little hands-on experience with computers, although I had overseen their introduction and use in our banks. Luckily, I had a number of friends and associates who helped me get set up and started using a personal computer. In this process,

I picked up several pointers, primary among them, which I had known from other areas, was the K.I.S.S. principle of keeping it simple. I have on my computers only the programs I want to use frequently, and I have found that the simpler the set of folders I use, the easier it is to find what I need. It is easier to search through a number of files in a single folder then it is to search through a number of folders.

Bob O., 76, Washington

Chapter 9

Managing and Maintaining Windows 8.1

Windows 8.1 facilitates whatever you want to do on your computer. It is the means by which you can run other apps, access the Internet, print documents and photos, capture digital pictures from your camera, send faxes, and connect to other computers. In this chapter we'll look at managing and maintaining many of the facilities of Windows 8.1 not discussed elsewhere, including managing apps in several different ways, as well as the maintenance and enhancement of Windows 8.1 and the setting up of Remote Assistance so that you can have someone help you without that person actually being in front of your computer.

MANAGE APPS IN WINDOWS 8.1

Previous chapters discussed starting and using apps in various ways with both the Start screen and the desktop. Here we'll look at how to handle the situation where you have several apps running at the same time, various ways of stopping apps, and other tasks aimed at managing apps.

▶▶ Switch Apps

You can switch apps that are running on the Start screen and on the desktop. You can do this using the app list on the left of the screen, using the desktop itself or the taskbar, and using the task list. You can also switch them using the Task Manager.

Switch Start Screen Apps

To start several apps on the Start screen, simply select one to open it, select the **Start** button in the lower-left corner to open the Start screen, and then select another app to open it. You can do that as many times as you wish, but the size and resolution of your screen will determine how many you can see and control in the app list. (I can get six apps in the app list on a 13-inch screen and nine on a 23-inch screen, both at 1920 × 1080 resolution.) As you open more apps than you have room to display, the earliest apps you entered are closed and you must reopen them to continue to work with them. If you have several apps open, the question becomes how to switch from one to another to get back to one you started earlier. The answer is the hidden app list on the left of the screen showing the apps that are open, as you can see in Figure 9-1. To open and use the app list:

1. Swipe from off the screen on the left on to the screen, or move the mouse to the lower-left corner of the screen and then move the mouse up to open the running app list. You can also move the mouse to the upper-left corner to display the most recently opened app (which can be the desktop if you are on the Start screen) and then move the mouse down to display the remainder of running apps.

2. Select the app that you want to switch to. You can switch among your open apps as much as you want and come back to previously opened apps unless you have more apps opened than can be displayed.

Figure 9-1: *An open app list can be displayed on the left of either the Start or desktop screen.*

3. Using the apps list on the left, you can also right-click (no touch equivalent) an app to open a context menu. If you do that from the Start screen, you get a single option: Close, but from the desktop, you get three additional options: Replace Desktop, Insert Left, and Insert Right (see the next section on displaying two or more apps on the screen, which you can do with Insert Left or Insert Right). Replace Desktop does just that—the app, which is a full-screen, Windows 8–style app, replaces the open desktop.

NOTE Only apps that are started on the Start screen are displayed in the running app list on the left.

Display Two or More Start Screen Apps

Windows 8.1 has enhanced the capability to display two to four Start screen apps on the screen at the same time and allow you to easily go back and forth between them. On my 23-inch monitor I can get three apps, as you see on the top of Figure 9-2, while I can only get two apps on my 13-inch laptop, shown on the bottom of Figure 9-2. To display multiple Start screen apps:

1. From the Start screen, successively open two to four apps.

2. Open the app list on the left (swipe in from the left, or move the mouse to the upper- or lower-left corner and then move the mouse down or up).

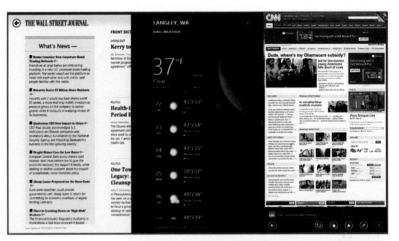

Figure 9-2: Your screen size and resolution will determine how many apps you can display.

3. Drag the apps from the app list onto the screen. The app that is on the screen will move to the right, making room for the new app, as shown on the top of Figure 9-3.

4. Try to drag a third app from the app list onto the middle of the screen. If your screen will support it, a space will open up between the existing two apps (see the bottom of Figure 9-3).

7. If you have a blank space on the screen between two apps or beside one app, or if you just want to expand one of the app panes, drag the three dots in the middle of the center app border to fill the blank area or enlarge the app.

Switch Apps on the Desktop

If you have several apps running on the desktop and arranged so that you can see all of them, switch from one to another by selecting the app you want to be active. If you have more than two or three apps running, it may be hard to see them on the desktop and, therefore, to select the one you want. See the taskbar technique next.

Switch Apps on the Taskbar

If you have up to five or six apps running, you should be able to see their tasks on the taskbar. Selecting the task will switch to that app.

If you have multiple instances of a single app open, they will, by default, be grouped in a single icon. For example, in the following illustration, the taskbar icon indicates (note the right edge of the icon) that there are multiple instances open for both Internet Explorer and Microsoft Word.

Figure 9-3: Dragging a second or more apps onto the screen will open up a space for it if the screen size and resolution allow.

5. Try a fourth app. When your screen can no longer support another app, it will no longer open a blank space and will simply allow you to replace one of the existing apps.

6. When multiple apps are displayed, you can close any one of them by dragging the app from the top to the bottom of the screen.

To select a particular instance of an app when there are multiple instances running, mouse over the icon on the taskbar to open thumbnails of the several instances, then mouse over the one you want to see enlarged. Finally, when you are ready to fully open one particular instance, select the thumbnail for it, as you can see in Figure 9-4.

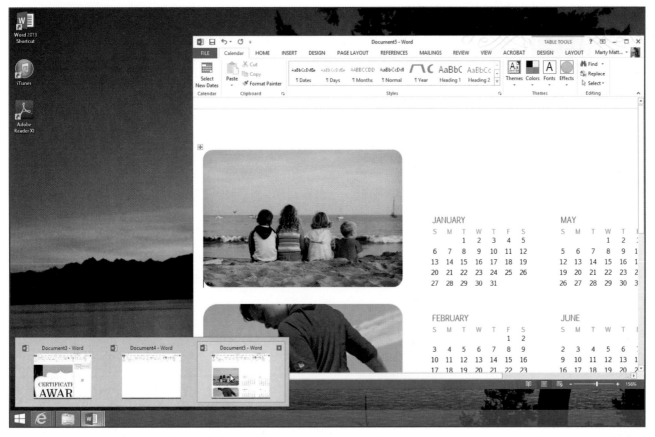

Figure 9-4: The taskbar icon allows you to select from several instance of a running app.

Switch Start Screen and Desktop Apps on the Task List

The oldest method of switching apps, which predates Windows 95 and the taskbar, is using the task list. *This is the only way that you can see and switch among both desktop and Start screen apps in one place.*

1. Press **ALT+TAB** and hold down **ALT**. The task list will appear.

2. While continuing to hold down **ALT**, press **TAB** repeatedly until the highlight moves to the app and instance you want or the desktop on the right. As an alternative, while holding **ALT**, select with either the mouse or finger the app you want to display.

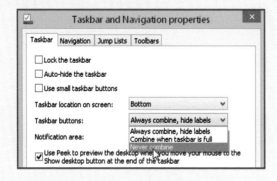

▷▷ Stop Apps

You may choose to stop an app simply because you are done using it or in an attempt to keep an app from harming your data or other apps.

Use a Desktop App's Close Button

The most common way to close/stop a desktop app is to select the **Close** button on the upper-right corner of all desktop windows.

Drag a Start Screen App Down

Close a Start screen app by dragging the app from the top to the bottom of the screen. Also, as mentioned earlier, right-click an app on the app list and select Close.

Use the Exit Command

Almost all desktop apps have an Exit command in a menu on the far left of the menu bar; often, this is the File menu or tab. Open this menu and select **Exit**. The "Close" option on this menu generally means to close the current document but leave the app running so you can open another document. In a few instances, "Close" means the same as "Exit" when there is only "Close" and no "Exit."

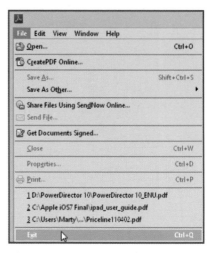

Close from the Taskbar

There are two ways to close an app from the taskbar.

Mouse over the icon, move the mouse to the red X that will appear in the upper-right corner of the thumbnail, and select it.

–Or–

Right-select a task on the taskbar, and select **Close Window** (or **Close All Windows** if there are multiple instances).

Close from the Keyboard

With either a selected desktop or Start screen app you want to close, press **ALT+F4**.

If none of these options work, see "Control Apps with the Task Manager."

> **NOTE** It could be that none of the options mentioned in "Stop Apps" will work if the app is performing a task or has some fault. In that case, if you want to force the app to stop, shut down Windows itself and select **Force Shut Down**.

▷▷ Control Apps with the Task Manager

The Windows Task Manager, shown in Figure 9-5, performs a number of functions, but most importantly, it allows you to see what apps and processes (individual threads of an app) are

running and to unequivocally stop both. A display of real-time graphs and tables also shows you what is happening at any second on your computer, as you can see in Figure 9-6. To work with the Task Manager:

1. From either the Start screen or the desktop, press **CTRL+ALT+DELETE** simultaneously and select **Task Manager**. Alternatively, you can open the **System** menu in the lower-left corner or right-select a blank area of the taskbar, and select **Task Manager**.

2. Select the **Processes** tab (if you don't see the Processes tab, select **More Details** at the bottom of the window). You'll

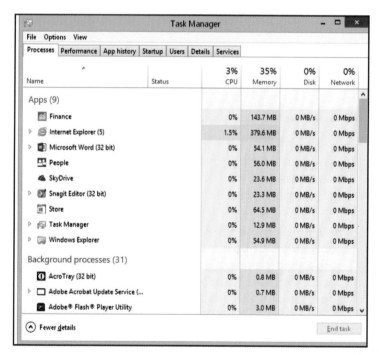

*Figure 9-5: **The Task Manager shows you what apps are running and allows you to stop them.***

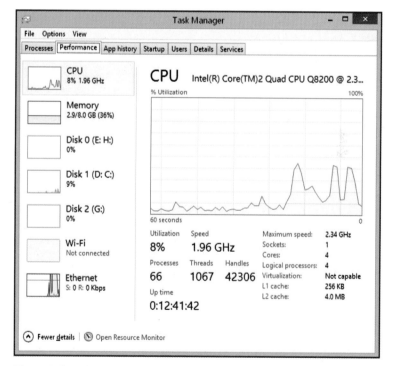

*Figure 9-6: **Under most circumstances, on a personal computer, only a small fraction of the computer's resources are being used.***

see a list of the apps and background processes that are running, as shown in Figure 9-5.

3. Select an app in the list. Select **End Task** in the lower-right corner to stop the app.

4. Right-select an app to open the context menu. Select **Switch To** to activate/display that app.

5. Under Processes, you see a list of those that are currently running and their central processing unit (CPU) (percentage) and memory (MB) usage. Many of these processes are components of Windows 8.1.

6. Select the **Performance** tab. This tab graphically shows the CPU and memory usage (see Figure 9-6), while the Networking tab shows the computer's use of the network. The Users tab shows the users that are logged on to the computer. You can disconnect them if they are coming in over the network or log them off if they are directly logged on.

7. Select the **Startup** tab and observe the apps that are automatically started when you start your computer and Windows. Select an app you don't want started and select **Disable.**

8. Select the **Services** tab. This is a list of the Windows 8.1 services that are active and their status. There is nothing that you can do here except observe it and open an enhanced Services window.

9. When you are done, close the Windows Task Manager.

Control Windows Indexing

Windows 8.1 automatically indexes the files that are stored on the computer to substantially speed up your searches of files and folders.

1. Open the **System** menu in the lower-left corner, select **Control Panel**, select **Large Icons** view if it is not already selected, and select **Indexing Options** to open the Indexing Options dialog box.

2. If you want to change what is being indexed, select **Modify**, select the triangle icon to open the drives on your computer, and select the folders, as shown in Figure 9-7. Then select **OK**.

3. If you want to change the types of files being indexed, select **Advanced**. Choose if you want encrypted files indexed, or if you want similar words that have different marks (diacritics such as the accent, grave, and umlaut) that change the sound and meaning of the word indexed differently. Select the **File Types** tab, and select the types of files you want included. When you are done, select **OK**.

4. Close the Indexing Options dialog box and close Control Panel.

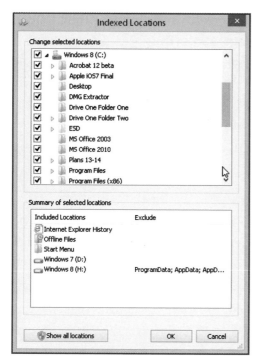

Figure 9-7: **Windows Indexing uses idle time to index your files and folders.**

 NOTE In Windows 8.1, you cannot turn off indexing—it is an integral part of the search facility. Windows Indexing has become quite efficient and seldom affects the performance of the computer. Also, you shouldn't index your full C: drive, as this includes app files that will slow down the search for your own data, music, and other personal files.

MAINTAIN WINDOWS 8.1

Windows 8.1 maintenance consists of periodically updating fixes and new features, restoring Windows 8.1 when hardware or other software damages it, getting information about it, and installing new hardware and software.

 # Update Windows 8.1

Microsoft tries hard to encourage you to allow Windows 8.1 to update itself, from the point of installation, where you are asked to accept automatic updates, to periodically reminding you to do that. If you turn on Automatic Updates, on a regular basis Windows will automatically determine if any updates are available, download the updates (which come from Microsoft) over the Internet, and install them. If Automatic Updates was not turned on during installation, you can do that at any time and control the updating process once it is turned on.

 CAUTION! It is important and strongly recommended that you allow Windows 8.1 to do automatic updates. Many of the updates are fixes for potential security loopholes that will help protect your system.

Turn On Automatic Updates

To turn on, off, and control Windows Update:

1. Open the **System** menu in the lower-left corner and select **Control Panel**. In Category view, select **System And Security**, and select **Windows Update**. Alternatively, in Large Icon view, select **Windows Update**.

   –Or–

   Some update maintenance is also available by opening Charms and selecting **Settings | Change PC Settings | Update And Recovery | Windows Update**.

2. Select **Change Settings**, and then select the down arrow on the right of the top option under **Important Updates**. Determine the amount of automation you want, and select one of the following four choices (see Figure 9-8):

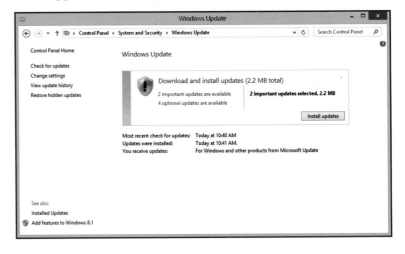

Figure 9-8: *Automatic Updates determines which updates you need and can automatically download and install them.*

- The first and recommended choice, which is what I use, is the default. It automatically determines if updates are needed, downloads them, and then installs them on a frequency and at a time when you are not using your computer.

- The second choice automatically determines if updates are needed and downloads them; it then asks you whether you want to install them.

- The third choice automatically determines if updates are needed, asks you before downloading them, and asks you again before installing them.

- The fourth choice, which is not recommended, never checks for updates.

3. Normally, updates are installed during a maintenance window, which by default is set for 2 or 3 A.M. daily. You can change that by selecting **Updates Will Be Automatically**

Installed and then selecting a different time. If you make this change, select **OK**.

4. Choose whether to include recommended updates when you are otherwise online with Microsoft and whether to get updates for other Microsoft products you have installed, like Microsoft Office.

5. Select **OK** when you are finished, and close Windows Update.

Apply Updates

If you choose either the second or the third option for handling updates, you will periodically see a notice that updates are ready to download and/or install. When you see this notice:

1. Select the notice. The Windows Updates dialog box will appear and show you the updates that are available.

2. Select the individual updates to see detailed information about them.

3. Select the check box for the updates you want to download and/or install, and then select **OK**.

4. After you have selected all the updates you want, select **Install**. You will see a notice that the updates are being installed.

5. When the updates have been downloaded and installed, Windows Update will reopen, inform you of this fact, and often ask to restart your computer.

6. Close any open apps, and select **Restart Now**, as required.

▷▷ Use the Action Center

The Windows Action Center contains messages that have been sent to you from Windows and other apps that, at least from the viewpoint of the app, you need to respond to. When a message is sent to you by an app, a flag appears in the notification area. 🏴

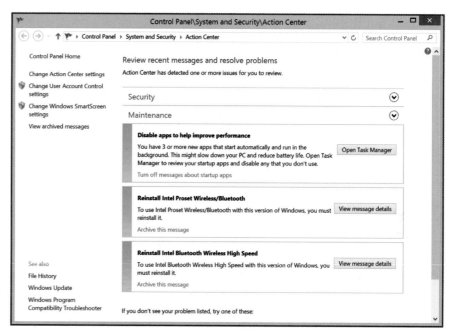

Figure 9-9: *The Action Center consolidates and maintains alert messages that are sent to you by the apps you run.*

Select the notification area Action Center flag to open the Action Center jump list. Select any option on the jump list to go directly to the window or dialog box, where you can view the

message and possibly take corrective actions.

–Or–

1. Select **Open Action Center** to review recent messages and resolve problems, as you can see in Figure 9-9.

2. Select the relevant item to address the issue, and when you are ready, close the Action Center.

Change Action Center Settings

You can change how the Action Center informs you of an alert message.

1. From the Action Center, select **Change Action Center Settings** in the upper-left corner.

2. Select the security and maintenance messages you want to see (all are selected by default. Open any of the related settings that seem pertinent, returning to the Action Center when you are ready.

3. When your Action Center settings are the way you want them, select **OK** and close the Action Center.

Restore Windows 8.1

System Restore keeps track of the changes you make to your system, including the software you install and the settings you make. If a hardware change, a software installation, or something else causes the system not to load or not to run properly, you can use System Restore to return the system to the way it was at the last restore point.

 NOTE System Restore does not restore or make any changes to data files, only to system and app files. Data files must be backed up, using the Windows 8.1 backup app, File History (see Chapter 3), or a third-party backup app, and then restored from a backup.

Set Up System Restore

In a default installation of Windows 8.1, System Restore is automatically installed. If you have at least 300MB of free disk space after installing Windows 8.1, System Restore will be turned on and the first restore point will be set. If System Restore is not enabled, you can turn it on and set a restore point.

 NOTE System Restore actually needs at least 300MB on each hard, USB, and memory card drive that has the feature turned on, and may use up to 15 percent of each drive. If a drive is smaller than 1GB, System Restore cannot be used.

1. Open the **System** menu in the lower-left corner and select **Control Panel**. In Category view, select **System And Security**, in any view select **System**, and finally select **System Protection** in the left pane. The System Properties

dialog box will appear with the System Protection tab displayed, as you can see in Figure 9-10.

2. By default, the disk on which Windows 8.1 is installed should have System Protection turned on, indicating that System Restore is operating automatically for that disk. Again by default, your other hard, USB, and memory card drives are not selected. If any drive does not have protection and you want it on, select the disk, select **Configure**, select **Turn On System Protection**, adjust the disk space usage as desired, and select **OK**.

3. When you have made the adjustments you want, select **OK**.

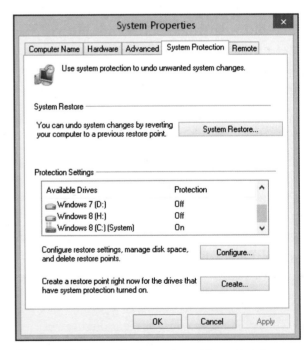

*Figure 9-10: **System Restore returns the system to a previous time when it was functioning normally.***

Create Restore Points

A *restore point* is an identifiable point in time when you know your system was working correctly. If your computer's settings are saved at that point, you can use those settings to restore your computer to that time. Normally, Windows 8.1 automatically creates restore points for the system drive on a periodic basis. But if you know at a given point in time that your computer was operating exactly the way you want it to, you can create a restore point.

1. Open the **System** menu in the lower-left corner and select **Control Panel**. In Category view, select **System And Security**, in any view select **System**, and select **System Protection** in the left pane. The System Properties dialog box will appear with the System Protection tab displayed.

2. Select **Create** and type a name for the restore point. The date and time are automatically added, and you cannot change the name once you create it.

3. Select **Create** again. You will be told when the restore point is created. Select **OK** and select **Close** to close the System Properties dialog box.

Run System Restore

Run System Restore to return to an earlier restore point.

1. Open the **System** menu in the lower-left corner and select **Control Panel**. In Category view, select **System And Security**, in any view select **System**, and select **System Protection** in the left pane. The System Properties dialog box will appear with the System Protection tab displayed.

2. Select **System Restore**; a message explains this feature. Select **Next**. Your recent restore points are shown. If you want to use one of them, select it, select **Next**, and go to step 4.

3. If you want to use another restore point, select **Show More Restore Points**. Select the restore point you want to use (see Figure 9-11), and select **Scan For Affected Programs**. This will tell you if any apps have been updated or had a driver installed after the restore point. If you go ahead with the restore, these apps will be restored to their state before the update. Select **Close | Next**.

4. You are asked to confirm the restore point the system will be returned to and given information about that point. If you do not want to restore to that point, select **Back** and return to step 2 or 3.

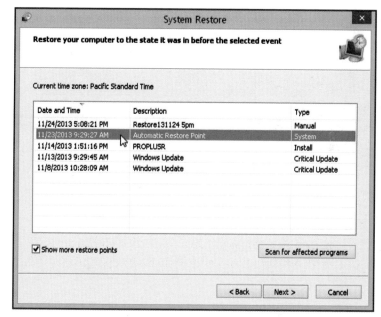

*Figure 9-11: **You can do a system restore at any of the restore points on the computer and return all of the Windows 8.1 settings and registry to that point in time.***

5. System Restore will need to restart your computer, so make sure all other apps are closed. When you are ready to restore to the described point, select **Finish**.

6. A confirmation dialog box appears, telling you that the restore process cannot be interrupted or undone until it has completed. Select **Yes** to continue. Some time will be spent saving files and settings for a new restore point, and then the computer will be restarted.

7. When the restore is complete, you will be told that it was successful. Select **Close**.

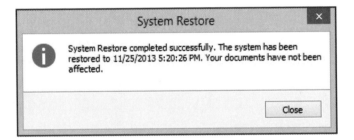

TIP You can restore from a system restore. Immediately before doing a system restore, a restore point is created and can be used to return to the point the system was at prior to performing this action. Simply rerun System Restore as described in the System Restore sections in this chapter, choose **Undo** for the last restore operation, and follow the remaining instructions.

Run System Recovery

Windows 8.1 has a System Recovery feature that allows you to refresh, recover, and restore your system without affecting any of your personal files (documents, music, photos, or videos).

Open **Charms** and select **Settings | Change PC Settings | Update And Recovery | Recovery** to display three options for recovering or restoring your computer:

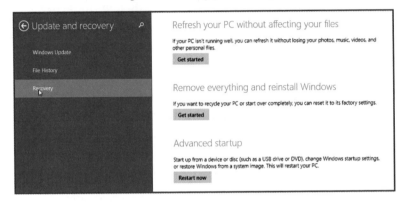

- **Refresh Your PC Without Affecting Your Files** will reinstall your Windows operating system (you must have your Windows installation discs) and all of your hardware drivers. This will not remove or change any of your personal files.

- **Remove Everything And Reinstall Windows** will completely wipe off everything on your computer and then install a new copy of Windows.

- **Advanced Startup** provides a number of alternative ways of starting your computer, including using a backup disk image of your computer or doing a system restore as describe in the previous sections. Select **Restart Now** (selecting this will cause an eventual restart of your computer) | **Troubleshoot | Advanced Options | System Restore**.

QuickFacts

Get System Information

When you are working on a computer problem, you, or possibly a technical support person working with you, will want some information about your computer. The two sources are Charms' PC Info and the Control Panel's basic information.

Get PC Info

Charm's PC Info is the least complete of the two, but it may be all you will need:

Open **Charms** and select **Settings | Change PC Settings | PC And Devices | PC Info** to display some information about your computer, as shown in Figure 9-12.

Get Basic Computer Information

Basic computer information provides general information about your computer that is similar to the information in Charms with a few added items (see Figure 9-13). To see the basic computer information:

Open the **System** menu in the lower-left corner and select **Control Panel**. In Category view, select **System And Security**, and in any view select **System**. The System window will open. After you have reviewed the information, select **Close**.

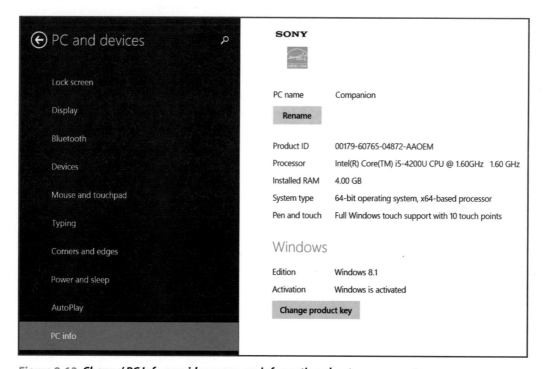

*Figure 9-12: **Charms' PC Info provides summary information about your computer.***

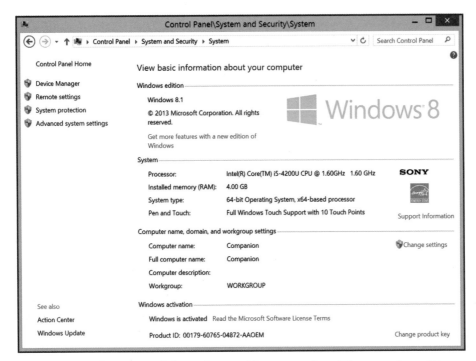

Figure 9-13: *Basic computer information provides an overview of the computer and its operating system.*

Set Power Options

Setting power options is important on laptop and notebook computers that run at least some of the time on batteries. It can also be useful on desktop computers to conserve power. Windows 8.1 has both Charms and Control Pane power options with several settings that allow you to manage your computer's use of power.

Use Charms Power Options

1. Open **Charms** and select **Settings | Change PC Settings | PC And Devices | Power And Sleep**.

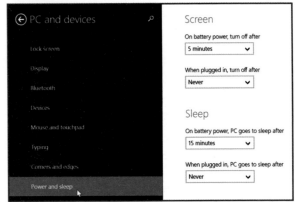

2. Select the drop-down arrow in each of the boxes to select the times that are correct for you for turning off the screen and putting the computer to sleep, both on battery and when plugged in, if you have the option.

Use Control Panel Power Options

1. Open the **System** menu in the lower-left corner and select **Power Options**.

2. Choose one of the power plans, depending on whether you want to emphasize battery life (energy savings on desktops), performance, or a balance between the two (select **Show Additional Plans** to display the High Performance plan shown in Figure 9-14).

You can also reduce the screen brightness on a laptop or notebook computer to reduce the power drain.

NOTE You could have two "recommended" plans, one from Windows and one from the computer manufacturer, making four plans instead of the three shown in Figure 9-14.

3. To see a more detailed setting, select **Choose When To Turn Off The Display**. If you are using a laptop or notebook computer, your power options will look like those in Figure 9-15. (A desktop computer won't have the battery or brightness settings.)

4. Select each of the drop-down lists, select the setting that is correct for you, and adjust the screen brightness.

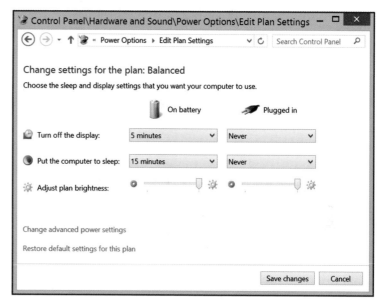

Figure 9-15: You can set the amount of idle time before the display and/or the computer are turned off or put to sleep, respectively.

5. When you are ready, select **Save Changes** to accept the changes you have made to your power options settings.

NOTE See Chapter 1 for a discussion of the differences between shutting down a computer and putting it to sleep.

Add and Remove Software

Today, almost all application and utility software comes in one of two ways: on a CD or DVD, or downloaded over the Internet, with the majority now being downloaded.

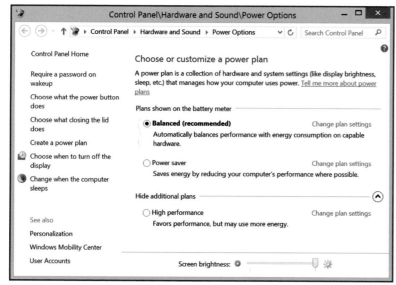

Figure 9-14: Windows 8.1 has three power plans that let you emphasize performance, energy consumption, or a balance between the two.

Install Software from a CD

If you get software on a CD or DVD, all you need to do is put the disc in the drive, select **Tap To Choose What Happens With This Disc**, select **Run Autorun.exe**, and follow the instructions as they appear, of which there are usually only a few. When

the installation is complete, you may need to acknowledge that by selecting **OK** or **Finish** and possibly restarting your computer. Then remove the disc from its drive. That is all there is to it.

 TIP If you are having trouble installing an app for no discernable reason, make sure you are logged on with administrative permissions. Some apps or installation situations require these permissions; without them, the app refuses to install.

Install Software from the Internet

To download and install an app from the Internet:

1. Select the **Internet Explorer** icon on the taskbar. In the address bar, type the URL (uniform resource locator, or Internet address) for the source of the download, and press **ENTER**. (For this example, I'm downloading the Firefox web browser whose URL is http://www.mozilla .org, but you don't need to type the "http://www"—just type "mozilla.org.") If you are not sure what the URL is,

go to Google.com or Bing.com and, in my example, type <u>firefox</u>, and then select the link to its parent.

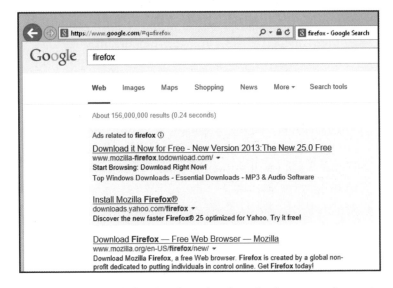

2. Locate the link for the download, and select it, as shown in Figure 9-16. You will need to approve the downloading in Internet Explorer in the bar at the bottom of the window by selecting **Run**.

3. A message box will appear, asking if you want to allow the program to make changes. Select **Yes**.

4. Depending on the app, there may be one or more intermediate steps. Mozilla thanks you for choosing Firefox and asks you to select **Install** to start the installation.

*Figure 9-16: **Mozilla's Firefox is a good alternative browser to Internet Explorer.***

5. Follow the app's installation instructions, making the choices that are correct for you.

6. When the installation is complete, you may need to select **Finish** or a similar term, you may be notified that the app will be started, File Explorer may be opened to show where the app is installed, and/or one or more shortcuts may be left on the desktop.

7. Close the File Explorer window and any other windows and dialog boxes that were opened by this process.

Remove Software

There are at least two ways to get rid of an app you have installed and one way not to do it. You do not want to just delete the app files in File Explorer. That leaves files in other locations and all the settings in the registry. To correctly remove an app, you need to use either the uninstall app feature that comes with some apps or Windows 8.1's Uninstall Or Change An App feature. To do the latter:

1. Open the **System** menu in the lower-left corner and select **Programs And Features**. The Uninstall Or Change A Program window will open, as you can see in Figure 9-17.

2. Select the app you want to uninstall, and select **Uninstall** on the toolbar. Follow the instructions as they are presented, which vary from app to app.

3. When the uninstall has successfully completed, close the Programs And Features window.

 NOTE The "change" part of the Uninstall Or Change An app window is used to install updates and patches to apps. It requires that you either have a CD with the changes or have downloaded them. With some apps you will get a third option: Repair.

⏩ Add Hardware

Most hardware today is ***Plug and Play***. That means that when you plug it in, Windows recognizes it and installs the necessary app automatically and you can shortly begin using it. Alternatively, when you first turn on the computer after installing new hardware, you see a message telling you that

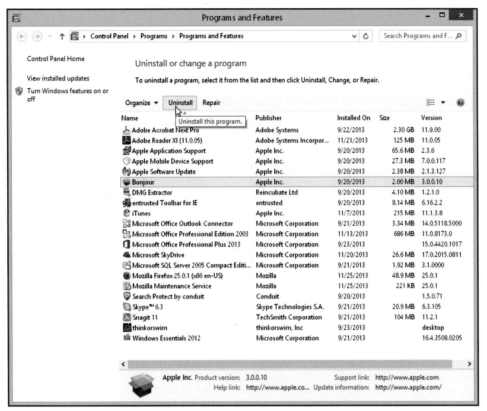

Figure 9-17: *Apps are removed through the Uninstall Or Change A Program feature.*

Problems may occur when you have older hardware and the apps that run it, called *drivers*, are not included with Windows 8.1. In that case, you will see a dialog box saying you must locate the driver and providing some suggestions:

- If offered, let Windows scan your computer and look on the Microsoft site to see what can be found. If a driver is found, go ahead and install it and see if it works.

- In some instances, Windows Update (discussed earlier in this chapter) can scan your system and see if it can locate a missing driver for you. The first step is to look at Windows Update by opening the **System** menu in the lower-left corner and, in Large Icons view, selecting **Windows Update**. Select **Check For Updates** in the upper-left area, and see if a driver for your device is found.

you have new hardware or that Windows is installing the device. Frequently, you need do nothing more; the installation will complete by itself. With other equipment, you must select the message for the installation to proceed. In either case, you are told when it has successfully completed.

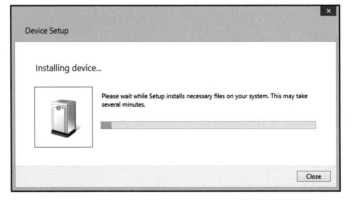

- The manufacturer of the device is sometimes a good source, but as hardware gets older, manufacturers stop writing new drivers for more recent operating systems. The easiest way to look for manufacturer support is on the Internet. If you know the manufacturer's website, you can enter it; or you may have to search for it. If you must search, start out by typing the manufacturer's name in the Internet Explorer address bar. This uses Bing search and gives you a list of sites.

- Third-party sources can be found using search engines like Google (google.com) and searching for "Windows 8.1 drivers for *your device.*" You often find several sources, as you can see in Figure 9-18. Some of these sources charge you for the driver; others are free. Make sure the driver will work with Windows 8.1.

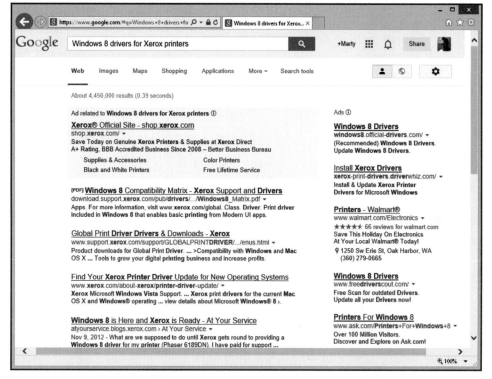

Figure 9-18: **Many device drivers can be found by searching the Internet, although you may have to pay for them.**

⟩⟩ Use Remote Assistance

Remote Assistance allows you to invite someone to remotely look at your computer and control it for the purposes of assisting you. The other person must be using Windows 8; Windows 7; Windows Vista; Windows XP; or Windows Server 2003, 2008, or 2012; in addition, it will be helpful if both of you have an email account. To use Remote Assistance, you must set it up, and then you can be either the requester or the helper.

Set Up Remote Assistance

Although Remote Assistance is installed with Windows 8.1, you must turn it on and set your firewall so that Windows 8.1 will allow it through. Both of these tasks are done in Control Panel.

1. Open the **System** menu in the lower-left corner and select **Control Panel**. In Category view, select **System And Security**, in any view select **System**, and select **Remote Settings** in the upper-left pane. The System Properties dialog box will appear with the Remote tab displayed (see Figure 9-19).

Figure 9-19: *Before using Remote Assistance, it must be turned on.*

2. Select **Allow Remote Assistance Connections To This Computer**, if it isn't already, and select **Advanced**.

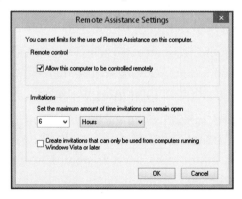

3. Determine if you want a person to control your computer, and select the check box under **Remote Control**

accordingly. Set the time an invitation for Remote Assistance is to remain open.

4. Select **OK** twice to close the two open dialog boxes. In Control Panel, select **Control Panel** in the address bar, select **System And Security**, and select **Windows Firewall**.

5. Select **Allow An app Or Feature Through Windows Firewall** in the upper-left corner. The Allowed Apps window will open and show the apps and features that are allowed through the firewall.

6. Select **Change Settings** toward the top-right area of the window, then scroll through the list until you see **Remote Assistance** and select it, if it isn't already selected (see Figure 9-20).

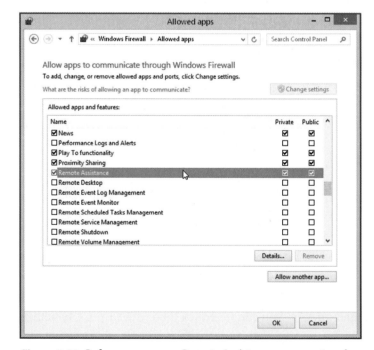

Figure 9-20: *Before you can use Remote Assistance, you must make sure that your firewall will let it through.*

7. Select **OK** to close the dialog box, close the Windows Firewall window, and then close Control Panel.

 NOTE Remote Desktop is different from Remote Assistance, even though it is on the same Remote tab of the System Properties dialog box. Remote Desktop lets you sit at home and log on and use your computer at work as though you were sitting in front of it.

Request Remote Assistance

To use Remote Assistance, first find someone willing to provide it and request the assistance. Besides the obvious invitation text, the request-for-assistance message will include a password to access your computer and the code to allow the encryption of information to be sent back and forth. All this is provided for you with Windows Remote Assistance. To begin a Remote Assistance session:

1. Open the **System** menu and select **Control Panel | System And Security**. Under System, select **Launch Remote Assistance** to open the Windows Remote Assistance dialog box.

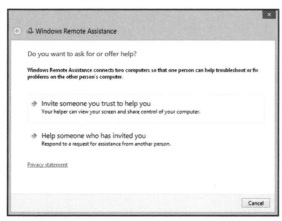

2. Select **Invite Someone You Trust To Help You**, select the person from a contacts list, and then select one of the following methods:

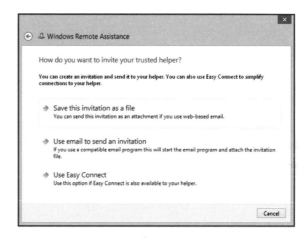

- **Save This Invitation As A File**   You can transfer the invitation as an attachment to an email message using any email app or web-based email such as Google's Gmail, or via a CD or USB flash drive.

- **Use Email To Send An Invitation**   Select this if you are using Windows Mail, Microsoft Office Outlook, or another compatible email package.

- **Use Easy Connect**   Select this if the other computer is using Windows 8 or Windows 8.1.

3. If you select **Use Email To Send An Invitation**, your email app will open and display a message to your helper and contain the invitation as an attachment, as shown in Figure 9-21. Address the email and select **Send**. Skip to step 6.

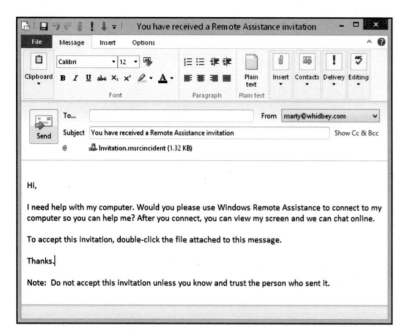

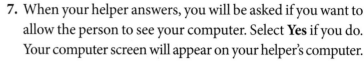

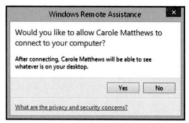

7. When your helper answers, you will be asked if you want to allow the person to see your computer. Select **Yes** if you do. Your computer screen will appear on your helper's computer.

8. Select **Chat** and then select the text box at the bottom and type a message to the other person, who can see everything on your computer (see "Provide Remote Assistance," next). Select **Send**.

9. If the other person requests control of your computer, you'll see a message asking if that is what you want to do. If you do, select the check box, and then select **Yes**. If you become uncomfortable, you can select **Stop Sharing** or press ALT+T at any time.

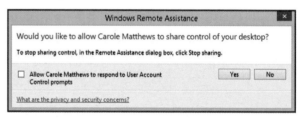

10. To end the session, send a message to that effect, and close the Remote Assistance window.

Figure 9-21: ***You need to send an invitation that asks a person for assistance and gives him or her the means to communicate in an encrypted manner.***

4. If you select **Save This Invitation As A File**, select the drive and folder where you want to store the invitation—it may be across a network on your helper's computer. Select **Save**.

5. Attach the saved file to an email message or store it on a CD or flash drive, and send or deliver it to your helper.

6. If you select **Easy Connect**, or in either of the other two cases, a Windows Remote Assistance window will open, providing you with the password you must also communicate to your helper, say, via phone. This window will wait for your helper to answer.

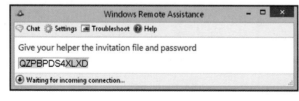

Provide Remote Assistance

If you want to provide Remote Assistance:

1. Upon receiving an invitation as a file, drag it to the desktop, and open it. Skip to step 3.

2. If you are using Easy Connect, open the **System** menu and select **Control Panel | System And Security**. Under System, select **Launch Remote Assistance** to open the Windows Remote Assistance dialog box. Select **Help**

Someone Who Has Invited You. It may take a couple of minutes to connect.

3. Enter the password you have been given, select **OK**, and, if the other person approves, you are shown his or her screen and can request control of the other person's computer. You can view the screen in its actual size or scale it to fit your screen, as shown in Figure 9-22.

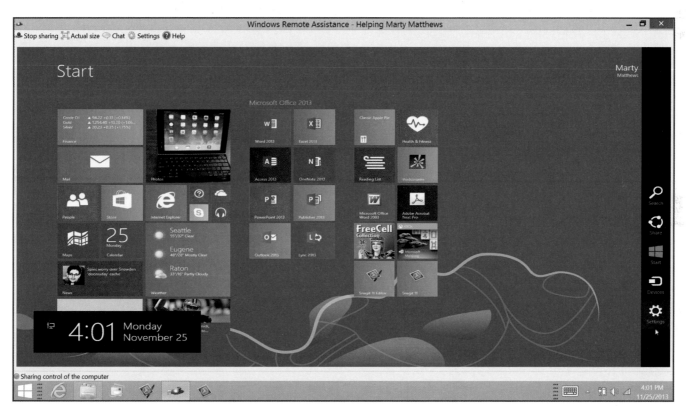

Figure 9-22: **The remote screen is shown on the assistance provider's screen.**

4. To request control of the other computer, select **Request Control**. Select **Stop Sharing** to give up control.

5. Select **Close** to end the session and close the Remote Assistance window.

NOTE You are protected from misuse of Remote Assistance in five ways: Without an invitation, the person giving assistance cannot access your computer; you can limit both the time the invitation remains open and the time the person can be on your computer; you can determine whether the person can control your computer or just look at it; you can select **Stop Sharing** or press **ALT+T** at any time to immediately terminate the other person's control; and you can close the Remote Assistance window to instantly disconnect the other person.

QuickQuotes

Ann Benefits from BOD Online Documents

The way I see it, the Internet has enormously benefited organizations with boards of directors. I have served on nonprofit boards for over 30 years, and staff always seems to scramble getting board packets out. They hustle around to copy, deliver, or mail the information, while board members hope they will receive it before the meeting. During the last couple of years, some of my boards have taken a different approach to distributing board packets that works well—the board members log on to organizational websites to get the materials they need for the meeting. The staff does have to post the information, but this takes far less time than before. Costs to the organization are reduced in terms of time and materials. In addition, I have trouble filing things so I can find them when I want them. The material available to me online solves the problem; I can find the budget or minutes from a previous meeting without spending hours shuffling through the piles of paper or requesting yet another copy. I am convinced this use of the Internet is a great way organizations and board members can be more effective.

Ann K., 65, California

Chapter 10

Controlling Security

Controlling computer security is a complex subject because of the many different aspects of computing that need protection. In this chapter you'll see how to control who uses a computer, control what users do, and protect data stored in the computer.

CONTROL WHO IS A USER

Controlling who uses a computer means identifying the users to the computer, giving them a secure way of signing on to the computer, and preventing everyone else from using it. This is achieved through the process of adding and managing users and passwords.

When you first use a new installation of Windows 8.1, either on a new computer or an upgrade of a prior Windows installation, you are asked to sign in with a Microsoft account such as Hotmail, Windows Live, or Xbox. If you do not have one of these accounts, you are asked to sign up for one. Your email address and password for that account become your ID and password for Windows 8.1. You can go to another Windows 8 computer, sign on with your email address and password, and be established as a new user on that computer. Many of your settings, preferences, and data will be synchronized across the computers.

Also in Windows 8.1, the first user of a computer is, by default, an administrator. An administrator has a number of permissions a standard user does not. For example, a Windows feature called *User Account Control* (UAC) can pop up and ask if you want to allow a program to make changes to your computer. An administrator can select **Yes** to proceed. A person who is not an administrator in the same circumstance would have to enter an administrator's password to continue.

 NOTE You may be asked to verify your identity on your PC by selecting **Verify**. A "Help Us Protect Your Account" screen then asks if you want to receive a text message with the security code, choose a call option, or use an existing received code. After selecting one of these and selecting **Submit** and then receiving and entering the code sent to you, you are returned to the Accounts screen.

⏵⏵ Set Up Users

If you have several people using your computer, each person should be set up as a separate user. To add users to your computer, or even to change your user characteristics (as well as to perform most other tasks in this chapter), you must be logged on as an administrator, so you first need to check on that. Then you may want to change the characteristics of your account, and, if you have multiple people using your computer, you may want to add user accounts and have each user sign in to his or her account.

Review Your PC Settings Account

Windows 8.1 has supplemented the Control Panel in several areas, including Users, with the PC Settings screen. Begin by looking at your information there and then review what is in Control Panel.

1. Open **Charms** and select **Settings | Change PC Settings** on the bottom right | **Accounts | Your Account** on the left. Your account will appear on the screen, as you can see in Figure 10-1.

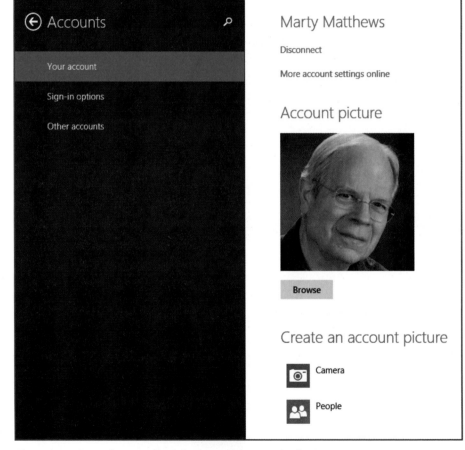

Figure 10-1: Some, but not all, of the user settings are in the Accounts screen.

2. You can change your current password by selecting **Sign-In Options** and selecting **Change** under Password. Enter your Microsoft password and select **Finish**. Enter your old Microsoft password again, enter your new password twice, and select **Next**. You are told you changed your password. Select **Finish**.

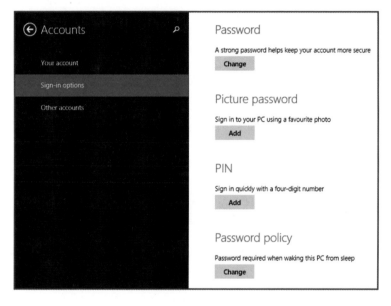

3. If you have a touch screen, you can create a picture password by once more entering your current password, selecting **OK**, and then selecting a picture and going through a set of three gestures twice to set the picture password.

4. You can also create a four-digit personal identification number (PIN) to use in place of your password by entering your current password, selecting **OK**, entering and confirming your PIN, and then selecting **Finish**.

5. If your computer is relatively safe when it is in Sleep mode, you can remove the requirement to enter a password or PIN when waking the computer after it has been put to sleep, but not when restarting it.

6. Close your Accounts screen.

Review Your Settings in the Control Panel

The Control Panel provides additional user-related settings, but fewer than it did in previous versions of Windows. To open the User area of the Control Panel:

1. Open the **System** menu and select **Control Panel | User Accounts And Family Safety | User Accounts**. The User Accounts window opens.

2. You can see next to your picture the type of account you are using—"Administrator" in the previous illustration—and change it by selecting **Change Your Account Type** | a different type | **Change Account Type**.

3. Select **Change User Account Control Settings** to change when the User Account Control dialog box appears (see the following section). Move the slider up to have

it appear more often; move it down to have it appear less often.

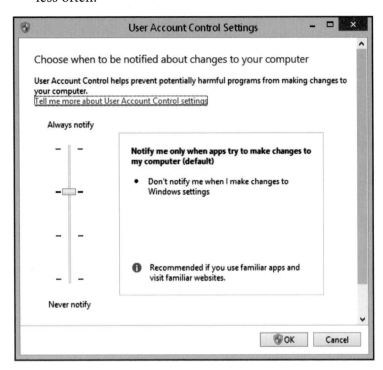

4. Select the other options in the User Account window to familiarize yourself with them. Some of these will be discussed in later sections of this chapter. Close the User Accounts window when finished.

Set Up Another User

To set up another user account:

1. Open **Charms** and select **Settings | Change PC Settings** on the bottom right | **Accounts** on the left. The user's account screen opens.

Understand User Account Control

Windows 8.1 has a feature called User Account Control, or UAC. UAC monitors what is happening on the computer, and if it sees something that could cause a problem, like installing an app, adding a new user, or changing a password, it interrupts that process and asks for physical verification. It also freezes all activity on the computer so that nothing can happen until verification is provided. If the user has administrator privileges, he or she is asked if they want to allow changes to the computer and to confirm this action. If the user doesn't have administrator privileges, he or she is asked for the administrator's password. By requiring a physical action, UAC ensures that an actual person is sitting at the computer and that malware is not attempting to modify it.

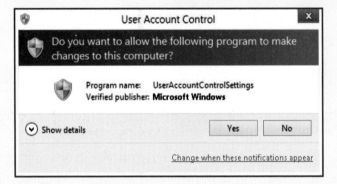

All operations that require administrative privileges have a little shield icon beside them, as shown in earlier illustrations.

If you are installing several apps, the UAC dialog boxes can be irritating. You can turn it off in the User Accounts Control Panel, but this is strongly discouraged. If you do turn it off while you are installing several apps, it is strongly recommended that you turn it back on when you are finished.

2. Select **Other Accounts** and then select **Add An Account** to open the Add A User panel, shown in Figure 10-2.

3. Type an email address for the new user that is tied to an account recognized by Microsoft. The email address can be with any Internet service provider (ISP), but it should be registered with one of the Microsoft services (Live.com, Outlook.com, or Hotmail.com). If the new user does not have a Microsoft account, see "Create a Microsoft Account," later in this chapter.

4. Select **Next | Finish**.

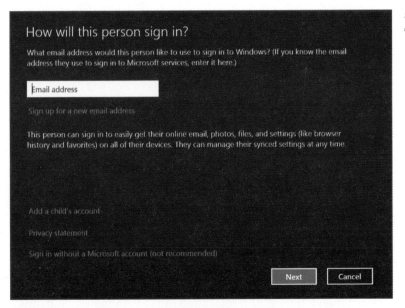

Figure 10-2: The Add A User panel starts the process for a new user.

⏩ Establish a New User Account

When setting up a new user on your computer with Windows 8.1, it is strongly recommended that the user have a Microsoft account, so the first step should be to create such an account.

Create a Microsoft Account

While you can use Windows 8.1 without a Microsoft account (see the bottom option in the Add A User panel shown in Figure 10-2), it is not recommended—you miss a lot of security, and the user can't use the Microsoft Store. With a Microsoft account, you can sync your settings across several computers so when you go from computer to computer, the look and feel will be the same. You can automatically get online content from Microsoft, and you can download free apps from the Microsoft Store without doing anything more than saying you want it. It is strongly recommended that new users get a Microsoft account. To create a Microsoft account and a password for Windows 8.1:

1. Follow the steps in "Set Up Another User" to open the Add A User pane. Select **Sign Up For A New Email Address** to open the sign-up panel.

2. Enter a name to be used as the first part of the email address, as you can see in Figure 10-3. Press **TAB** and select the Microsoft domain you want to use.

3. Press **TAB** and enter a password that is at least eight characters long and has any combination of at least two of the following: uppercase or lowercase letters, numbers, or symbols. For example, *seattle1962* works because it is over eight characters long and it has both lowercase letters and numbers. *Dogitdan* also works because it has

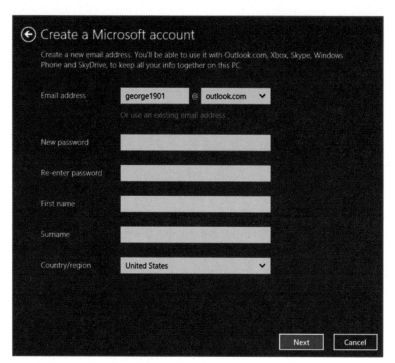

Figure 10-3: *Setting up a Microsoft account allows you to sync your settings over several computers.*

eight characters and both uppercase and lowercase letters. *12345678* does not work, although it is eight characters long, because it is just numbers.

4. Using **TAB** to go from field to field and **Next** to go from panel to panel, enter the requested information.

5. When you are told that your new user can now sign in to your computer, if this is a child's account, select the question to turn on Family Safety (see "Set Up Family Safety" later in this chapter), and then select **Finish**.

Set Up a New User

When the new user signs on, they may want to set their own password. Also, it is a good idea to change a password periodically in case it has been compromised.

1. If the new user has just set up a new email account with Microsoft, skip to step 4; otherwise, continue to step 2.

2. The first time a new user signs on to a computer, they are asked to verify their identity through either a text message to a cell phone or one or more email addresses. They then need to select one of the choices and select **Next**. Finally, the new user needs to enter the code sent to them and once again select **Next**.

3. The user is asked if they want to copy the settings they have on another computer, if they have them, and, if so, select that computer, or set up the current computer as a new PC instead. In the latter case, they can choose to sync their Start screen layout to their other computers, if they have them, and then select **Next**.

4. The new user is told that pictures that are taken on the computer and that go into their Camera Roll will be backed up to SkyDrive along with their PC's settings and new documents they create. They can choose to turn this off, but that is not recommended. They once more need to select **Next**.

5. They are welcomed to the computer and told that it is being set up for them and that apps are being installed.

Change a Password

It may be that a new user, or any user, may want to change their password, which we will assume has been registered with Microsoft. To do that:

1. Open **Charms** and select **Settings | Change PC Settings | Accounts**. The user's account screen opens.

2. Select **Sign-In Options | Change** under Password, type the old password, type a new password, type it again to confirm it, and select **Next**.

3. When you are told your password has been changed, select **Finish**.

 TIP You can see the actual characters in your password by selecting the icon on the right of the password text box.

Old password   g&rM1949

 TIP For a password to be *strong*, it must be eight or more characters long; use both upper- and lowercase letters; and use a mixture of letters, numbers, and symbols, which include ! # $ % ^ & * and spaces. It also should *not* be a recognizable word, name, or date. Instead of a password such as "mymoney23," consider using something like this: "my$Money23."

Remove a User Account

To remove a user account from a computer:

1. Open **Charms** and select **Settings | Change PC Settings | Accounts | Other Accounts**. The list of accounts on the computer opens. (You must be an administrator to view Other Accounts.)

2. Select the account you want to remove and select **Remove**. Choose whether to delete the user's data or not, and select either **Delete Account And Data** or **Cancel**. If you want to keep the data but remove the account, cancel

at this point, open the user's account, back up the data, and then try again

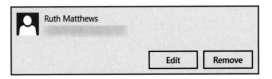

Ruth Matthews

Edit   Remove

3. Close the Accounts window.

CONTROL WHAT A USER DOES

User accounts identify people and allow them to log on to your computer. What they can do after that depends on the permissions they have. Windows 8.1 has two features that help you control what other users do on your computer: Family Safety and the ability to turn Windows features on and off for a given user.

 ## Set Up Family Safety

If you have a child or grandchild as one of the users on your computer and you are an administrator with a password, you can control what your child can do on your computer, including hours of usage, apps he or she can run, and access to the Internet. When your child encounters a blocked app, game, or website, a notice is displayed, including a link the child can select to request access. You, as an administrator, can allow one-time access by entering your user ID and password.

 NOTE A child for whom you want to set up Family Safety must have a Standard User account. To set up Family Safety, you must have an Administrator account with a password.

1. Open **Charms** and select **Settings | Change PC Settings | Accounts | Other Accounts**.

2. Select **Manage Family Safety Settings Online** under the list of accounts. Internet Explorer will open and ask you to sign in with your password.

3. Enter your password and select **Sign In**. The Family Safety site opens.

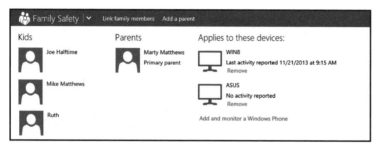

4. Select the user for whom you want to set restrictions to open the Overview settings for that user, as shown in Figure 10-4.

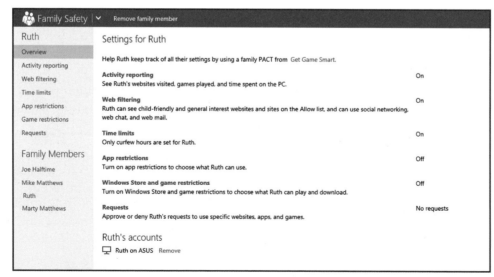

5. Select each of the options in the list on the left, review the settings, and implement the ones that are correct for your child. Several of the more prominent settings are discussed in the following steps.

6. Select **Web Filtering | Restriction Level** to review how you can restrict Internet usage. If you have specific websites you want to block, select **Allow Or Block List** and enter the sites to be blocked.

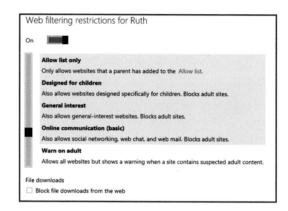

Figure 10-4: Family Safety allows you to determine what a child can do and see on your computer.

7. Select **Time Limits | Curfew** to select the times of day and the days of the week that the computer is blocked for the user by selecting and dragging across the squares to be blocked, or selecting and dragging across them again to unblock them, as you can see in Figure 10-5.

8. Select **App Restrictions** to open a list of all the apps on your computer. Select **On** to activate the list and then select the apps you want blocked.

9. Select **Game Restrictions | Rating** to turn on restrictions based on the ratings of the games and then select the rating level you want to use, as shown in Figure 10-6. You can also select **Game List** and block specific games on the computer.

▷▷ Control What Parts of Windows Can Be Used

As an administrator, you can control what parts of Windows 8.1 each user can access.

1. Log on as the user for whom you want to set Windows feature usage.

2. Open the **System** menu and select **Programs And Features**.

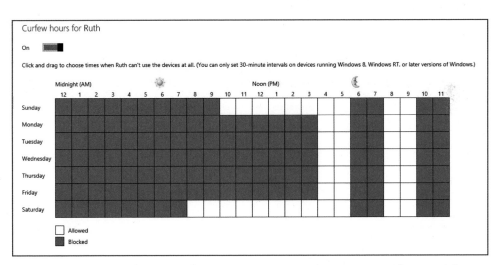

Figure 10-5: Setting the hours of a day that a child can use the computer provides even tighter control of computer use.

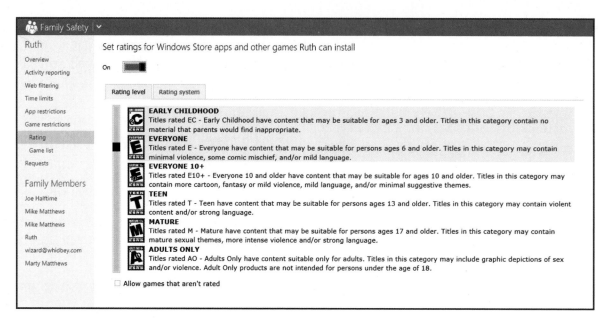

Figure 10-6: You can control computer games both through ratings and by individual games.

3. Select **Turn Windows Features On Or Off** in the left column. If needed, type a password and select **Yes**. The Windows Features dialog box appears.

4. Select an unselected check box to turn a feature on, or select a selected check box to turn a feature off. Select the plus sign (+) where applicable to open subfeatures and turn them on or off.

5. When you have selected the features the user will be allowed to use, select **OK**.

6. Close the Programs And Features window.

PROTECT STORED DATA

Protecting stored data is another layer of protection. It works by making unusable whatever is found on the computer by someone who managed to break through the other layers of protection.

Protect Files and Folders

You can protect files and folders by hiding them and encrypting them. The easiest way is to hide them, but it is also the weakest protection. Start by opening the Properties dialog box for a file or folder.

1. On the desktop, select the **File Explorer** icon on the toolbar. In the navigation pane, open the disk and folders necessary to locate and select in the right pane the file or folder you want to protect.

2. In the Home tab Open section, select the **Properties** icon. The Properties dialog box will appear, as shown here for a folder (there are slight differences among file and folder Properties dialog boxes).

Hide Files and Folders

Hiding files and folders lets you prevent them from being displayed by File Explorer. This assumes the person from whom

you want to hide them does not know how to display hidden files or how to turn off the hidden attribute. To hide a file or folder, you must both turn on its hidden attribute and turn off the Display Hidden Files feature.

1. In the file or folder Properties dialog box, on the General tab, select **Hidden | OK**. If needed, type a password and select **Yes** (the object's icon becomes dimmed or disappears). Select **OK** to close the Properties dialog box.

   If you are hiding a folder, you are asked if you want to do this to the folder only, or if you want to do this to the folder, subfolders, and files. Make your choice and select **OK**

   –Or–

   In the File Explorer window, select the **View** tab | **Hide Selected Items**, as you can see in Figure 10-7.

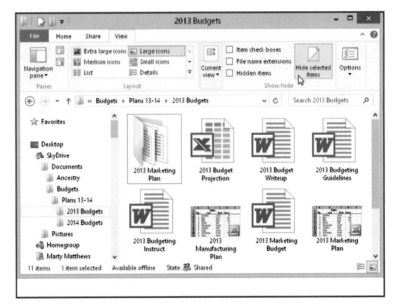

Figure 10-7: Hiding files is not a very secure form of protection.

2. In the File Explorer window, select the **View** tab | **Options** | **Change Folder And Search Options** | the **View** tab | **Don't Show Hidden Files, Folders, Or Drives**. Select **OK** to close the Folder Options dialog box. Close and reopen the parent folder, and the file or folder you hid will disappear.

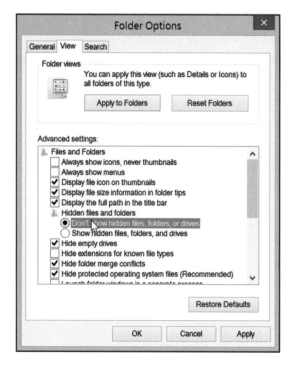

–Or–

In the File Explorer window, select the **View** tab | **Hidden Items** to unselect (uncheck) it.

3. To restore hidden files and/or folders to view, in the File Explorer **View** tab, select **Hidden Items** to check it.

Encrypt Files and Folders

File and folder encryption, called the *Encrypting File System* (EFS), is built into Windows 8.1. Once EFS is turned on for a

file or a folder, only the person who encrypted the file or folder will be able to read it. However, you can back up the encryption key and use that to access the file or folder. For the person who encrypted the file, accessing it requires no additional steps, and the file is re-encrypted every time it is saved.

To encrypt a file or folder from File Explorer, starting with files:

1. On the desktop, select the **File Explorer** icon on the taskbar. In the navigation pane, open the disk and folders necessary to locate in the right pane the file or folder you want to encrypt.

2. In the Home tab Open section, select the **Properties** icon | **Advanced**. The Advanced Attributes dialog box appears.

3. Select **Encrypt Contents To Secure Data** | **OK** twice.

4. If you are encrypting a file, you will see an encryption warning that the file is not in an encrypted folder, which means that when you edit the file, temporary or backup files might be created that are not encrypted. Choose whether to encrypt only the file or to encrypt both the file

and its parent folder, and then select **OK**. The filename will turn green.

5. If you are encrypting a folder, the Confirm Attribute Changes dialog box that you saw earlier appears, asking if you want to apply the encryption to this folder only or to both the folder and its contents. If you select **This Folder Only**, *existing* files and folders in the folder will *not* be encrypted, while files and folders later created in or copied to the encrypted folder will be. If you select **This Folder, Subfolders, And Files**, all files and folders will be encrypted. Choose the setting that is correct for you, and select **OK**. If needed, type a password and select **Yes**.

6. Restart your computer, and log on as another user. Open the desktop, select **File Explorer**, and open the drive and folders necessary to display in the right pane the file or folder you encrypted. You can see that the file exists, but is shown in green while everything else is in black. When

you try to open it, edit it, print it, or move it, you will get a message that access is denied.

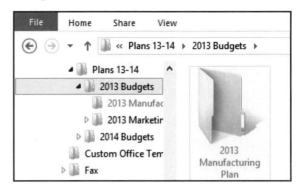

7. To decrypt a file or folder, log on as yourself (given you're the person who encrypted it), reopen the file or folder Properties dialog box, select **Advanced**, deselect **Encrypt Contents To Secure Data**, and select **OK** twice (three times with folders).

 TIP Because many apps save temporary and secondary files during normal execution, it is recommended that folders rather than files be the encrypting container. If an app is then told to store all files in that folder, where all files are automatically encrypted upon saving, security is improved.

 CAUTION! If you encrypt a shared folder and select This Folder, Subfolders, And Files, any files or subfolders belonging to others will be encrypted with your key, and the owners will not be able to use what they created.

Back Up Your Encryption Key

If you use file encryption, it is important to back up your file encryption key so that you do not lose the information you have, and you may be reminded of this. It is also important, of course, to keep the media that you back up on to safe so that it can't be used. The key is part of a digital certificate, so this section refers to backing up the certificate.

1. Open the **System** menu and select **Control Panel | User Accounts And Family Safety | User Accounts**. Your User Account window opens.

2. Select **Manage Your File Encryption Certificates** in the left column. If needed, type a password and select **Yes** to open the Encrypting File System dialog box.

3. Read about what you can do with this wizard, and select **Next**. By default, a certificate was automatically created when Windows was installed—that certificate or a more recent one will appear in the Certificate Details area, as shown in Figure 10-8. Select **Next**.

4. The Back Up The Certificate And Key dialog box will open. Select **Browse** opposite Backup Location, and navigate to the removable disc or USB flash drive and folder you want to hold the certificate (it is not recommended to save the key on the same machine where the encryption is located). Type a filename and select **Save**.

5. Type a password and confirm it, and then select **Next**. Select **All Logical Drives**, or select the plus sign and then select the individual drives and/or the folders with encrypted files that you want the new certificate and key applied to, and select **Next**. Your files will be updated with the new key.

Figure 10-8: A security certificate is required to use file encryption.

6. When you are told the files have been updated and where the key is stored, select **Close** and close the User Accounts window.

7. Store the removable disc or USB flash drive in a safe place.

 TIP To use a backed up encryption key, insert the removable media with the key, open the drive in File Explorer, and browse to and open the file with the key. In the Certificate Import Wizard that opens, select **Next**, confirm that you have the right file, and select **Next**. Type the password used to back up the key, select how you want to use the key | **Next**. Select the certificate store you want, and select **Next | Finish**.

Use Encrypted Files and Folders

If you are the person who encrypted a file or folder and you log on as yourself, you can use the file or folder exactly as you would if it hadn't been encrypted. The only way you know the files or folders are encrypted is that File Explorer shows them in green, as you saw earlier. If you log on as someone else, or if someone else logs on as anyone other than you, they will not be able to use the files or folders. Copying and moving encrypted files and folders, however, has a special set of rules:

- If you copy or move a file or folder into an encrypted folder, the item copied or moved will be encrypted.

- If you copy or move a file or folder to an unencrypted folder, the item moved remains as it was prior to being moved. If it was unencrypted, it remains so. If it was encrypted, it is still encrypted after being moved.

- Someone other than the owner who tries to copy or move encrypted files or folders to a different computer sees an error message that access is denied.

- If the owner copies or moves an encrypted file or folder to another file system, the encryption is removed, but a warning message is generated before the copy or move is complete.

- Backing up encrypted files or folders with Windows 8.1 File History leaves the items encrypted.

 ## Explore the Microsoft Store

Windows 8 introduced the Microsoft Store, and it has grown substantially with Windows 8.1. Get started with the store, and then explore it on your own.

Back Up Your Information

Computers are a great asset, but like any machine, they are prone to failures of many kinds. Once you have started using your computer regularly, it becomes important to make a copy of your information and store it in another location should your hard drive fail or something else happen to your computer.

There are several solutions to copying and saving your information. The term normally used for this is **backup** (or to back up—the verb form). This means storing a copy of your information in a location other than on your computer. You can back up to other disks connected to your computer or to cloud services on the Internet. In Chapter 3 we discussed using Windows 8.1's File History app to automatically back up files and folders on your computer, as well copying files and folders to CDs and DVDs. In Chapter 8 we discussed using SkyDrive to copy files to the Internet. There are many third-party (non-Microsoft) apps that help you back up either to other drives connected to your computer or to other cloud services. Some of these are available from the Microsoft Store, as you'll read in the next section. You can search for other apps using Google or Bing and entering "Windows backup apps" or "Cloud backup."

1. On the Start screen, select **Store**. The Store screen opens, as you see in Figure 10-9. Scroll the screen from right to left to view a sample of apps that you can get, some for free and some for a price.

2. To get an app, select it. A page opens describing the app (see Figure 10-10). If you want to go ahead and get the app, select **Install**. If the app you are installing is free and it is one of your first apps, you are asked if you still want to enter payment information to use later. If so, select **Add Info**; otherwise, select **Ask Me Later**.

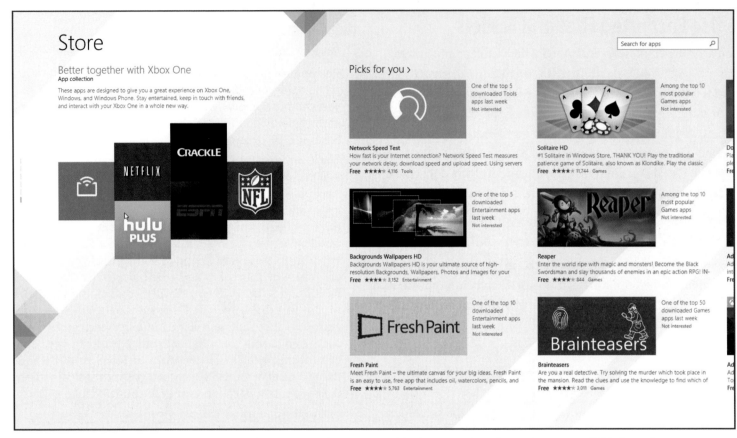

Figure 10-9: The apps shown on the opening Store screen are a few samples of the large number of apps that are available from the Store.

3. If you are getting an app that is not free, the price and terms are displayed both initially and after you select **Buy**, and again when you are asked to select **Confirm**. You then need to enter your Microsoft password to verify your account. Next, you must enter payment information. If you have previously entered a credit card, you can choose to use that, or enter a new one, or use PayPal. Select **Submit**. A message will appear in the upper-right corner telling you the status of the installation.

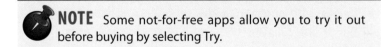

NOTE Some not-for-free apps allow you to try it out before buying by selecting Try.

4. You will find most apps by searching for them, either for a specific app or for a category of apps to get a number of choices. Scroll to the far right. In the upper-right area, enter your query in the box provided, and select **Search**

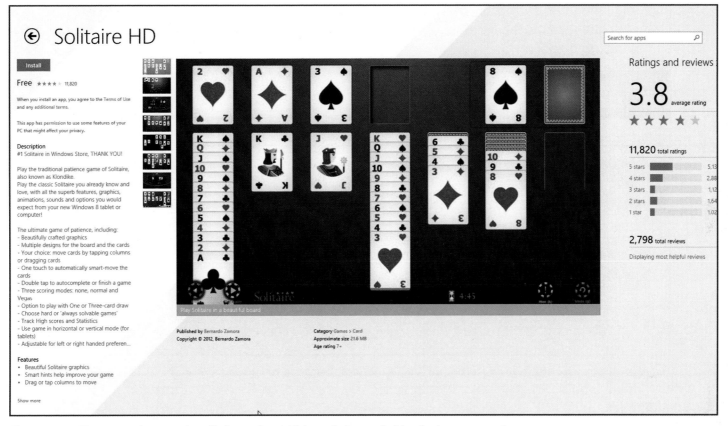

Solitaire HD

Install

Free ★★★★ 11,820

When you install an app, you agree to the Terms of Use and any additional terms.

This app has permission to use some features of your PC that might affect your privacy.

Description
#1 Solitaire in Windows Store, THANK YOU!

Play the traditional patience game of Solitaire, also known as Klondike.
Play the classic Solitaire you already know and love, with all the superb features, graphics, animations, sounds and options you would expect from your new Windows 8 tablet or computer!

The ultimate game of patience, including:
- Beautifully crafted graphics
- Multiple designs for the board and the cards
- Your choice: move cards by tapping columns or dragging cards
- One touch to automatically smart-move the cards
- Double tap to autocomplete or finish a game
- Three scoring modes: none, normal and Vegas
- Option to play with One or Three-card draw
- Choose hard or 'always solvable games'
- Track High scores and Statistics
- Use game in horizontal or vertical mode (for tablets)
- Adjustable for left or right handed preferen...

Features
• Beautiful Solitaire graphics
• Smart hints help improve your game
• Drag or tap columns to move

Show more

Published by Bernardo Zamora
Copyright © 2012, Bernardo Zamora

Category Games > Card
Approximate size 21.6 MB
Age rating 7+

Search for apps

Ratings and reviews

3.8 average rating

★★★★☆

11,820 total ratings

5 stars		5,13
4 stars		2,88
3 stars		1,12
2 stars		1,64
1 star		1,02

2,798 total reviews

Displaying most helpful reviews

Figure 10-10: Most apps give you a lot of information, which can help you decide whether you want it.

(the magnifying glass icon). The results will be displayed as you can see in Figure 10-11.

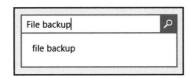

5. After the app you got has completed downloading, you should see it on the Apps view screen with the word

"New" under the name. You can right-select the app and select **Pin To Start** if you want the app on your Start screen.

 TIP It is normally worthwhile looking at the ratings and reading the reviews before purchasing an app. Also, the initial prices may be misleading because there often are in-app purchases that are needed to get the full use of the app.

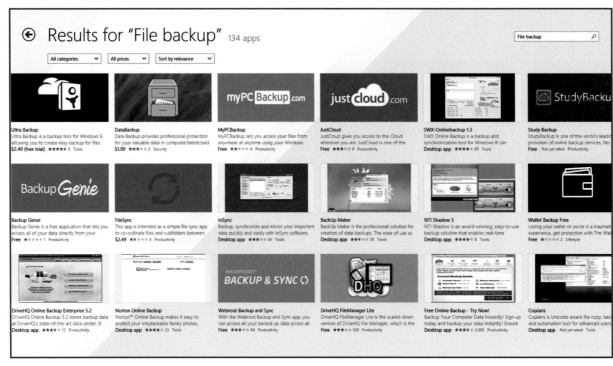

Figure 10-11: Many searches turn up a lot of apps you can consider. Look at the ratings and reviews.

QuickQuotes

Jeremy Is Comfortable with His Security Precautions

I am a small book publisher working out of my home. I depend very heavily on my computer and do a large part of my business over the Internet, frequently using PayPal for handling payments and keeping all my records on my computer. You would think in that situation I would be very concerned about computer security. I'm actually not. I do all the prudent things like using the latest software, doing all the recommended updates, running the latest antivirus software—again with the latest updates—doing recurring backups of my files, and maintaining the recommended security settings. None of these steps, though, is extreme, and none take much effort to implement and maintain. I believe that I have moderate-to-low exposure to security risks by working out of my home, where only my wife has access to my computer, and by following the basic security steps just mentioned. I believe that it is easy to get overly concerned about computer security, but if you look at what is the real risk if someone got control of your computer, generally, if you have taken the basic precautions, the answer is not much.

Jeremy B., 64, Michigan

Index

Numbers

3G/4G
  data plan, 94
  wireless connection, 95

Symbol

| (pipe) character, use of, 15–16

A

accessory apps. *See also* apps
  Calculator, 201–202
  Character Map, 202
  Notepad, 202
  Paint, 202–203
accounts. *See* user accounts
Action Center
  accessing, 19, 217
  changing settings, 218
address bar, navigating with, 77–78
administrator
  accounts, 235
  permissions, 241–242
Adobe Reader app, using, 204–205
Aero Peek, using, 25–27, 49
Aero Shake, described, 25, 27
Aero Snaps
  described, 25
  using, 27–28
airline tickets, shopping for, 119, 121–122
all-in-one computers, 2
ALT key combinations, 11. *See also* keyboard shortcuts
App bar
  displaying, 12, 14, 38
  hiding, 24
app icons, adding to desktop, 45. *See also* desktop
  icons; icons

apps. *See also* accessory apps; desktop apps; Start
  screen apps
  Adobe Reader, 204–205
  buying from Microsoft Store, 247–250
  Classic Windows, 22
  closing, 21–22, 212–213
  controlling with Task Manager, 213–214
  pinning to Start screen, 38
  ribbon, 22
  searching for, 12, 83–86
  splitting, 30
  starting, 14, 20–21
  starting on desktop, 16
  stopping, 212–213
  switching among, 12
  switching between, 53
  switching to, 14
  terminology, 7
  title bar, 22
  using Exit command, 212
Apps view, opening, 14, 20–21, 38
audio CDs, playing, 162. *See also* CDs
audio files, playing on Internet, 112. *See also* sounds
Automatic Updates
  applying, 216–217
  using, 215–216

B

background
  changing for Start screen, 40
  restoring for Start screen, 40
backing up
  encryption key, 246
  files, 86–89
  folders, 86–89
  information, 247
Bing, searching for songs, 167

browser navigation
  Back button, 99
  Forward button, 99
  Pages recently entered, 99
Burn Files To Disc option, 89
burning music CDs, 175–176

C

Calculator app, using, 201–202
Calendar app, using, 135–138
camcorder, importing video from, 179–180
camera images, importing, 146
cameras, installing, 143–144
Category view, 55
CDs. *See also* audio CDs; music CDs
  copyright laws, 172
  versus DVDs, 180
  playing, 162–163
  ripping, 170–172
  writing to, 89–91
Change PC Settings control, described, 20
Character Map app, using, 202
Charms
  opening, 8–9, 11, 14, 19
  Settings, 19
  showing, 53–54
clicking mouse, explained, 6
clock, adjusting, 58
Close button, identifying, 23
closing
  apps, 21–22
  apps from keyboard, 212–213
  apps from taskbar, 212
  windows, 12
cloud, overview, 183–184
colors
  changing for desktop, 42–43
  changing for objects, 44–45

email. *See also* Mail app; Web mail
  attaching files to, 130–131
  attaching signatures, 130
  Bold button, 129
  changing default formatting, 129–130
  Clear Format button, 129
  creating, 126–127
  Emoticons button, 129
  fonts, 129
  formatting, 128–129
  handling spam, 132
  Highlight button, 129
  Italic button, 129
  List button, 129
  opening People, 127
  options for addressees, 127
  receiving, 127
  Redo button, 129
  responding to, 127–128
  sending, 126–127
  Underline button, 129
  Undo button, 129
  Web Link button, 129
encrypted files, using, 247. *See also* files
encrypted folders, using, 247. *See also* folders
encryption key, backing up, 246
events, adding to Calendar, 136–138
Excel Web App
  editing in, 201
  worksheets, 199–200

F

Family Safety feature, setting up, 239–241
favorite folders, accessing in IE, 107
favorite sites. *See also* sites
  creating folders, 105–106
  deleting, 107
  opening, 102
  saving, 100
favorites, placing in folders, 106
Favorites bar, adding sites to, 106
Favorites list, rearranging, 105

File Explorer
  address bar, 69
  appearance, 69
  Back button, 69
  changing icons, 52
  changing panes, 52
  Computer tab, 72
  contextual tabs, 73
  control menu, 69
  customizing, 70–71
  Details pane, 69–70
  File tab, 71
  Folder Details view, 73
  Folder Options dialog box, 73–74
  Folders list, 69
  Forward button, 69
  Home tab, 72
  layout options, 70
  manipulating panes, 51
  Navigation pane, 69–70
  New folder, 69
  opening, 51, 68–70
  Preview pane, 69–70
  properties, 69
  push pins, 72
  Refresh button, 69
  ribbon, 51, 69, 71–72
  Search box, 69
  Search ribbon, 84
  Share tab, 72
  subfolders, 69
  Subject pane, 69
  tabs, 69
  Up a level, 69
  using SkyDrive in, 190
  View buttons, 69
  View tab, 72
File History app
  restoring from, 88–89
  setting up, 87–88
  starting, 87–88
files. *See also* encrypted files
  attaching to email, 130–131
  backing up, 86–89

  copying, 82–83
  copying to SkyDrive, 187–188
  creating, 85
  deleting, 79–80
  encrypting, 244–245
  hiding, 243–244
  locating, 16
  moving, 82–83
  moving to SkyDrive, 188–189
  opening, 16
  protecting, 243–246
  renaming, 79
  searching for, 11, 83–86
  selecting, 80
  storing, 68
  writing to devices, 89–91
  zipping, 86
flash memory, explained, 4
floating windows. *See also* windows
  left-aligning, 28
  maximizing, 27
  right-aligning, 28
focus, moving, 78
Folder Details view, 73
Folder Options dialog box, 73–74
folders. *See also* encrypted folders
  adding to SkyDrive, 186–187
  backing up, 86–89
  copying, 82–83
  creating, 79
  creating for favorite sites, 105–106
  deleting, 79–80
  encrypting, 244–245
  hiding, 243–244
  moving, 82–83
  navigating, 76–78
  navigating with, 77
  placing favorites in, 106
  protecting, 243–246
  renaming, 79
  selecting, 80
  selecting and opening, 75–76
  sharing on SkyDrive, 194–196

minimizing windows, 12
mirror touch, 8
motherboard, explained, 4
mouse
  buttons, 7
  explained, 2
  Start screen, 16
  switching buttons, 61
  switching pointers, 61
  using, 5–8, 14–15
mouse actions
  highlighting objects, 8
  mirror touch, 8
  moving objects, 8
  opening context menus, 8
  opening objects, 8
  selecting objects, 8
mouse pointer
  changing, 61–62
  described, 17
  explained, 18
moving
  files and folders, 82–83
  objects, 8, 14
  objects in multi-touch, 10
multimedia, explained, 161
multi-touch screens
  finger gestures, 10
  moving objects, 10
  opening context menus, 10
  opening controls, 10
  opening objects, 10
  opening windows, 10
  scrolling, 10
  selecting objects, 10
  support for, 9
  turning pages, 10
  zooming in, 10
  zooming out, 10
music
  adding to playlists, 174
  controlling volume, 165
  finding online, 166–167

getting account information, 170
  organizing, 172–175
  Shuffle option, 178
  storing on cloud service, 173–174
  Xbox app, 165–166, 170
music CDs, burning, 175–176. *See also* CDs
music players, copying to, 177

N

navigating
  using address bar, 77–78
  using folders, 77
  using libraries, 76–77
navigation. *See also* site navigation
  changing, 52–54
  showing Charms, 53–54
  switching between apps, 53
Network control, described, 20
Network icon, identifying, 19
newspapers, reading online, 114
Notepad app, using, 202
notification area
  changing, 49
  closing taskbar properties, 50
  customizing icons, 49
  described, 17
  displaying system icons, 50
  icons in, 19
  turning off icons, 49
  using, 18–19
Notifications control, explained, 19

O

objects
  changing appearance of, 44–45
  highlighting, 8
  moving, 8, 14
  opening, 8, 14
  opening with keyboard, 11
  resizing, 44
  selecting, 8, 14

selecting in subject pane, 80
  selecting with keyboard, 11
On-Screen Keyboard, 80. *See also* keyboards
OneDrive, 184. *See also* SkyDrive
opening
  App bar, 14
  Charms, 8–9, 11, 14, 19
  context menus, 8, 11, 14
  Devices pane, 12
  documents, 15
  drives, 75–76
  favorite sites, 102
  File Explorer, 68–69
  files, 16
  folders, 75–76
  objects, 8, 14
  objects in multi-touch, 10
  objects with keyboard, 11
  screen magnifier, 12
  Settings pane, 12
  Share pane, 11
  system features, 18
  System menu, 12
  Windows Help, 12
optical disc
  explained, 4
  inserting, 5

P

pages, turning in multi-touch, 10
Paint app, using, 202–203
passwords
  changing, 238–239
  entering, 6
Paste command, 83
PC info, getting, 221
PC Settings, 55, 65, 234–235
People app
  opening in email, 127
  using, 133
Personalization window, opening, 42

Quick Reference

Actions Taken with Various Windows Key Combinations

Key(s)	Description	Key(s)	Description
WINDOWS	Switches to the Start screen from the desktop or Start screen app, and to the desktop from the Start screen once the desktop has been otherwise opened.	**WINDOWS+R**	Switches to the desktop and opens Run.
WINDOWS+1, 2...	Switches to the desktop and opens the first, second, etc., application on the taskbar.	**WINDOWS+U**	Switches to the desktop and opens the Ease of Access Center.
WINDOWS+B	Switches to the desktop and selects the notification area.	**WINDOWS+W**	Searches for settings.
WINDOWS+C	Opens Charms.	**WINDOWS+X**	Opens the System menu.
WINDOWS+D	Shows the desktop, hiding open windows.	**WINDOWS+Z**	In a Windows 8–style window, displays the App bar.
WINDOWS+E	Switches to the desktop and opens File Explorer.	**WINDOWS++** **WINDOWS+–**	Opens the screen magnifier and increase or decreases the magnification of the current screen.
WINDOWS+F	Searches for files.	**WINDOWS+TAB**	Switches among Windows 8–style apps.
WINDOWS+H	Opens the Share pane.	**WINDOWS+HOME**	Closes all but the selected window on the desktop. When pressed a second time, it reopens all windows originally open.
WINDOWS+I	Opens the Settings pane.	**WINDOWS+F1**	Opens Windows Help.
WINDOWS+K	Opens the Devices pane.	**WINDOWS+PRT SCN**	Saves an image of the screen to the Clipboard; +**ALT** saves just the open window.
WINDOWS+L	Locks the computer and displays the Lock screen.	**WINDOWS+UP ARROW**	Maximizes the selected window. If this is followed by **WINDOWS+DOWN ARROW**, the window is restored to its original size.
WINDOWS+M	Switches to the desktop and minimizes all open windows.	**WINDOWS+DOWN ARROW**	Minimizes the selected window, unless the window was originally maximized, in which case the window is restored to its original size.
WINDOWS+O	Turns a tablet's autorotate between portrait and landscape on or off.	**WINDOWS+LEFT ARROW**	The selected window fills the left 50 percent of the desktop. If this is followed by **WINDOWS+RIGHT ARROW**, the window is restored to its original size.
WINDOWS+P	Opens the settings to display on a second screen.	**WINDOWS+RIGHT ARROW**	The selected window fills the right 50 percent of the desktop. If this is followed by **WINDOWS+LEFT ARROW**, the window is restored to its original size.
WINDOWS+Q	Searches for apps.	**WINDOWS+SHIFT+UP ARROW**	The selected window fills the desktop vertically, but maintains its previous width. If this is followed by **WINDOWS+SHIFT+DOWN ARROW**, the window is restored to its original size.

Quick Reference

Implementing Common Terms with a Mouse, Touch, and a Keyboard			
Action Term	**With a Mouse**	**With Touch**	**With a Keyboard**
Select an object on the desktop, in a window or dialog box, or on a menu	**Click** the object	**Tap** the object	Use **TAB** or the **ARROW KEYS** to highlight the object and press **ENTER**
Start an app in the Start screen	**Click** the tile	**Tap** the tile	Select the tile and press **ENTER**
Open an object on the desktop, such as a window or folder	**Double-click** the object	**Double-tap** the object	Select the object and press **ENTER**
Start an app on the desktop	**Double-click** the app	**Double-tap** the app	Select the object and press **ENTER**
Open an object's context menu	**Right-click** the object	**Touch** and hold for a moment, then release	Select the object and press the **CONTEXT MENU** key
Open the App bar for an app	**Right-click** the app	**Touch** and hold for a moment, then release	Select the object and press the **CONTEXT MENU** key
Move an object on the screen	**Drag** the object with the mouse	**Drag** the object with your finger	Select the object and press **ALT+SHIFT+ARROW KEYS**
Switch to the desktop from the Start screen	**Click** the desktop tile	**Tap** the desktop tile	Press **WINDOWS+D**
Switch to the Start screen	**Click** the **Start** button	**Swipe** from the right edge and tap the **Start** button	Press **WINDOWS**
Switch to another running Windows 8–style app	**Point** to the upper-left corner, move down, and click the app	**Swipe** from the left edge until the app opens	Press **WINDOWS+TAB**
Open Charms	**Point** to the lower-right corner and move up	**Swipe** from the right	Press **WINDOWS+C**
Open Apps view	**Click** the down arrow on the Start screen	**Swipe** up from the vertical middle of the Start screen	Press **CTRL+TAB** from the Start screen